DONNA KOOLER'S

encyclopedia *of* quilting

A LEISURE ARTS PUBLICATION

DONNA KOOLER'S

encyclopedia *of* quilting

3

Library of Congress Control Number: 2010922701

Library of Congress Cataloging-in-Publication Data
    Kooler, Donna
    Donna Kooler's Encyclopedia of Quilting
    "A Leisure Arts Publication"

ISBN-13: 978-1-60900-086-8

contributors

produced by

KOOLER
DESIGN
STUDIO
BOOKS

published by

the art of everyday living
www.leisurearts.com

If you have questions or comments
please contact:

LEISURE ARTS CUSTOMER SERVICE
5701 RANCH DRIVE
LITTLE ROCK, AR 72223-9633
www.leisurearts.com

KOOLER DESIGN STUDIO, INC.
399 TAYLOR BLVD., SUITE 104
PLEASANT HILL, CA 94523
www.koolerdesign.com

PRINTED IN THE UNITED STATES

---

photography/color separations
DIANNE WOODS, BERKELEY, CA

photo stylist
BASHA KOOLER
SONDRA DANIELS

models
THEA HANNER, ALYSSA PAKIN, ZACK PAKIN,
COURTNEY THOMPSON

creative director
DONNA KOOLER

editor in chief
JUDY SWAGER

encyclopedia editor
LAURA NOWNES

writers
RESEARCH, INSTRUCTIONAL TEXT AND
PATTERN GALLERY: LAURA NOWNES, JEAN LEWIS
HISTORY: SHELLEY CARDA
CHAPTER INTRODUCTIONS: SHELLEY CARDA,
JENNIFER CANNON ROUNDS

project coordinators
MARSHA HINKSON, PRISCILLA TIMM

proofreaders
LORALEE WINDSOR, MARY HUTCHESON

indexer
JANET RUSSELL

book design & production
NANCY WONG SPINDLER, RHONDA SHELBY,
JACOB CASLETON, BECCA SNIDER, JANIE WRIGHT

illustrations
JOHN HEISCH, NAOMI HOLT, MARIA RODRIGUEZ

projects designed by
NANCY BUSBY, CARA GULATI, SHERRY HUTCHENS,
GWEN MARSTON, JUDITH BAKER MONTANO,
VIVIENNE MOORE, VERNA MOSQUERA, SUE NICKELS,
APRIL OLIVEIRA-WARD, JOHN SERRAO,
PAT SLOAN, ANITA GROSSMAN SOLOMON,
ANNE SUTTON, LINDA TIANO, LYNNE TODOROFF

projects made by
LAURIE GRANT, JANICE E. PETRE, JAMIE SCHANTZ,
W. CISSY SERRAO, CHERYL SIMPSON, PAT SLOAN,
ANNIE SMITH, LINDA TIANO, JOHN WILLCOX

Leisure Arts is pleased to bring you the revised *Encyclopedia of Quilting*. This comprehensive guide to the history and techniques of quiltmaking has been updated with information on what's popular in quilting today.

editor's notes

When I joined the Kooler Design team as writer/editor of this book, I admit I was skeptical as to how we would ever be able to include all the information we wanted to share about quilting in a single book. Quilting is such a vast and ever-changing art form and our goal was to cover traditional as well as the many modern methods which have developed in recent years.

I feel that the *Encyclopedia of Quilting* has successfully accomplished what we set out to do— to serve as a reference book containing information about the wide range of topics within the field of quilting. The History section is well researched by Shelley Carda with great care and attention to detail. She examined and reviewed numerous sources to ensure a comprehensive look at this beloved pastime. Her selection of antique quilts presents an engaging and illustrative history of quilt styles popular during different eras. Her thorough research into the history of quilting is informative and intriguing, while providing food for thought as to the origin of the first quilt.

The how-to sections, Basics and Beyond the Basics, appeal to me as a long time teacher of beginning techniques. Researching them provided me the opportunity to become more familiar with many techniques and styles that I have yet to try. I now have a better understanding and new appreciation for the variety of ways in which we as quilters approach the making of a quilt. The talented contributing artists were handpicked and have graciously allowed us to include their work in the Projects section. It contains a wide variety of wonderful designs from simple appliquéd wool pillows to an elaborately stitched Victorian crazy quilt. Each project is complete with color photographs, diagrams and clear step-by-step instructions that will assist you in making it.

Finally the Gallery of quilt block patterns contains eighty pieced patterns, ten appliqué patterns and 14 quilting designs. I especially like the format of presenting each pattern not only as a single block but also as four joined together. It was fun sifting through numerous pattern books in search of our favorite designs.

It was a joy to be a part of this project, and I hope you will not only find inspiration but also a sense of connection to the beautiful art of quiltmaking that has been my passion and that of thousands of quilters for centuries.

Laura Nownes
Encyclopedia Editor

acknowledgments

I am forever grateful to Laura Nownes; without her tireless pursuit of fact and detail, this book would never have happened. Laura's passion for the art of quilting, her sense of design, and, of course, her patience as a teacher provided us with the perfect researcher, writer, and editor for the Encyclopedia of Quilting. *Also my thanks to all who contributed their knowledge, talents, resources, and hard work to bring you this beautiful book.*

I hope you find the material within these pages useful and informative, while perhaps, enticing you to venture down a road to your own creative projects.

Enjoy,
Donna Kooler

contents

beginnings

quilting basics

beyond the basics

projects

pattern gallery

for your information

QUILTING, for many was the demure art of thrifty women, loving keepers of hearth and home. The smallest scraps of precious cloth were carefully stitched into color-rich folk art, to warm us for generations. That vision, pieced into our cultural memories, is too limited. Quilting is a practical everyday craft, where ancient roots lie beneath the notice of most cultures, connecting remote parts of the world by a single strand. Quilt making limited to a housewife's craft is a myth, indeed.

In its most basic form a quilt has two layers of anything, held together with stitching. We are most familiar with two layers of fabric stuffed with something soft. For thousands of years people have kept warm with quilted clothing or burrowed under quilted bed covers. From ancient Egyptians to nomadic tribesmen who still travel Arctic lands, quilted goods layer the lives, resources, and aesthetics of the quilters. The different tastes among world cultures guide the artistic traditions of quilting, but the practical considerations draw us together, like a thread through cloth and batting.

Modern quilt making is an artful pursuit, ranging from traditional tastes to the most refined or avant garde innovations. Quilters come in all ages, sexes, and levels of skill and choose from an equally broad range of techniques. The wealth of modern quilting materials is boundless and intoxicating. Quilt makers can choose natural fibers from anywhere in the world or unbelievably fine synthetics. In our high-tech age, computerized sewing machines and customized quilting tools can compress time, so that heirloom-quality quilts can be made in hours rather than years. Yet for the purist, quilts can be assembled by hand, catching in amongst the layers the unhurried pace of a timeless rhythm. In the world of quilting there is a place for all.

10

Sicilian quilt, scenes from Tristan legend, c. 1400, linen, quilted with brown and white linen thread, 122" x 106". Victoria & Albert Museum/ V & A Images, London, England.

LAYERS IN HISTORY

When you think of quilts, do you think of beautiful, colorful bed coverings made by American women of generations past? You are correct, at least in part. Humans long ago discovered that layers provided protection, and layers held together were more convenient to use.

Quilting was always a practical craft, using layers of fabric, feathers, straw, leather, or other materials for armor, shoes, soles, insulation on draughty walls, bedcovers, and even church doors.[1] Practicality does not limit creativity, it focuses it. Once you have determined that there shall be more than one layer, creativity is required to fasten the layers together. Holding layers together is the actual quilting, and it is done in many different ways: with lines of stitching, ties placed at regular intervals across the piece, or—in some cases—rivets. Still more creativity is needed in constructing the individual layers.

If you have a top layer, there will also be a back layer, often quite different. In bed quilts the back can be a plain, whole-cloth piece that clearly shows the quilting stitches. Some quilts are so beautifully quilted that they are displayed back up. Other quilt backs are pieced with large fabric scraps, haphazardly arranged just to make a big enough back to fit the front. No elegant pattern was required: the front was the important part,

even if great skill was used in the quilting. Backs are as rich with information about the date of the quilt as the front, and it may be easier to interpret from the large pieces of fabric.

Of course we all think of soft, plump quilts, but the thicker the stuffing, the less intricate the quilting stitches must be. Some quilts had no stuffing at all: just a top and a back. These were often used for summer, and may be very beautifully quilted. Even the most intricate quilting stitches are primarily functional. The stability of the stuffing determines how successful a quilt is: stuffing that shifts easily will create a quilt with cold spots and ugly lumps. Very thick quilts are called comforts or comforters, and have minimal decorative stitching. The stuffing may be down, well-prepared wool or cotton, old woven blankets, or worn-out quilts. There are occasional surprising discoveries of ancient quilts inside worn-out heirlooms.

Most modern, whole-cloth quilted bedcovers are really comforters, filled with stable, glazed polyester batting. We value them for their warmth while enjoying their beauty. When they are tattered, lumpy, and no longer warm, we take them camping or use them for dog beds. Such was the fate of many excellent handmade quilts that saw hard daily use. Special quilts kept "for best" had a better chance of becoming heirlooms.

In some quilts the top is not stitched to the back. A top can be stitched to the padding alone. Some quilts have a lined top, in addition to the visible backing fabric. This is true of trapunto, where a very loosely woven piece of cloth is stitched in a pattern to the top, and bits of stuffing are inserted between the threads only where a raised design is desired. Then the back is put on, and all the layers are quilted together.

PATCHES OR PIECES?

The terms *patchwork* and *pieced quilts* are synonymous. Both are made of fragments of cloth sewn together to make a larger single layer of cloth, usually a quilt block. Blocks are then pieced together to form the quilt top. Piecing is the technique most often used for eye-catching geometric quilts. Many of the earliest pieced quilt patterns only have straight seams, such as the 1-patch, 4-patch, and 9-patch. These are the easiest to stitch smoothly, and are often recommended for beginners. Diagonal seams require more skill because fabric cut on the bias tends to stretch, leaving it prone to puckering. Even more demanding is a pattern with curved seams. Many deceptively simple-looking pieced patterns have curved seams, but a curved seam has both bias fabric and different amounts of fabric on the edges being joined. A smooth, curved seam without puckers shows great skill with the needle.

Sometimes quilts contain both pieced and appliquéd techniques. Geometric quilt blocks may have some appliquéd patches, or a quilt of appliqué blocks may have a pieced border.

LAYER UPON LAYER

The ancient Egyptians, textile experts at the dawn of history, may have had quilted garments, as seen in a First Dynasty (3100 B.C.) carved ivory pharaoh figure. The pharaoh is wrapped in a robe "covered with a diamond pattern which suggests soft, quilted layers".[2]

A tomb discovered at Hunan Province, China, from about 193-141 B.C., yielded a treasure trove. The contents of grave goods interred with the wife of the Marquis of Tai include a perfectly preserved silk jacket padded with silk floss for warmth.[3] History is scarcely being recorded and quilting already appeals to the upper classes. Some things are intrinsically luxurious.

There were few luxuries that didn't eventually find their way to the Middle Ages. In the 1100s St. Bernard of Clairvaux commented on ladies' quilted cloaks and gowns, which had costly fur sandwiched between two layers of the finest silk.[4]

IN THE HEAT OF BATTLE

Quilted clothing was the first and sometimes the only defense a soldier had against spears and arrows. Leather, straw, and coarse cloth have been used to make various layered protective garments from Egyptian times up to the present. Kevlar vests and flak jackets—the current version of quilted armor—can even stop bullets. So-called armored cars use the same Kevlar material, and are really quilted cars!

Medieval knights who wore metal armor used quilted clothing as a second line of defense, to protect skin and skull

Military Bases (soldier's quilted war kilt, worn over armor), 16th century. The Metropolitan Museum of Art, New York, NY, Rogers Fund, 1921 (21.142).

from the assaults of their own armor. But quilted military garments protected not just the heart and head. Other vital areas, such as the royal posterior, were protected by thickly padded, quilted skirts called bases.[5] (See photo above.)

As is often the case, boudoir and battlefield have much in common, and ladies adopted quilted petticoats to battle bone-numbing cold and damp. When they were warm enough, (about 1750) fashionable ladies divided their outer skirts and hiked up their hemlines to display beautifully quilted satin petticoats.[6] This fashion was particularly popular with the Dutch settlers of New Amsterdam (New York). When the fashion passed, such garments were frequently cut up and used in bed quilts.

BIG AND DRAUGHTY

Castles are notoriously hard to heat, so quilting became décor. The oldest extant European quilt is Sicilian, from about 1400 A.D. (See photo, page 10.) It is a linen wall hanging of scenes from the tragic love story of Tristan and Iseult, decoratively quilted with brown and white linen thread. More often, to brighten the walls as well as insulate them, narratives were worked as colorful tapestries with multiple layers of colored threads, drawn individually to the surface as needed in the design. The inability of weavers and dyers to make brilliant printed fabrics of only one layer was responsible for the high development of tapestry and brocade weaving, but it really didn't matter. The added warmth was most welcome. However, being squashed flat as you sleep is about as unpleasant as being cold. Because quilts weighed less than tapestries, they found their true niche as bedclothes.

Quilts for beds are found in inventories of wealthy households. Such quilts were of whole cloth, or broad panels of cloth seamed together for width, lightly padded and backed with whole cloth, then covered with close, decorative stitching in colored silk threads. A gift of 23 sarsenet (silk) quilts from Henry VIII to Katherine Howard,[7] his unfortunate fifth queen, were not enough to keep his affections warm.

People without enough possessions to require inventories may also have had quilts; we may never know. At any rate, they knew about quilts by the time that they traveled to create colonies in the New World, because as soon as there was wealth to spend, quilts were imported to the colonies.

OLD WORLD STYLE

Early American quilts were luxury items. The tastes of southern aristocratic colonists were firmly based in European tradition, including the tradition of great wealth.[8] Southern plantations, established in the late 1500s and early 1600s, sold tobacco to England and were soon highly prosperous. Wealthy plantation owners imported tasteful, upper class goods from England, including whole cloth quilts of the most fashionable fabrics.

Puritan settlers who arrived in the 1620s did not make quilts, nor did they bring them. The standard bed coverings for two generations were thick, practical woven blankets and bed rugs. Building houses, providing food and heat, keeping tattered clothes mended, and collecting things to trade with England left no time for decorative textiles. Patches were placed over holes in the most efficient way possible. But the Puritans did not come to America seeking holy poverty. They wanted freedom from the Church of England, but certainly had no wish to be free of wealth or comfort. The practical Puritans established the new colonies specifically to do an enormous amount of highly profitable export trade to England, and once a steady food supply was ensured they got down to business. Soon Massachusetts Bay colonists also imported whole-cloth quilts from England. At first these were practical, plain wool quilts, or hard-wearing worsted or glazed worsted, called foulard.

ON THE SURFACE

The part of a quilt that first catches the eye—the top—has a long history, too. The Egyptians, artistic just for the joy of it, created appliquéd works, some of which have survived to modern times. A beautiful gazelle leather canopy from the tomb (980 B.C.) of Egyptian Queen Esi-Mem-Kev shows that weaving was not the only craft to reach early heights. Naturally, you cannot weave any designs into leather, so appliqué was used. Hides dyed pale blue, blue-green, pink, and deep and pale yellow were cut into shapes of scarabs, ducks, gazelles, flowers, and snakes, and affixed to white gazelle hide backing.[9]

Appliqué permitted decoration as an afterthought, giving more freedom of design. Egyptian textiles frequently were highly decorated during the weaving process, and techniques abounded. The invention of rigid-heddle looms allowed greater efficiency in some areas of weaving, but made some woven decorative techniques more difficult. Appliqué became a highly adaptable fiber art, and the ancient technique of appliqué is still a lively art in Egypt.

Of course everyone used appliqué for decorative as well as mending purposes. If you had to patch a hole, a few similar patches created a design. Such a useful technique spread along Egyptian trade routes across the rest of the African continent and through the Near East. Sometimes holes were created and appliqué patches were sewn into the holes, a technique called inlaid appliqué. This is especially useful for flags or other items which show both sides simultaneously, and is occasionally used for quilting. Appliquéd surcoats and banners[10] traveled from one continent to another during the Crusades, essential when coats of arms identified friend and foe.

Crusaders' ladies and Renaissance princesses entertained themselves by needlework. Sometimes appliqué showcased the needlework of the lady of the manor and her companions. Vast expanses of both winter quilts and velvet bed hangings were brightened by small motifs worked in delicate silk embroidery and appliquéd to the hangings and quilts. The time for making such beauty was a luxury the common people did not have. Wealthy merchants invested in textiles and wore them as a statement of rank, choosing practical velvet and brocade yard goods to display their success. For ambitious merchants, whole cloth was an essential statement of cash worth.

Multicolored clothing (called parti-colored) became common during the Crusades,[11] and color-block fashions were popular in Medieval and Renaissance Europe. A gentleman might have one blue leg and one red, or a lady might have sleeves of gold and a bodice of green, and a skirt half green and half gold. An occasional Renaissance prince wore bases (quilted military skirts) with color-pieced borders or inverted pleats in a complementary color. Color-block fashions were not really geometric textiles because the only geometry was the tailoring required to fit the human body. It was just fashion feeling frisky.

LOTS OF CHOICES!

Early quilts were of solid color wool, silk, or (rarely) linen. Protein fibers, such as silk and wool, are easy to dye. England was famous for its wools. China held the secrets of silk for centuries, shipping by caravan to Persia and Byzantium along the Silk Road. The secrets of silk worms were smuggled to Byzantium along this route, becoming famous as damasks from Damascus, then falling to Muslim conquerors. They sold their fabrics willingly, but not their secrets.

In the late 16th century, Jesuit missionaries went to China and Japan in Portuguese ships. The captains exchanged missionaries for exotic cargo, giving Europeans a glimpse of oriental elegance. "Chinese madness" swept the Continent. All things oriental were imported, then copied. In 1685 a single ship brought in 8,000 bolts of Chinese silks to France. By the 18th century many Chinese dye techniques—unknown even in the Middle East—had been "borrowed" by European fabric industries, who were shamelessly producing their own brilliant silks.[12]

Plantation ladies of the warmer climes wore and slept beneath European silks as soon as they were available. Puritan ladies of the early 17th century wore plain wool dresses and hoods in a number of colors—reds, browns, greens, purples, and blues—rather than the black that we usually think of.[13] (Those who could afford silk in the early years used it to line their hoods.) Wool quilts also came in various colors. At the end of the century, when they were wealthier, Puritan ladies had plain European silk dresses and quilts, too.

Tree of Life quilt, 1-piece, c. 1700-60, Courtesy of Winterthur Museum, Wilmington DE, gift of Miss Gertrude Brinckle.

Linen, the only cellulose fiber known to 17th century Europe, doesn't accept dye readily. (Even the Egyptians were known for their white linen.) In the late 15th[14] century the Portuguese (on their way to China) investigated the coasts of Africa and India and established merchant colonies. The Portuguese sold exotic European cloth and bought the equally exotic African and Indian cloths. Africa and India had long traditions of decorative cellulose textiles, both cotton and raffia (palm tree fibers). During centuries of working with fine cottons, the Indians had developed dyes and sophisticated methods for making multicolored cotton prints, as beautiful as the tapestries of Europe but light as a feather. Soon the dream textiles for dresses and truly dazzling quilts were fabulously beautiful Indian chintzes. Fabric merchants had numerous variations of the most popular floral patterns made specifically for colonial markets.

Such exotic fabrics were enormously expensive. Extremely wealthy colonists could afford bed-sized, whole-cloth Indian chintz quilts (see photo, above). If you could afford only a small piece, that small piece was stretched. Frequently the method used was an appliqué technique called broderie perse, or Persian embroidery. A small chintz panel (such as the ancient Persian "Tree of Life" design) would be cut apart and the individual motifs spread out and appliquéd onto plain, bed-sized fabric. The piece was then lined, backed, and quilted to emphasize the lovely motifs. Sometimes small amounts of different chintzes were assembled into a single quilt, mixing and matching random motifs into larger compositions. Encouraged by the wildly enthusiastic acceptance of expensive Indian cottons, southern tobacco producers tried growing some cotton.

WICKED WEALTH

Costly textiles were not the only luxuries that English colonists wanted. Whatever was available in Europe was fair game, and that included servants—and slaves. The new colonies were established by freemen and indentured servants. Freemen paid the passage and expenses (and sometimes debts) of poorer folk, who became indentured servants, usually for five to seven years. Naturally it was very good business to have servants helping to establish your fortune in the colonies. As soon as settlers became prosperous enough to pay for indentured servants, they did so. Female servants customarily did much of the endless domestic sewing.

In 1641 it was decided in the Massachusetts Bay Colony that though the indentures of all white servants legally expired, there was no legal end to the indentures of black servants brought from Europe: they became slaves for life, and the children of enslaved mothers were slaves, too.

Slavery was not legal in the English southern colonies, though it already existed in French territories (which later became the Louisiana Purchase). But when cotton grew vigorously in the southern colonies, moral constraints were laid aside: more hands meant more money. In 1689 slavery became legal in the southern English colonies, and the slave trade burgeoned. An Infernal Triangle was established between the New World, Europe, and Africa. Africans were snatched and sold as slaves to cotton growers, who (via slave ships) sold raw cotton to European mills, who (via slave ships) sold the cotton fabric to Africa.

Newly enslaved Africans brought their aesthetics and textile expertise to fertile new lands. In New England both thrift and fashion were a habit, in that order. When thrift met with African aesthetics an amazing thing happened—beauty.

BITS OF HISTORY

"Straight is the line of duty, Curved is the line of beauty,"[15] was stitched on early American samplers because people believed it. It seems unlikely that the inspiration for pieced geometric quilts sprang from stylized gardens of Indian chintz, or from brocade, which was the other admired textile art of the time. Brocade, a silken descendant of tapestry weaving, used several colors to weave motifs with graceful, curved lines. Geometric textiles for the less wealthy tended to be of two colors at a time (limiting thickness) in designs based on stripes, such as checks and plaids, or designs that attempted to copy graceful curves with octagons and polygonal patterns. Even the common taste preferred curves.

Art in Europe was also figural, using recognizable motifs such as plants, humans, animals, etc. Figural art has been popular from prehistoric times because people enjoy making and seeing art about familiar things. Western civilizations

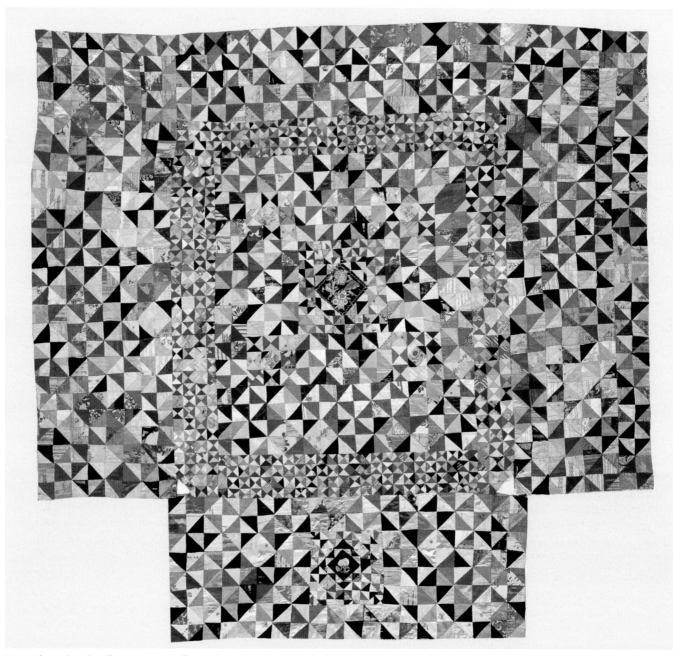

Hour Glass pieced quilt, c. 1788-90, silk, 100" x 104". Courtesy of Winterthur Museum, Wilmington, DE, bequest of Henry Francis de Pont.

didn't have much purely geometric art, though geometric borders were used to frame wall paintings, mosaic floors, fabric, and the like. But the earliest geometric quilt patterns celebrate straight lines and angles, glory in the piecing of corners, and are a beloved symbol of America. Where on earth did they come from?

The earliest extant geometric quilt is the Saltonstall quilt, from Massachusetts, dated to about 1704.[16] Solid color silk triangles were pieced together to form squares in the pattern commonly known as Hour Glass. A similar quilt from the end of the century has the same pattern of triangles. In this later quilt the squares vary in size, creating a highly unusual abstract effect, quite different from the balanced, formal patterns of the European tradition, and different even from the orderly Saltonstall quilt. (See photo above.)

PLAIN GEOMETRY

The Amish, like the Muslims, avoided figural art for religious reasons. The first few Amish arrived in Pennsylvania in 1683, invited by William Penn because of the frightful persecutions they suffered in Germany. Many more Amish came in the 18th century. But the Amish preferred woven blankets and avoided the artistic customs of their new neighbors for a long time. It was not until the last quarter of the 19th century[17] that Amish women began to make quilts in sedate geometric patterns, using large squares and rectangles of unpatterned cloth. By this time geometric quilt blocks were a flourishing American art form, with hundreds of variations. Clearly the Amish were not the originators of geometric quilt blocks.

But there were in the colonies people with a living tradition of geometric textile art, including dyed, appliquéd, and pieced textiles. Throughout Africa displays of cloth were a form of wealth and status, and cloth was used as money[18], as well as for healing.[19] Egyptians had been producing dyed cellulose fabrics prior to 3000 B.C., and cotton textiles were woven in the Sudan from at least the 5th century A.D.,[20] and by Nigerian weavers before the 9th century A.D.[21] Africans had also been enthusiastic purchasers of European fabrics which were treasured as exotic luxury goods, or reprocessed into luxury African fabrics, though they also processed their own wild silk.[22] Some European cloth was dyed and used for appliqué, (see photo below) some was raveled for thread which was used to weave new fabrics, and some was resist dyed into patterned textiles.[23] Equatorial African embroidered, dyed, and appliquéd cloths were legendary and highly prized throughout the world, until the justification of slavery required that the technical achievements of an entire continent be defamed. For slavery to proceed unabated, Africans must be dismissed as savage primitives. Nevertheless, the Hour Glass pattern seen in the earliest pieced quilts of colonial America was a traditional symbolic pattern in African textiles. We must seriously consider the likelihood that African slaves were the source of the pieced quilt, symbol of American creativity and thrift.

LINES OF DESCENT

Symbolic art uses shapes to hide a multitude of meanings and has been used in ceremonial art for centuries. Sometimes the symbols are recognizable, such as wreaths, crowns, and fishes. But in societies that avoid figural art, symbols are simply shapes, such as spirals and triangles. Nevertheless, they have meaning within their own cultural context, and that meaning may be more profound because it is hidden in abstraction.

The 7th century birth of Islam spurred the development of abstract geometric art because of strict prohibitions against figural art. Geometric art allowed sumptuous decoration of mosques and palaces, and traditional symbolic art of tribal Africa enriched the geometric art of Muslim Africa.[24] There was even a traditional Muslim pieced wall hanging—the qibleh—for which antique textiles and embroideries were precisely cut and stitched to indicate the mihrab, the direction of prayers to Mecca.[25]

Itinerant artisans carried the designs and techniques into the Byzantine Empire, then into Moorish Spain. Returning Crusaders brought beautiful objects from the East. Wealthy Europeans wanted such beauty in their homes but preferred figural art, so geometric art lapsed into the background. Some 300 years before we find it in a Massachusetts quilt, the Hour Glass quilt pattern can be seen as a tile floor in the illuminated manuscript Grandes Heures of Jean, Duke of Berry, painted in 1409.[26] In the 16th century a textile mat from Equatorial Africa was used as the background in a Portuguese painting of the Annunciation to the Virgin Mary.[27] But though African geometric patterns were known in Europe, they did not become part of the European artistic vocabulary.

FANCY GEOMETRY

African designs relegated to the background in Europe were still at the forefront of the living African artistic tradition. When newly enslaved hands were filled with scraps of textiles too precious to be discarded, Africans drew on generations of geometric wealth and expertise. Taking in hand their traditions and their realities, they made something to be proud of—something that spoke of home.

African geometric art is hinted at in a number of quilting traditions, and while it is easy to see similarities in simple geometric patterns from widely separated regions, sometimes influences are too overt to be ignored. It is unlikely that geometric textile influences went from America to Africa because American quilts were made strictly for home use, so no one was exporting them anywhere. Yet among the earliest American quilts it is easy to see design elements very different from the European norm, but very similar to the African.

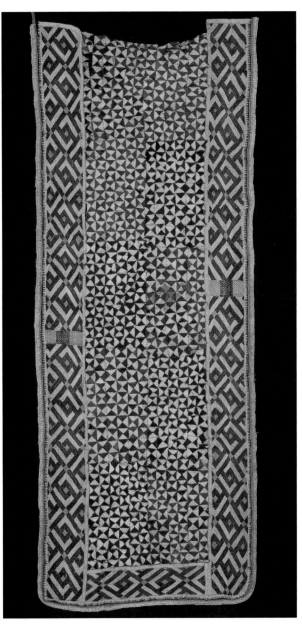

Beaten bark cloth with appliqué, Hour Glass pattern, Kuba, Republic of Zaire, 58½" x 27½". ©Indiana University Art Museum: Gift of Dr. and Mrs. Henry R. Hope.

Spiky Tree of Life quilt, courtesy of Winterthur Museum, Wilmington, DE, museum purchase.

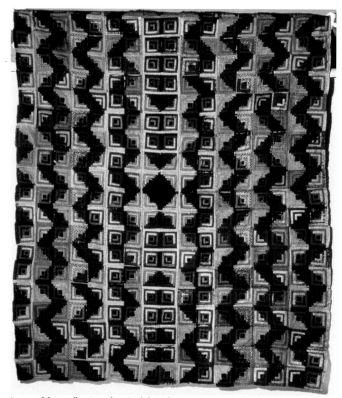

Log cabin quilt–Streak o' Lightening pattern. Made by Dolly Jackson, c. 1860-1870. Courtesy of the Louisiana State Museum, New Orleans, LA.

The Log Cabin pattern (see photo above right), made of layered thin fabric strips with sloped corners, looks remarkably similar to Ashanti kente cloth. (See photo, page 17.) A familiar pattern may also contain decorative shapes that are symbolic, such as the zigzag. In some African cultures "a vocabulary of semi-abstract symbols, essentially geometric in nature, is used to decorate both men's and women's clothing."[28] It represented the snake symbol of fertility to some African cultures, and wisdom to a specific group of African priestesses. Even long after an esoteric meaning has been lost, the familiar symbol may be repeated.

Other traditional African textiles suggest quilt patterns familiar to us. Narrow strip textiles, traditionally woven in Africa by men, were sometimes sewn together with offset geometric patterns. Echoes of such textiles can be seen in strip quilts such as Wild Geese Flying and Roman Columns.

From strip textiles it is only a small step to highly practical quilt blocks of all kinds, which allowed discrete sections of quilts to be composed, worked, and set aside as time or materials demanded. Blocks of appliqué solved the problem of having to acquire whole cloth to display the designs, while the aesthetics of balance were unchanged. Indeed, many appliqué block quilts are far more stiff and formal than broderie perse chintz quilts. This may stem from the European aesthetic that asymmetry equals informality, and informality equals poverty.

When purchasing ready-made goods, Americans preferred to buy imports in the European style. Besides, it would be moral confusion to import as luxuries the traditional textiles from a continent you characterized as savage and raided for human chattel. But utilizing the creativity of everyone—even slaves—was normal colonial behavior, and geometric pieced quilts from scraps were warm and beautiful. They had always been luxury textiles: they still were. The startling beauty of the geometric patterns and practicality bridged cultural chasms. Quilts become a shared creative endeavor of ladies and their slaves.[29]

Because of their ease, designs with straight vertical and horizontal seams were often chosen for little girls' first attempts at piecing, but many pieced designs demanded the highest technical skills, and were obviously made because the beautiful design made difficulties worthwhile.

The origin of pieced quilts from slaves might explain the lingering tendency to think of pieced quilts as having been worked for reasons of unavoidable thrift, and even as faintly lower class than appliquéd quilts. But when thrift was essential, it was not limited to pieced quilts. Vast numbers of appliquéd quilts were made during times of tremendous economic hardship, such as the American Revolution, the Civil War, and the Depression. Scraps and old clothes were cut up and used for appliqué quilts, too. Pieced or appliquéd, quilt makers chose patterns for their intrinsic beauty. Some quilts combined the two techniques and had the best of both traditions. From this time on both pieced and patchwork designs developed at the speed of sight, displaying the tastes and skills of the makers.

ENTERTAINING WITH NEEDLES

There was always an expectation that women would amuse themselves with their needles. Thomas Jefferson exhorted his daughter to depend on her needle skills to allow her polite distraction in boring company,[30] while young men looked askance at young ladies who lacked "needle wisdom."[31] Any needle art that allowed a woman to be creative and expressive

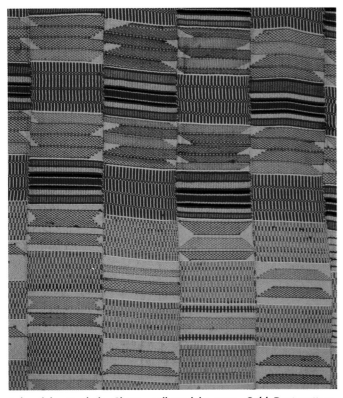

Ashanti kente cloth, Ghana, collected in 1951, Gold Dust pattern. Image Number 1870 (1), The American Museum of Natural History, New York, NY, courtesy of the Library Special Collections.

could expect to become popular. Making quilts also became an entertainment that women used to share time with each other. Women spent time sewing the blocks for their quilt tops while exchanging essential local information. After a woman had completed one or more quilt tops, she might treat herself to a "quilting," now called quilting bees. Often these were in preparation for a wedding, but any reason to take a day for pleasant accomplishment was a good reason. At these large parties friends from near and far could gather and finish several quilts while eating and talking. Sometimes husbands and admirers stayed to help thread needles, sometimes they stayed away until evening, returning to dine, dance, and escort the ladies home.

Fashions of the times in fabric and composition can be traced through three centuries of American quilts. Each advance of science and industry can be seen in the fronts and backs of quilts, and each advance spurred renewed creativity in quilters. The cotton gin allowed American short-staple cotton to be swiftly and efficiently cleaned. Illegally imported spinning machine technology and steam mechanized weaving made cottons far more affordable than ever before.

Block prints from India were countered with French engraved copper plates producing delicate monochrome toile prints (see photo right). Copper plates were followed by copper rolls, which could print yards of fabric with as many as 20 separate colors, so the infant chemical industry was shoved along by demands for more colors and colorfast dyes. Coal technology, burgeoning with the steam engine technology, led to the discovery of aniline (coal tar) dyes. The range of colors from vegetable dyes was expanded each decade, adding more

and more to the wealth of textile choices available. Each new hue discovered makes it easier for us to date antique quilts.

The invention of the sewing machine was a blessing dropped straight from heaven. With essential sewing completed in a matter of hours (rather than days), women could actually use needles for pleasure for a change. They turned to machine-piecing of quilts with enthusiasm. While this limited the time spent in pleasant groups sewing quilt blocks, it increased the number of quilt tops that could be an excuse for a big party, and it allowed women to make lots more quilts. Lest we become too wistful for the good old handmade quilts of long ago, the women who handmade everything from underwear to overcoats were profoundly grateful for sewing machines, and even after they pieced a quilt by machine there was plenty of hand quilting to become wistful over. Never be cavalier about your conveniences. Your treasured antique quilts probably came from their new "free" time.

FADS AND FASHIONS

Despite limitations of time and money, there were a number of distinct fads in quilting that make quilt history even more interesting. The death of George Washington in 1799 made mourning embroideries, replete with doves and willows, highly fashionable.[32] The fashion lasted about 30 years, and its effects hung in parlors until the Civil War spawned an odd parallel in quilts. Memory quilts were made of fabrics worn by the dear departed, often with the person's name and death date embroidered in the center of the block. Mourning quilts were used during the period of mourning itself (which could last for a decade), using a subdued palette of black, white, and grey, in dart or cross and star motifs.[33] One truly morbid quilt has a starry top surrounding a center square representing

Detail of traditional French Toile print fabric.

Kentucky Coffin quilt, Kentucky Historical Society, Frankfort, KY.

the family plot. Small coffins embroidered with the names of family members are arranged around the outer edge, and were moved into the center as required.[34] One wonders if it was used in the guest room. (See photo, above.)

Many more cheerful memorial and commemorative traditions existed. Album or presentation quilts were gifts to friends and honored members of the community (see photo, page 19). They might be made of assorted blocks, allowing the contributors to express themselves through various designs. Sometimes signatures and quotations were embroidered onto matching theme blocks. The Baltimore album quilts, famous for both their beauty and their numbers, were made of quilt blocks from groups of friends. The pieced and appliquéd blocks of different designs were united into a pleasing whole, sometimes formally arranged around a central medallion.

Usually each member of such a group received an album quilt, often as a wedding gift.

As more and more Americans moved west, album and presentation quilts became memories of the friends and families the women left behind. They also took with them the quilt designs of their homes, spreading regional patterns across the country. This makes a fascinating study of quilt pattern migrations which started new regional traditions.

Some patterns are found in so many places that identifying the donor state is impossible. Other patterns are so rare as to be a neon arrow pointing to the place of origin. Because quilt patterns were simply household art, no one claimed ownership over designs. Ideas were shared among friends, changed at will, and have become the cultural property of the nation, a continuing source of creative wealth. Often, though the names

Pratt Family Album Quilt, United States (Delaware River Valley) about 1842, glazed cotton appliqué, silk embroidery, and ink drawing on cotton; cotton fringe; 118" x 132" (including fringe). Denver Art Museum Neusteter Textile Collection, Denver, CO. Funds from Nancy Lake Benson and Bruce Benson and the Anonymous Acquisition Challenge Grant 1985.300.

have been changed to suit new circumstances, the faces are very familiar.

The Star of Bethlehem pattern, (see photo, top page 20) popular at the beginning of the 19th century, has made itself at home in all states and essential in many. In Texas, the Lone Star State, it became the Lone Star pattern for obvious reasons. It also traveled with missionaries to the Indian schools of the Great Plains, and is now the traditional presentation pattern of Lakota (Sioux) quilters.

UNDER COVERS

Some less desirable traditions migrated, too. Slavery, that social bane, moved out of the colonies into states, and out of states into territories. Quilts played a fascinating, if little known role in this chapter of America.

The underground railroad was set up to help slaves flee to areas where slavery was forbidden, whether a neighboring state or even a neighboring country. There is evidence from statements made by slaves who followed these routes at the time, and from later inherited oral tradition, that quilts with specific designs, quilting patterns, and colors were used to guide fleeing slaves along safe routes to safe houses. Quilts were hung out in the open as if to air them out, and people who were not aware of the codes took no notice. The patterns used may have been drawn from traditional African geometric textile designs, but since different African cultures had different meanings for various patterns, this area of quilting history is still a rich field for researchers.[35]

Rising Sun or Star of Bethlehem. Made by Mary (Betsy) Totten of Tottenville, Staten Island, New York, c. 1810, 94" square. National Museum of American History, Behring Center. ©2004 Smithsonian Institution, Washington DC.

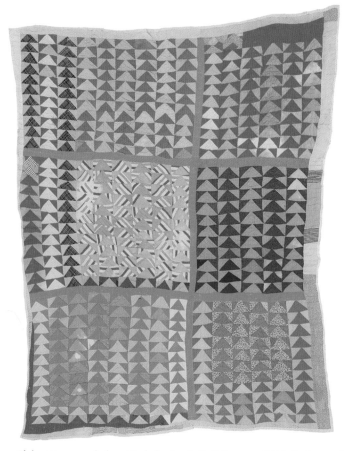

Flying Geese variation. Made by Annie E. Pettway, c. 1935. Cotton and wool, 86" x 71". Collection of the Tinwood Alliance.

NO COVERS

In the early 1800s missionaries took quilting skills to islands that required quilts not at all, but that didn't dissuade them from teaching Hawaiians to appliqué and quilt in missionary schools. But because traditional Hawaiian clothing was minimal and the new style of modest missionary clothing used whole widths of unshaped cloth, there were no scraps. Undeterred, they bought bolts of whole cloth, cut out silhouettes of the beauties around them for inspiration, and appliquéd repeated motifs around an intricate central medallion. No amount of pieced calicoes could improve on the shape of a pineapple (long admired in the colonies), or of an orchid, so appliquéd silhouettes remain the quilting tradition of the islands.[36]

Other islands, too, have adopted this approach to their natural beauty. In New Zealand, where quilts are welcome, they have copied their own flora and fauna to appliquéd quilts.

CRAZY COVERS

Perfection can be a burden at times, and even the most disciplined quilters got bored with perfect lines, perfect corners, perfect curves. They went crazy, and their quilting went with them. Victorian exuberance of design encouraged lots of everything, layered if need be. Beautiful silks and velvets and ribbons were taken in whatever shape they came and stitched next to other random shapes. The seams were embroidered with fancy stitches in silk threads, and blocks of this millinery madness were assembled into throws and edged with silk ruffles…not often quilted, but lined with silk. Women who had never quilted also took the opportunity to go crazy, and for a quarter of a century or so, everyone was happily demented under a mountain of glowing silk fragments and soft velvet scraps. After such wild self-indulgence people set aside quilts and began to do other things for awhile.

Dedicated quilters quietly continued their work, often in poor rural areas.[37] The quilters were often descendents of slaves, continuing the traditions they had inherited. Here we find the lasting aesthetic traditions of African textiles, and they are profound: variations of a pattern vying with the original, just like musical variations on a theme; asymmetry used as visual syncopation; vibrant colors in astonishing combinations; and symbols rich with centuries of meanings, sometimes unknown even to the artists.

Again Europe embraced the African aesthetic, this time in paintings of Paul Klee and Piet Mondrian. Much of the radical stuff of art galleries was really the continuum of African art, and the daily visual fare of sharecroppers. (See photo, left.)

RECOVERS

Though quilting never really dies out, sometimes we take it for granted for a few generations, just until the old quilts wear out. This allows us to rediscover quilting and have exciting revivals. Scrap bags had become full to bursting during the quilting hiatus toward the end of the 19th century. In true American fashion, the revival of 1910 opened new territory. The first history of quilting was published.[38] Quilt patterns

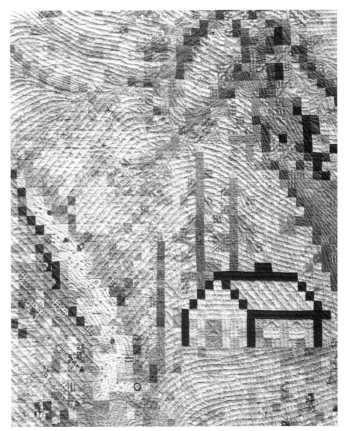

The Matterhorn made by Myrtle M. Fortner, c. 1934, pieced cotton quilt; 104" x 85½" in Denver Art Museum Neusteter Textile Collection, Denver, CO. Gift of Melvin Dorsett, 1967.89.

Detail of the Matterhorn quilt, depicting the many small pieces used and close quilting lines. Today's quilters are replicating this style with computer-generated pixelated designs.

that should have been handed down had become mislaid, so newspapers published weekly quilting columns and women's magazines began to publish new or rediscovered quilt designs, both pieced and appliquéd. Carefully orchestrated designs were published and appeared on hundreds of beds, in their original or in revised forms (helpful for quilting historians). Competitive quilting became an American pastime. When beautiful original designs were not enough to take the prize at state fairs, women began piecing quilts and counting the pieces, some of which numbered well above 60,000 for one quilt (see photos, above). Despite this, the quality of quilts was extremely fine, and many of those revival quilts are treasured heirlooms, used for best or saved for posterity.

The popularity of quilting continued through the poverty of the Dirty '30s. Quilting was a comfort when the country was suffering and people were desperate to get another turn from a piece of fabric. Appliqué quilts allowed a person to take the few inches of good cloth from a shirt and use it to warm a child or commemorate a triumph. Creativity and making something beautiful out of nothing gave them hope. But time got short and quilting went into hibernation during World War II. Precious fabric scraps were put aside for the peaceful quilting times that were sure to come after the war. Old quilters never die: they just fold away.

After the war, manufacturers made fluffy blankets and comforters far too beautiful for war weary women to resist, and they bought their bedding rather than spend hours stitching.

In the 1960s young men and women who remembered sleeping under granny's quilts got quite nostalgic and tried to recapture those memories. They began to buy old quilts and examine them, to copy and analyze them, and to write histories about them. Color printing allowed people to see volumes of more fabulous quilts than anyone imagined existed, in all their glory and variety. Similarities have been found and traced, family trees of both quilt patterns and their quilters flourish, while new designers travel farther and farther into the lands of geometric abstraction or infinite appliqué.

Bits of history gleaned from quilts still tell us secrets about the transmission of technology, beauty, and culture by anonymous quilters of centuries past. It is interesting to consider how much of the way Americans see the world—and how the world now sees the world—was formed by the geometry of bedclothes. Instead of balanced, formal design, Americans rich and poor, in all regions of the country woke up and went to sleep with abstract, asymmetrical, fractured fabric art surrounding them. Pieces from the scrap bag could be made into anything with a pair of scissors and a needle and thread, and if it was good enough for you, it was good enough. The creative freedom of that kind of thinking has brought us a very long way. Let it take us a long way, too. 🌀

quilting basics

BEGINNING A QUILT STARTS WITH SIMPLE items—fabric, needle, thread, and cutting tool. A plan would be nice, but it's not essential, since many creative quilts have grown from spontaneous inspiration. The basics are easily understood, and you will quickly increase your repertoire of skills, all the while making the language of quilting your own. Everything needed to begin the experience is explained in detail here. After only a few pages you will want to venture headlong into the realm of quilting, whether in stores, or catalogs, or on the Internet. There you will find a myriad of instructions, gadgets, fabric, patterns, teachers, friends, and mentors, all in abundance no matter where you live.

What used to be simply "the basics" now becomes the springboard for your imagination as you take a simple pattern and turn it into a geometrical, colorful, one-of-a-kind work of art. Do not wait a moment longer, turn the pages, learn the basics, plan a project, and begin the adventure. Early efforts will quickly transform into accomplishments and become lifelong treasures. Who would have thought that a few snippets of fabric could become something so wonderful? The door will open and invite you into a world of quilting where everyone is welcome.

parts of a quilt

binding

outer border

middle border

pieced inner border

lattice/sashing

appliqué

post

pieced block

batting

backing

quilting stitches

quilt top

At the start of each new class for first time quilters I am reminded of the line from a song in the Sound of Music, "Let's start at the very beginning." It is important to have some understanding of what a quilt is before we can begin to plan, design, and make it. Knowledge and familiarity with the names of the parts of a quilt will assist with the construction process. The diagram above will help you attach a name to each of the different parts that make up the whole quilt.

PARTS OF A QUILT

APPLIQUÉ: A cut-out shape that is stitched onto a background fabric either by hand or machine.

BACKING: The fabric on the backside of the quilt. The backing can be either one fabric, pieced to the needed size, or several fabrics sewn together. This can be a way to use leftover lengths of fabrics or simply to add interest to the backside of the quilt.

BATTING: The filling layer between the quilt top and the backing of the quilt. It adds warmth and gives thickness to the quilt.

BINDING: The strip of fabric sewn around the outer edge of the quilt. It encases the edges of the three layers: quilt top, batting, and backing.

BLOCK: The basic unit of a traditional pieced quilt. Quilt blocks can be pieced, appliquéd, stenciled, embroidered, or any combination of these techniques. A solid, unpieced block that is incorporated into the quilt top is called an alternate block.

BORDER: A strip or strips of fabric that form a frame around the outer edge of a quilt top. The strips can be plain, pieced, appliquéd, stenciled or any combination of these techniques. Some quilts have multiple borders while others have none at all.

LATTICE/SASHING: Strips of fabric that are sewn in horizontal or vertical rows, or both, within the body of the quilt top. The strips can be plain, pieced, appliquéd, or any combination of these techniques.

POST: Corner posts or corner stones are pieces of fabric either plain or pieced that meet at the intersections of sashings or corners of border strips.

QUILTING STITCHES: Hand or machine stitches that hold the three layers of the quilt together. The quilting stitches add texture to the overall design of the quilt.

QUILT TOP: The front or top layer of the quilt.

SLEEVE: A tube of fabric that is attached to the top edge of the backing of the quilt. It is used for hanging the quilt.

quilting supplies

As you look through the following pages you may ask yourself how so many supplies could be needed to make a quilt. The reality is that one could make a wonderful quilt with only fabric, scissors, needle and thread, and a quilting hoop. Why, then, all the "stuff?" Over the years, as quilting gained popularity in a society that is fast-paced and likes quick results, designers and manufacturers searched for ways to make the process easier and faster. How could one truly make "a quilt in a day" without a little help from tools to speed up the process? While perusing stacks of catalogs and attending shows featuring the newest and best items on the market, it became difficult to decide which items to include. In this book you'll find our favorites, but it is important to know that new items are being introduced every day. Use these as a guideline and find what works best for you.

PLANNING, DESIGNING, AND PREPARATION

The inspiration for making a quilt can come from a variety of sources. Perhaps you want to make a quilt for a new baby or an upcoming wedding. You begin to look for ideas to help with planning. Looking through pattern books and magazines and visiting fabric stores can assist with the first step in the quiltmaking process. Often an exciting new line of fabric will provide the inspiration for a new quilt.

TOP ROW: Fabric, proportional scale, 3-in-1 Color Tool.
MIDDLE ROW: Pattern and design books, foundation piecing paper, photo transfer sheets, quilt design software, light table, design paper.

BOTTOM ROW: Fabric bundles, acrylic templates, vellum sheets, template plastic, pins, permanent marking pen, fabric view finder, reducing glass.

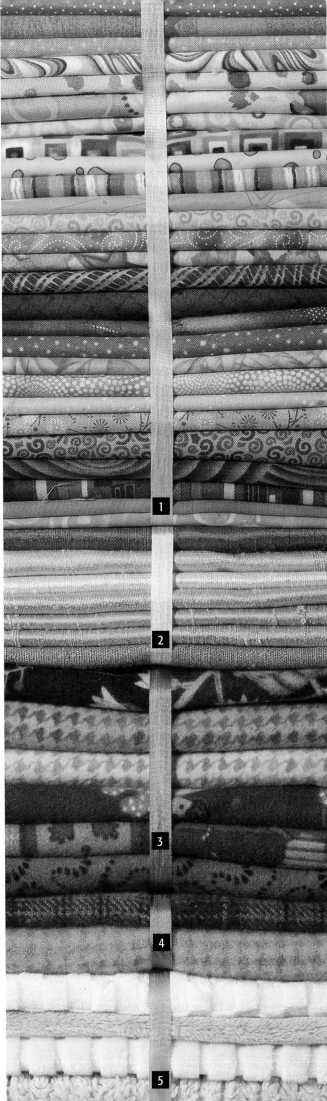

LEFT: An assortment of fabric: 1-cotton, 2-silk, 3-flannel, 4-wool, 5-velour.

FABRIC

It is difficult to find a quiltmaker who doesn't love fabric. The look, feel, colors, and designs of a fabric draw us in and entice us to take it home with us. Shopping for fabric is an exciting part of the quiltmaking process. Devoted quilters are always searching for just the right piece or something new to add to their already extensive collections. Fabric and quilt shops offer an abundance of choices, so the quiltmaker can find almost anything she wants. Most of us like to see and feel the fabric before making the purchase, but if you enjoy a quick online shopping trip, there are many websites that are ready at the click of a mouse to meet your every need. Mail order catalogs offer yet another alternative.

Throughout the years quilts have been made from a variety of fabrics. In times when fabrics were scarce, scraps from old clothing and blankets were used to make utility quilts for bed coverings. We're fortunate today that so many fabrics are readily available. For most traditional quilters, 100% cotton is the fabric of choice. Cotton fibers are natural, easy to wash, and durable.

Choosing good quality fabrics for your quilt project is well worth the investment in time and money. As you begin shopping you may find a wide price range for what appears to be the exact same piece of fabric. A quiltmaker should become an educated consumer and learn to distinguish a good piece of fabric from a lesser piece. A higher price does not always mean better quality, however, it can be an indicator. There is good-quality cotton as well as poor-quality cotton. Quality issues are generally not a concern while shopping at the local quilt shop, which carries top-quality fabrics especially suited to quilting. When shopping at other stores that carry a wide range of fabrics, you need to be a little more discriminating. Here are a few points to help you with the decision-making process.

• Read the end of the bolt for information such as fabric content, width, and care instructions. If the fabric is sold off the bolt in "flat folds," check any labels, read the signs, or ask a salesperson for this information.

ABOVE: The end of the fabric bolt provides valuable information, including fabric content, width of fabric, and care instructions.

- What is the feel of the fabric (called the "hand")? As you begin touching fabrics you will find they are not all created equal. You will quickly discover the hand of different fabrics can vary from being thin and flimsy to stiff with almost a glazed feel.
- Check the clarity of the printed designs and colors. Are they consistent throughout the fabric? If you are considering a fabric with a directional design such as a plaid, look closely at the selvage edges. Is the pattern printed straight and parallel to the selvages? A lesser grade of fabric may not be.

The amount of fabric needed for a quilt is referred to as the yardage required. In some countries, such as the United States, fabric is cut and sold in increments based on the 36" yard. Countries in Europe sell fabric based on the 39" meter. Following is a chart of the most commonly cut yardages. Most quilt-weight, 100% cotton fabrics measure approximately 42" from selvage to selvage. After shrinkage (if pre-washing) and trimming selvages away, fabric will have a "usable width" of approximately 40". Actual usable width will vary slightly from fabric to fabric.

YARDS	INCHES	METERS	CENTIMETERS
1/8	4½"	0.11	11.4
1/4	9"	0.23	22.9
1/3	12"	0.31	30.5
3/8	13½"	0.34	34.3
1/2	18"	0.46	45.7
5/8	22½"	0.57	57.2
2/3	24"	0.62	61
3/4	27"	0.69	68.6
7/8	31½"	0.80	80
1	36"	0.91	91.4

When selecting fabric for a quilt, the types of prints, size of the prints and color all play a part in the look of the finished quilt. Choose a variety of fabrics including solids and prints, and to make your quilt even more interesting visually, vary the size (scale) of the prints. To learn more about the importance of color when selecting fabric for a quilt, turn to page 72.

RIGHT: 1-small prints, 2-medium prints, 3-large prints, 4-stripes, 5-plaids, 6-dots, 7-batiks, 8-tone-on-tone prints.

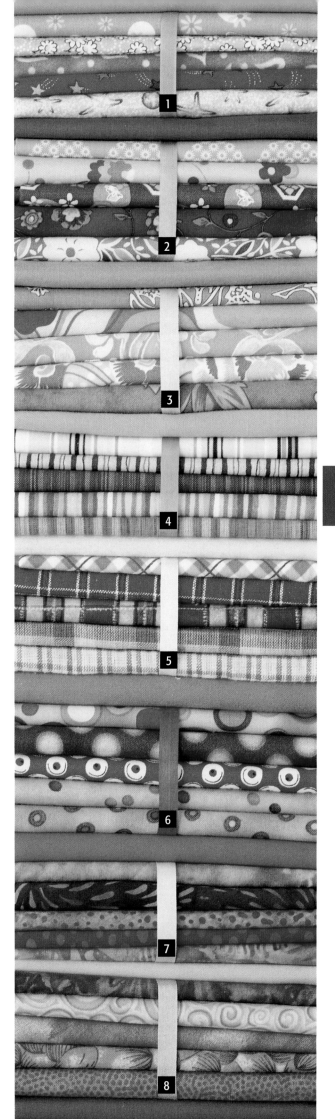

PRE-CUT FABRICS

Ready-to-purchase fabric bundles made from fabric pieces cut to a uniform size and shape are commonly referred to as "pre-cuts." They are usually packaged by fabric manufacturers and contain one piece of each fabric in a line or collection. Pre-cut shapes include rectangles, strips cut from the width of the fabric, squares, and triangles. Due to the popularity of these handy bundles, many quilt shops are now custom cutting, blending, and packaging pre-cuts by color, theme, or collection. Many quilters like using pre-cuts for the following reasons:

- Pre-cuts take the guess work out of planning a quilt. Because the bundles are composed of one fabric collection or fabrics specifically selected to be used together, there is no question of "will these fabrics look good together?"

- Pre-cuts are a real time saver. Depending on the design of your quilt, some pre-cuts can be used "as is" and some will require only minor sub-cutting thus eliminating several cutting steps.

- Pre-cuts offer a lot of variety for quilters for a reasonable price. Also, there is usually less waste when using pre-cuts than there is when shapes are cut from yardage.

TYPES OF PRE-CUTS

Fabric manufacturers frequently add new sizes and shapes to their pre-cut lines so the styles of pre-cuts on the market are continually increasing. Because manufacturers choose their own names for pre-cuts, two packages of $2^1/2$" wide strips from different manufacturers may have different names. For example, one company may call their strips Jelly Rolls while another might use the name Sushi Rolls. But names aren't nearly as important as the size of the cut.

Below are some of the most common names and sizes of pre-cuts. If there are a standard number of pieces in a bundle, that number has been included. Always check the number of pieces in a pre-cut against your pattern requirements.

NAME	CUT SIZE
Fat Quarter Bundles	approx. 18" x 22"
Fat Eighth Bundles	approx. 9" x 22"
Petit Fours	$2^1/2$" x $2^1/2$"
Charm Packs	5" x 5" or $5^1/2$" x $5^1/2$"
Layer Cakes	10" x 10"
Jelly Rolls	$2^1/2$" x width of fabric
Honey Buns	$1^1/2$" x width of fabric
Dessert Rolls	5" x width of fabric
Bali Pops	$2^1/2$" x width of fabric
Sushi Rolls	$2^7/8$" x width of fabric
Twice The Charms	$5^1/2$" x 22"
Turnovers	6" x 6" x $8^1/2$"
Jelly Cakes	1 Jelly Roll and 1 Layer Cake
Charming Jelly Cake	1 Charm Pack, 1 Jelly Roll and 1 Layer Cake
Sweet Box	1 Honey Bun from each of 2 different collections

Purchasing bundles of fabrics in coordinating colors can take the challenge out of selecting fabrics for quilt projects.

SUB-CUTTING PRE-CUTS

While pre-cuts can be used as purchased, there may be times when you want to sub-cut the pieces. The following diagrams show a few of the different ways of sub-cutting, the cutting and finished size of sub-cuts, and the number of pieces each pre-cut piece will yield.

From a 5" Charm square:

Cut 2¹/₂"x 2¹/₂" to yield four 2" x 2" squares.

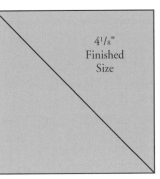

Cut once diagonally to yield two 4¹/₈" triangles.

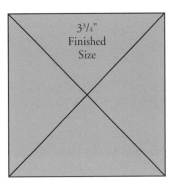

Cut twice diagonally to yield four 3³/₄" triangles.

Cut once 2¹/₂"x 5" to yield two 2"x 4¹/₂" rectangles.

From a 10" Layer Cake square:

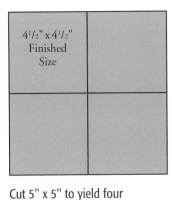

Cut 5" x 5" to yield four 4¹/₂"x 4¹/₂" squares.

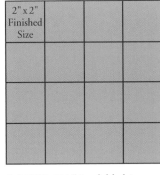

Cut 5" x 5" and 2¹/₂"x 2¹/₂" to yield two 4¹/₂"x 4¹/₂" squares and eight 2" x 2" squares.

Cut 2¹/₂"x 2¹/₂" to yield sixteen 2" x 2" squares.

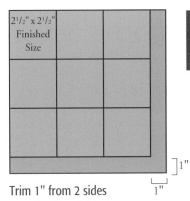

Trim 1" from 2 sides
Cut 3"x 3" to yield nine 2¹/₂" squares.

29

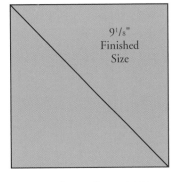

Cut once diagonally to yield two 9¹/₈" triangles.

Cut 2"x 10" to yield five 1¹/₂"x 9¹/₂" rectangles.

Cut 5" x 5" to yield four squares. Cut each square once diagonally to yield eight 4¹/₈"x 4¹/₈" triangles.

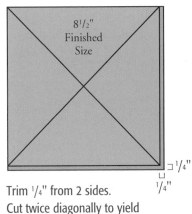

Trim ¹/₄" from 2 sides. Cut twice diagonally to yield four 8¹/₂" triangles.

HELPFUL HINTS FOR WORKING WITH PRE-CUTS

- The fabric pieces in pre-cut packages are usually not pre-washed. Washing is not recommended because pre-cut shapes are delicate and may distort when washed. If pre-cuts must be pre-washed, hand rinse them very gently. Lay them flat on a towel and pat to remove excess water. Gently smooth the pieces, air dry, and press.

- Some pre-cut pieces have pinked edges. Do not trim off the points. Most manufacturers include the points in the measurement given on the package. For example, the measurement across a 10" square from one outside point to the opposite outside point (not from valley to valley) should be 10". Be sure to measure your pre-cuts just in case they are different.

- To sew an accurate $^1/_4$" seam allowance, first measure across the fabric piece as described above. Then, align the points, valleys, or any point in between with your $^1/_4$" seam guide as needed to sew an exact $^1/_4$" seam. If your fabric piece measures larger than 10", trim as needed to make the squares exactly 10".

QUILT DESIGN SOFTWARE

If you are computer savvy, you may enjoy designing your quilt projects with one of the quilt design software programs available. They are useful for pieced and appliquéd blocks, paper piecing, and quilting stencils. They allow you to design patterns, print templates, provide cutting charts, and estimate yardage. You can also add color and even the latest fabrics or scan your own fabrics into the shapes. The programs have a library full of patterns from which to choose, or you can draw and print your own original ones. Embroidery designs are also an added feature.

INKJET FABRIC SHEETS allow you to print sharp, photo quality images directly from the computer.

FOUNDATION SHEETS are perfect for printing paper patterns. They run through the printer just like paper.

FOR APPLIQUÉ PATTERNS SELF-ADHESIVE TEMPLATE SHEETS allow you to print the individual pattern pieces from the computer directly onto the paper. The patterns are self-adhesive and reusable.

ADDITIONAL SUPPLIES

QUILT PATTERNS: Often found in books and magazines or sold in packets.

COLOR WHEEL OR COLOR TOOL: Designed specifically for quilters, they can be very helpful when selecting color combinations for a quilt project.

LIGHT TABLE: Provides a fast and easy way to trace designs and patterns.

DESIGN WALL: Design walls are large vertical surfaces made from a material you can pin into (such as Celotex®) or covered with a fabric such as flannel or felt that fabric pieces will adhere to without pinning. Design walls are very useful for auditioning fabrics, arranging pieces in a block, or planning block placement for a quilt top. They can be small and portable or large and stationary.

To make a removable design wall, simply tack a length(s) of white flannel to a wall or door. For best results, pull the fabric taut and tack the bottom corners in place.

For a small design wall, staple flannel over artist stretcher strips or simply cover a piece of foamcore with flannel.

For a large, durable design wall, nail a 4' x 8' sheet of foamcore, Celotex®, or wallboard to a wooden frame made from 1" x 8' boards. Cover the design wall with flannel if desired. The design wall can either be leaned against or secured to a wall.

REDUCING GLASS AND VALUE FINDER: Provide the viewer with a better sense of color and balance and even a distinction between value (light, medium, and dark), which is extremely helpful when selecting fabrics and planning the layout of a quilt.

PROPORTIONAL SCALE: Helpful if you wish to resize a quilt pattern, stencil, or anything from ½" to 50".

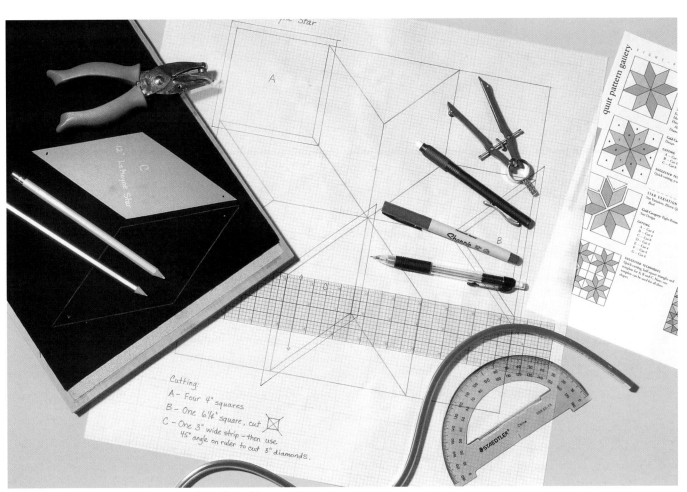

CLOCKWISE FROM LEFT: Sandpaper board, marking pencils, template, 1/16" hole punch, graph paper, pattern, compass, marking pens, drafting ruler, flex design ruler, protractor.

DRAFTING SUPPLIES

GRAPH PAPER: 8-to-the-inch graph paper works well for drafting patterns.

DRAFTING RULER: Clear, thin ruler with accurate markings used for drafting.

TEMPLATE PLASTIC: Clear or gridded plastic used to make patterns of individual shapes. Marks best using an ultra fine-point permanent marker.

FLEX DESIGN RULER: Used for creating curved lines when drafting patterns.

COMPASS AND PROTRACTOR: Used for drafting curved lines.

1/16" HOLE PUNCH: Used for marking dots on templates.

SANDPAPER BOARD: Keeps fabric from slipping while marking. Make your own by gluing a large sheet of fine-grit sandpaper to a lightweight board or purchase one ready-made at your local shop.

CUTTING SUPPLIES
ROTARY CUTTERS

The rotary cutter was first introduced in 1979 by Olfa. This cutting tool revolutionized the world of quilting. The rotary cutter is a hand-held tool with a rolling, stainless steel, razor-sharp blade. Cutters are made in a variety of sizes, styles, and handle shapes. Up to four layers of fabric can easily and accurately be cut into straight, curved, and even scalloped edges. This cutter needs to be respected as a sharp tool and must ALWAYS be kept out of the reach of children.

With proper use the blades will last through several projects; however, over time they will dull or become nicked. There are both replacement blades and blade sharpeners available. The sharpeners will help with a dull blade but a badly nicked blade should be replaced. Save old blades for paper cutting, scrapbooking, or wallpapering. When disposing of blades, always wrap well in paper before tossing into a trashcan.

CUTTING MATS are used as the cutting surface for the rotary cutter. They are made from a self-healing material and are designed to withstand the pressure of the sharp rotary blades. They come in a variety of convenient sizes: larger ones

SUPPLIES FOR CUTTING: Mat, rotary cutter, replacement blade, blade sharpener, Alto's Quilt Cut Cutting System, acrylic rulers, Invisi-Grip®, fabric scissors.

ROTARY CUTTERS (From top to bottom): Includes 28 mm., 45 mm., 60 mm., as well as slashing cutter.

for working at home and smaller ones that are perfect for taking to classes. They are clearly marked with overall grid lines and often angle lines for easily aligning fabric and accurately cutting a variety of shapes. These mats are very heat sensitive and are best stored flat and out of the way of direct sunlight to prevent warping.

CUTTING RULERS, available in a variety of sizes, shapes, and colors are made from clear or frosted ⅛" thick acrylic. They are marked with grid lines and angle markings with easy-to-read numbers for both right- and left-handed use. The rulers are designed to be used with the rotary cutter and cutting mat and assist with accurate cutting of fabric shapes. Some of the newer rulers now have gripper marks on the backside to prevent slipping. Gripper dots and InvisiGrip™, a clear, nonslip material, can be applied to rulers, cutting mats, and templates to prevent slipping while cutting.

An assortment of scissors including dressmakers, appliqué, paper, embroidery, and thread clips.

SCISSORS

A good pair of 5", 6", or 8" scissors with a knife-edge is essential for cutting fabric. Scissors are available for both right-, and left-handed cutters. A less-expensive pair of scissors is needed for cutting paper and batting. Small thread clips are convenient for trimming unwanted thread tails. If you are planning to do any hand appliqué, quilting, or embroidery, you will also want to invest in a good pair of embroidery scissors.

SEWING/PIECING SUPPLIES
SEWING MACHINE

If you want to use a sewing machine for constructing your quilt, maintaining it in good working condition is a must. It's important that your machine runs smoothly, has even tension (no thread loops on either the front or back), and makes straight, even stitches. An extension table that attaches to the machine provides a supportive surface while sewing.

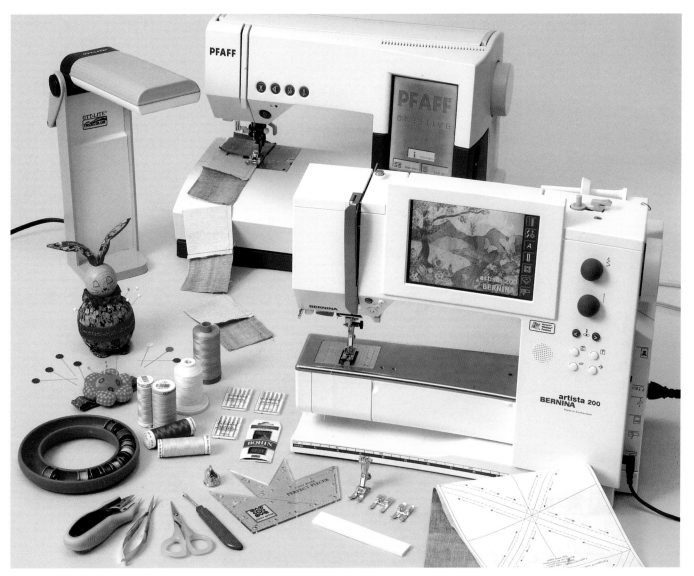

SUPPLIES FOR SEWING: Natural light desk lamp, sewing machines, decorative pin cushion, thread, sewing machine and hand sewing needles, bobbin keeper, thread clips, perfect piecer ruler, presser feet.

There are many good-quality machines available today. Purchasing a new machine is a big investment, and it is always best to do your homework before making the final decision. Some features that quilters look for in machines may not be as necessary for other types of sewing, such as dressmaking, crafts, or machine embroidery. So it is best to be clear about your intended use when you are researching and test-running different machines.

ASK THESE QUESTIONS WHEN SHOPPING FOR A MACHINE:

- Will the machine easily stitch an accurate ¼" seam allowance? Easily is the operative word here. Check to see if there is a presser foot designed specifically for this purpose.
- Does it have any decorative stitches? Quilters often use the blanket stitch for machine appliqué. If this stitch is available, see if the machine will allow you to override the setting. This simply means, are the stitch width and length programmed into the setting or can you adjust the length and width of the decorative stitches to meet the needs of your project? Being able to adjust the setting is a great feature. An open toe embroidery foot is also helpful to allow good sewing visibility while machine appliquéing.
- If you are interested in machine quilting, ask if the machine has a walking foot and darning foot designed specifically for the model. Generic feet don't always give the best results. Some of the *Pfaff* machines have a built in walking mechanism, eliminating the need for an additional foot.
- The *Bernina Aurora* has a new stitch length regulator that assists in making even stitches when free-motion quilting. Some manufacturers, such as *Brother* and *Juki*, have more high-powered industrial type models that are strictly for straight stitch sewing with a longer bed to accommodate the bulk of the quilt during machine quilting. Often there is a thread cutter available at the push of a button.
- Other options to look for in a machine include a needle down option which allows you to pivot easily, ease of refilling and changing the bobbin, adjustable speed control, and ease of dropping or covering feed dogs for machine quilting. Another thing to consider is where to get service after the sale.
- The most important question of all is do you LOVE the look and feel of the machine? This is a must.

PRESSER FEET

¼" OR PATCHWORK FOOT: This foot is designed specifically to allow the sewer to align the edge of the fabric with the right edge of the presser foot and accurately stitch a ¼" seam allowance. It is used for simple straight-stitch sewing.

OPEN TOE EMBROIDERY: This foot is designed for machine appliqué as the cut-out space in the center allows for clear visibility while sewing.

WALKING FOOT: This is a larger foot that is most often used for machine quilting. It allows the three layers of a quilt to feed evenly through the machine, preventing pleats and puckers on both the front and back of the quilt. It is also helpful when attaching binding to the edge of the quilt. Generic walking feet are available for some machines. Have the dealer fit the foot properly to your machine to be sure the correct pressure will allow for even feeding.

DARNING FOOT: This foot is used for free motion quilting. Darning feet come in a variety of styles made from both metal and plastic. They are available in generic styles to fit many different machines. Choose a foot that offers the clearest visibility while stitching. Test the foot to make sure there is enough space below it to allow for free movement of the layered quilt when in the down position.

NEEDLES AND PINS
HAND SEWING NEEDLES

The most commonly used sewing needles for hand piecing are "Sharps" and "Betweens." SHARPS are long and thin with round eyes and are good for general sewing and basting as well as hand quilting and hand piecing. BETWEENS are shorter and are generally the needles of choice for hand quilters. They have small eyes, so using a good quality needle threader will ease any frustration that may result from trying to thread them. Both types of needles range in sizes from 4–12 (the larger the number, the smaller the needle).

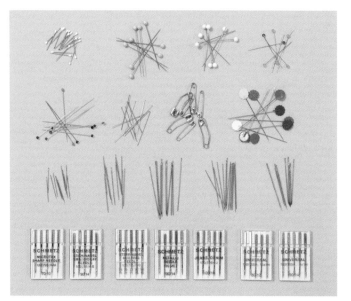

PINS AND NEEDLES: (Top to bottom) Row 1: Sequin/appliqué, quilting (2), glass head. Row 2: Glasshead, silk, safety pins, flowerhead. Row 3: Betweens, Sharps, cotton darners, straw, embroidery. Row 4: Embroidery (2), quilting, metallic, jeans/denim, universal (2).

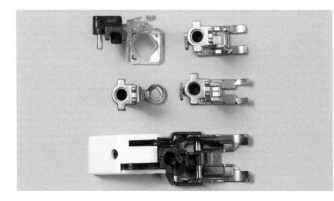

PRESSER FEET: (Left to right, top to bottom) quilting, open toe embroidery, darning, patchwork, walking.

DARNING NEEDLES, which are very long and thin, are used for basting a quilt by hand in preparation for hand quilting. These thin sharp needles can easily glide through the three layers which are being basted (quilt top, batting, and backing). The long length helps to speed up the process of making long stitches.

STRAW NEEDLES, sometimes called "milliners" are also long with round eyes. These are especially good for hand appliqué. Embroidery needles are also long but have a larger oval eye to make threading multiple strands of embroidery floss easier.

HAND SEWING NEEDLES

TYPE	SIZE	USE
Sharps	4–12	Hand piecing, hand quilting, and general sewing
Betweens	4–12	Hand piecing and hand quilting
Darners	1–11	Hand basting
Straw/Milliners	4–10	Hand appliqué
Embroidery	1–10	Hand embroidery

MACHINE SEWING NEEDLES

TYPE	SIZE	FEATURES/USE
Universal	60/8 to 120/19	All purpose, machine piecing, machine appliqué, and quilting
Metallica	80/12 to 90/14	Large, elongated, Teflon-coated eye for use with metallic and embroidery threads
Jeans/Denim	70/10 to 110/18	Sharp point with slender eye for use on heavy fabrics like denim and canvas
Quilting	75/11 to 90/14	Special tapered point for quilting through thick areas and across seams
Topstitch	80/12, 90/14, 100/16	Larger eye for use with heavier threads or fabrics; also useful for machine quilting
Embroidery	75/11 and 90/14	Deep thread groove and larger eye for use with synthetic embroidery threads

SEWING MACHINE NEEDLES

Using the correct needle in your sewing machine can improve the outcome of the finished project. To prevent thread breaks and a frayed look, it is wise to always use a clean needle. Sewing machine needles can become dull, bent, or damaged through normal use. Since they are relatively inexpensive it is good advice to change the needle when starting each new project.

It is important to use the correct needle and size for your fabric. In general sewing machine needles can be used by all makes and models of sewing machines. They range in size from 60/8 to 120/21. The number on the left of the slash is the European sizing and the number on the right of the slash is the American sizing—the larger the number, the stronger

the needle. The main difference in the needles revolves around the point: round (ballpoint) vs. sharp. Also, larger needles have larger eyes which can create holes in the fabric. It is important to use them only when working with heavy-weight fabrics which won't be damaged by the thickness of the needle.

In the left column is a list of sewing machine needles most commonly used by quiltmakers.

PINS

In days past quilters had to make do with "stubby" and nail-like pins. Today there are specific pins for each step of the quilting process—long ones, short ones, thick ones, thin ones, even the heads differ from flower-shaped to plastic and glass. As with all supplies, for best results purchase a good quality to match the need of your project. Following is a list of pins most commonly used by quiltmakers.

QUILTING PINS: These pins are longer and stronger than most. They have a large plastic head and work well for pinning blocks or pieces of fabric onto a design wall. Their strength is also helpful when going through multiple thicknesses for layering and basting or binding a quilt. The large head makes removal easy. Since the heads are made of plastic, it is best to keep them away from the iron to prevent melting.

GLASSHEAD PINS: These pins are a favorite for holding shapes together for piecing. They are long and thin and will not create large holes in the fabric. Some quilters prefer extra-fine dressmaker's silk pins.

APPLIQUÉ PINS: These short pins which are also called "sequin pins" are best used for securing small fabric shapes for hand appliqué.

SAFETY PINS: These pins are used when layering and basting a quilt for machine quilting. They, too, come in a variety of styles, from the familiar nickel-plated steel pins to curved and even colored pins. If you are machine quilting, you will need a large supply of 1" long (size 01) rustproof safety pins for pin-basting. Pins may remain in the quilt for some time (unless you are a speedy quilter), so it is best to use ones made of brass or nickel-plated steel to prevent rust and tarnishing.

THREAD

As with other tools and supplies, it is important to use the best quality thread in the correct size appropriate to the project you are making. Thread is made from either natural or synthetic fibers. Natural fibers come from plants and animals and are either spun or twisted into yarns. We are most familiar with cotton and wool, but other common thread products are made from silk, hemp, jute, and linen.

Synthetic fibers are made from various chemicals or a combination of chemicals and natural products. Some synthetic fibers are rayon, polyester, acrylic, and nylon. In most cases, a synthetic fiber has greater strength than a natural fiber. Threads are not only labeled by content but also by weight. The most common thread weights are 30 wt., 40 wt., and 50 wt.—the smaller the number, the heavier the thread.

Use general-purpose 50 wt. sewing thread for basting, piecing, and some appliquéing. Choose high-quality cotton or synthetic thread in light and dark neutrals, such as ecru and grey, for your basic supplies. Quilting thread, made from cotton or cotton-poly blend, is stronger than general-purpose sewing thread. Some brands have a coating to make them slide more easily through the quilt layers, which is helpful for hand quilting. For machine appliqué quilts, you may want to use transparent monofilament (polyester) thread. Use a very fine (.004 mm) soft thread that is not stiff or wiry. Choose clear thread for white or light fabrics or smoke color thread for darker fabrics.

Below is a list of threads most commonly used by quilt-makers.

COTTON: Safe, durable, easily adjusts to changes in fabric (such as shrinkage), available in a variety of weights, easy care. Low quality is linty and top quality has very little lint. Extra-long staple cotton is the top quality. Beware of a smooth, wiry, lint-free cotton, as it is coated with wax or starches and is not recommended for machine work. Use 30 wt. for creative machine quilting, 40 wt. for hand piecing, 50 wt. for machine piecing, machine embroidery for hand and machine appliqué, and quilting for hand and machine quilting.

POLYESTER: Strong, resistant to stretching and shrink-ing, resistant to most chemicals, quick-drying, crisp and resilient when wet or dry, wrinkle resistant, mildew resistant, abrasion resistant, retains heat-set pleats and creases, eas-ily washed, colorfast, retains shape, recovers stretch. Use for machine quilting and appliqué, and in the bobbin for machine embroidery, polyester monofilament for machine appliqué and machine quilting.

RAYON: Soft, high sheen, not known for its colorfastness and not as strong as polyester. Use for machine embroidery, machine appliqué, and machine quilting.

METALLIC: High sheen metallics are made with silver foil. Metallics with less sheen are made with aluminum. The highest quality metallics have a protective outer coating to prevent shredding; best used with a 90/14 metallica needle. Use for machine appliqué and machine quilting.

SILK: Good but very expensive and has some lint. Use for hand appliqué and machine quilting.

NYLON: Melts, gets brittle, and discolors. It is best to avoid using 100% nylon thread for quilting.

An assortment of threads including cotton, polyester, rayon, metallic, silk, monofilament, and quilting in a variety of solid and variegated colors.

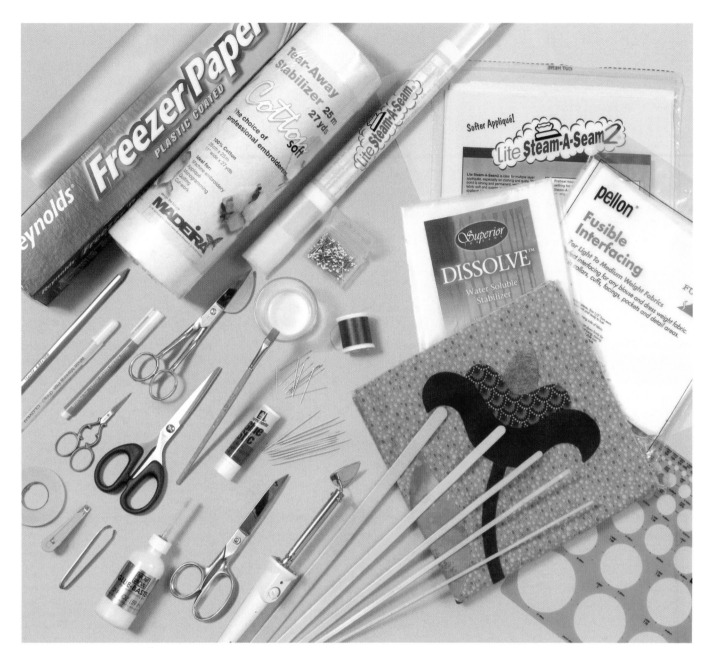

SUPPLIES FOR APPLIQUÉ: Vinyl, plastic coated freezer paper, tear away stabilizer, fusible web, wash away stabilizer, fusible interfacing, marking pens and pencils, embroidery scissors, appliqué scissors, fusible tape, bias tape maker, small paint brush, liquid starch, sequin (appliqué) pins, thread, glue stick, Glue Baste-It™, mini iron, bias bars, circle template.

ADDITIONAL SEWING SUPPLIES

SEWING LIGHT/LAMP: Try to find a lamp with a full spectrum light source for true colors.
SEAM RIPPER: For removing unwanted stitches.

APPLIQUÉ SUPPLIES

SCISSORS: A good pair of 5" or 8" fabric scissors for cutting fabric shapes, small embroidery scissors for cutting thread and small shapes; optional appliqué scissors with a sheath to protect the background fabric from being cut.

APPLIQUÉ PINS: Short pins used for securing small shapes to the background fabric; also called sequin pins.

THREAD: 100% cotton machine embroidery or silk for hand appliqué; cotton, polyester, or metallic for machine appliqué.

PLASTIC-COATED FREEZER PAPER: Use for making paper templates of individual shapes. The plastic coating will adhere to the fabric when pressed.

SUPPLIES FOR PRESSING: (Clockwise from left) spray starch, hot iron cleaner, pressing board, pieced fabric, iron, appliqué pressing sheet.

GLUE-BASTE-IT™ AND GLUE STICK: Used in preparing shapes and securing them to the background fabric.

LIGHTWEIGHT IRON-ON INTERFACING: Used in preparing shapes for appliqué.

BIAS PRESSING BARS: Used for making narrow strips for vines and stems; comes in a variety of widths.

BIAS MAKER AND FUSIBLE TAPE: This tool is used for folding and pressing narrow strips of bias cut fabric; also useful for Celtic quilting, as the fusible tape runs through the tool, making it ready for stitching to the background fabric.

APPLIQUÉ PRESSING SHEET: A Teflon-coated, non-stick sheet used in preparing shapes, especially multiple layers before stitching onto the background fabric.

MINI IRON: Helpful when working with small projects such as appliqué shapes.

EMBROIDERY FLOSS: Used for stitching hand blanket stitches around the edges of shapes.

SPRAY STARCH: Used to stiffen fabric when preparing shapes for either hand or machine appliqué.

HAND APPLIQUÉ

NEEDLES: #10 straw needles (milliners).

TWEEZERS: Used for removing paper patterns after shape is stitched to the background fabric.

CLEAR UPHOLSTERY VINYL: The entire design pattern is marked onto the vinyl then used for placing individual shapes onto the background fabric.

MACHINE APPLIQUÉ

NEEDLES: See page 34.

OPEN TOE EMBROIDERY PRESSER FOOT: See page 34.

FUSIBLE WEB: A product that bonds two fabrics together, used for raw edge machine appliqué.

STABILIZER: Used between the backside of the fabric and the feed dogs to prevent puckering and give stability to the fabric during stitching. It is torn away after the stitching is complete.

PRESSING SUPPLIES

IRON: A good quality iron is essential. Some quilters prefer using a steam iron.

PRESSING BOARD: An ironing board or piece of plywood covered with cotton batting and either light-colored canvas or flannel.

ADDITIONAL SUPPLIES

HOT IRON CLEANER: Helpful for removing excess glue or fusible web which may become attached to the bottom of the iron.

SPRAY STARCH OR SIZING: Used to restore crispness to prewashed fabric and give a finished look to completed blocks.

MARKING, LAYERING, AND BASTING SUPPLIES

Marking is the process of transferring quilting designs onto the quilt top. If a quilt will be quilted by hand with outline quilting or by machine with free-motion or all over meandering stitches, marking is generally not necessary. Designs that are intricate or must be precisely placed are best traced onto the quilt top. After any necessary designs are transferred, the quilt top is ready to be layered with the batting and backing in a process called layering and basting. The quilt "sandwich" will then be ready for quilting.

SUPPLIES FOR MARKING, LAYERING, AND BASTING: (Clockwise) design paper, masking tape, basting gun, batting, safety pins, thread, darning needles, marking pens and pencils, templates, perle cotton, spray adhesive.

BATTING

The middle layer between the quilt top and the backing is most commonly called the batting. Other names for batting are wadding and filling. Batting is made from both natural and synthetic fibers, the most common being cotton, polyester, wool, and silk. Batting can be purchased in packages of precut sizes for wall and bed size quilts or by the yard. For best results, it is wise to purchase a good quality batting. An inexpensive batting can not only be difficult to quilt but may not hold up to wear. There are a few considerations before deciding on the type of batting used for your quilted project. How do you want the finished quilt to look—flat or puffy? Do you want to quilt by hand or machine, and how far apart will the quilting stitches be? Will the quilt hang or be used as a bed quilt? Read the manufacturer's suggested use on the packaging and talk with experienced quiltmakers to see what they have used in similar projects. The selection of the batting should be as important a decision as the fabric used on the quilt top and backing. Harriet Hargrave's book, *From Fiber to Fabric, The Essential Guide to Quiltmaking Textiles,* has a wealth of information for anyone interested in learning more about this subject. It is worth investigation.

Here are some of the characteristics of different battings.

COTTON: A natural fiber, not as flammable as synthetic battings, breathes well, made in pure white (bleached) and natural (unbleached). It's often dense and hard to hand quilt unless it has been through a process called needlepunching which makes quilting easier. Holds the layers together without shifting for machine quilting.

POLYESTER: A synthetic fiber made in white, grey, and black, doesn't breathe as well as natural fibers so can become warm. It's lightweight, easy to wash and quilt through. Layers don't hold together as well as natural fibers for machine quilting. Fibers can travel or migrate through fabric layers causing "bearding" on the quilt top and/or backing.

WOOL: A natural fiber, lightweight, breathes easily, good for both hand and machine quilting. Fibers can migrate through fabrics.

SILK: Natural fiber, breathes well, is expensive and not as readily available as other battings.

An assortment of batting including cotton, cotton-polyester, polyester, silk, and wool.

BATTING SIZES

BED TYPE	MATTRESS SIZE	SUGG. QUILT SIZE*	PACKAGED BATTING	BATTING: PER YD AT 90" WIDE**
Crib	27" x 52"	35" x 56"	45" x 60"	1⅛
Twin	39" x 75"	63" x 87"	81" x 96"	2
Long Twin	39" x 80"	63" x 92"	120" x 120"	2¾
Double	54" x 75"	78" x 87"	90" x 108"	2⅜
Queen	60" x 80"	84" x 92"	120" x 120"	2¾
King	76" x 80"	100" x 92"	120" x 120"	5⅜
Cal King	72" x 84"	96" x 96"	120" x 120"	5⅝

*Allows for a 12" extension on three sides except for the crib which has 4" extra on three sides.
** Allows for a 2" extension beyond the edge of the quilt top all the way around.

MARKING, LAYERING, AND BASTING FOR HAND QUILTING

To secure the layers of the quilt in preparation for hand quilting, baste by hand with long stitches.

QUILTING STENCILS: Plastic templates with cut-out designs are marked onto the quilt top before layering and basting. They come in a variety of sizes and designs for blocks and borders. Books and magazines often feature designs that are appropriate for hand quilting. Occasionally it is necessary to draft your own design to fit the need of your quilt. Use a long-lasting marking pencil rather than a chalk marker for designs that need to remain on the quilt for an extended period of time. It is always best to test the marking pencil on a piece of fabric before using on the quilt.

DARNING/BASTING NEEDLES: Long, thin needles used for hand basting.

THREAD: Use a light-colored thread for hand basting.

PINS: Use long, straight quilting pins to secure the three layers in preparation for hand basting.

MARKING, LAYERING, AND BASTING FOR MACHINE QUILTING

Securing the layers of the quilt in preparation for machine quilting is much the same as for hand quilting but can be a faster process using either safety pins, adhesive spray, or a basting tool.

QUILTING DESIGNS: There are many continuous line quilting designs available that come on a roll with press-on tape for temporarily securing to the quilt. Other designs can be marked onto design paper, pinned to the quilt top and used as a guide for stitching.

DESIGN PAPER: This lightweight and easy to remove paper is used for tracing quilting designs. It is pinned onto the quilt top after layering and basting. Stitches are made through the paper along the marked lines. It is pulled away when the stitching is complete.

MARKING TOOLS: There are a variety of tools made for marking designs onto quilt tops. The pencils are more long lasting than some of the chalk markers, which work well for short-term marking projects. Water-soluble pens are also available, but use them with caution as the marks can become permanently set if not used properly.

SAFETY PINS: Use small (size 00, 0, or 1) brass or nickel-plated pins for basting. These work best as they will not create large holes in the fabric or rust/tarnish over time.

ADHESIVE SPRAY: This secures layers of fabric or batting and fabric together; it has a variety of uses, including basting quilts.

BASTING GUN: A tool designed for holding multiple layers together for quilting. It looks much like a gun and releases plastic tacks which are inserted through the layers. They are similar to those used for clipping tags to garments.

Storing supplies in a wooden container keep them organized for easy use.

QUILTING SUPPLIES
HAND QUILTING

It is important that the layers of the quilt be held taut for hand quilting. This can be achieved with either a hoop or a frame.

HOOPS are available in a variety of styles and sizes (oval, square, circle). Choose one that will be comfortable for you while hand quilting.

THIMBLE: The thimble should fit comfortably on the middle finger of your quilting hand. Try out the many different styles: metal, leather, flat top, rounded top, open top, plastic and even some of the beautiful designer thimbles. A thimble shouldn't be too tight or too loose. It should fit comfortably on your finger and not slip off. For the best control while stitching, the end of your finger should just touch the end of the thimble.

FINGER COT: Also called a "finger protector" is used on the index finger of the quilting hand. The finger cot will assist in grasping the end of the short quilting needle when pulling it through the thicknesses of the quilt. Quilters have also used the tip end of rubber gloves or pieces of a balloon but the convenience of the finger cot makes not having to pick up a separate tool an advantage.

TIGER TAPE: This narrow self-stick tape is marked with striped lines and designed to help with making evenly spaced quilting stitches. It is also good for blanket stitch appliqué. It

SUPPLIES FOR QUILTING: (Clockwise) quilting hoop, label and marking pen, gloves for machine quilting, continuous machine quilting designs, walking foot, quilting foot, thread, binding hem clips, sewing machine needles, marking tools, thimbles, embroidery scissors, needle threader, tiger tape, beeswax, thread, marking pencils, udder cream, quilting needles, small ruler, leather thimble, finger cot.

is cut to any needed length and applied to the quilt top next to the line of quilting. Quilters can stitch up and down following the lines on the tape. It is easily removed when quilting is complete.

BAG BALM OR UDDER CREAM: An antiseptic, nongreasy cream used for sore fingers after a full day of quilting. It soothes and heals damaged skin from needle pricks.

NEEDLES: See page 34.

THREAD: See page 35.

MACHINE QUILTING

QUILTER'S GLOVES: These snug fitting gloves are designed with rubber gripper dots on the palm side of the glove. These are helpful in feeding a large and bulky quilt through the sewing machine at an even rate without slipping.

PRESSER FEET: See page 34.

SEWING MACHINE NEEDLES: See page 35.

THREAD: See page 35.

quilting techniques

PLANNING, DESIGNING, AND PREPARATION
DRAFTING

Using computer software to draft and design patterns is fun for anyone who enjoys working on the computer. It is a perfect way to preview a quilt and make quick decisions about designs before investing too much time in the sewing process.

The traditional method of drafting patterns involves the use of graph paper, ruler and pencil. Just the word "drafting" may intimidate quilters who feel they are not good with numbers. You don't have to be expert at math to enjoy drafting. In fact, drafting will open the door to endless design possibilities. You need to begin with some simple blocks to see how the process works and soon you may be designing your own original quilt blocks and patterns. Let's begin by drafting a 10" finished Pinwheel Square block.

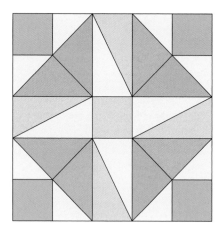

This block is called a Five-Patch block because the underlying grid is 5 squares across and 5 squares down.

1. Use a ruler and pencil to mark a 10" square onto a piece of eight-to-the-inch graph paper.

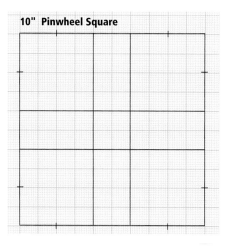

2. Mark points every 2" around the outer edges of the square. Next mark straight lines from top to bottom and side to side.

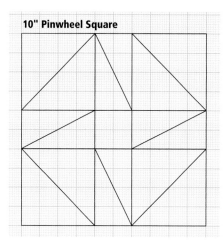

3. Mark diagonal lines in the side rectangles and corner squares, exactly as shown.

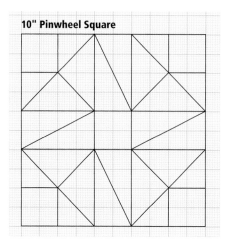

4. Mark the final lines in the corner squares to complete the drafted pattern of this block.

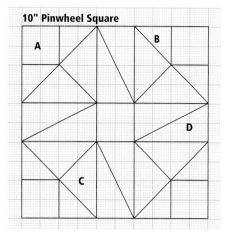

5. There are four shapes in this pattern: a square and three triangles. Label each A, B, C, and D, as indicated.

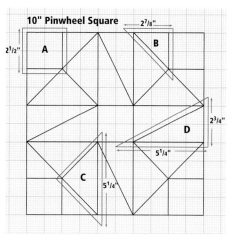

6. Use a red fine-line permanent pen to mark a ¼" line around the outer edges of each of these shapes. Next measure around the marked red lines of each shape to determine the cut size of the fabric.

- A: Measures 2½", therefore cut 2½" squares for each of the A shapes.
- B: Measures 2⅞" along one of the legs, therefore cut 2⅞" squares. Then cut the squares in half diagonally to make triangles for the B shapes. Note that this keeps the straight grain of the fabric along the outer edges of the block.
- C: Measures 5¼" along the longest side. Therefore cut 5¼" squares. Then cut the squares into quarters diagonally to make triangles. Note that this keeps the straight grain of the fabric along the outer edges of the unit.

- D: measures 2¾" x 5¼", therefore cut 2¾" x 5¼" rectangles. Then cut the rectangles in half diagonally for the D shapes.

MAKING TEMPLATES FROM A DRAFTED PATTERN

Let's consider the Around the World pattern with both straight and curved sides. This pattern is a perfect candidate for making templates.

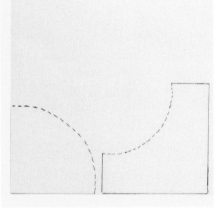

1. Use a pencil to mark a 12" square onto a piece of graph paper. Then mark a grid of sixteen 3" squares.

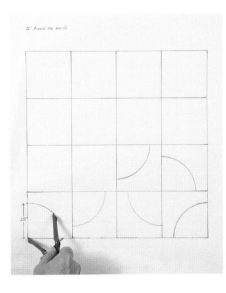

2. To make the curves, place the point of the compass in the corner of a square. Extend the compass so the pencil tip is 2¼" from the corner. Draw the quarter circle.

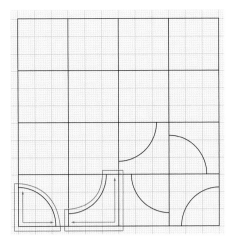

3. Use a red fine-line permanent marking pen to mark a ¼" seam allowance around one of the larger shapes as well as one of the smaller shapes.

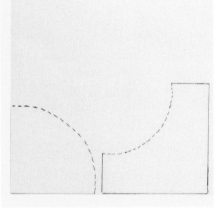

4. Place a piece of template plastic over the drafted pattern and, using a black fine-line permanent pen, trace around the red shapes.

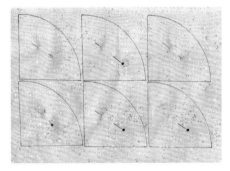

5. Use a small rotary cutter and mat or a pair of paper scissors to cut out the individual templates, cutting just inside the black lines. For easy identification, label each shape with the block name, finished size, and grain line arrows.

MAKING FABRIC SHAPES USING TEMPLATES

Template patterns are helpful for accurately marking a shape onto a piece of fabric. Double check the template pattern against the original drafted pattern to be certain it is the accurate size before marking the fabric.

1. Place the fabric wrong side up onto a sandpaper board.

2. Lay the template pattern on the fabric and hold it firmly in place while tracing around it with a marking pencil. Use a pencil that will clearly show marks on the fabric: silver, white, and yellow are often good choices.

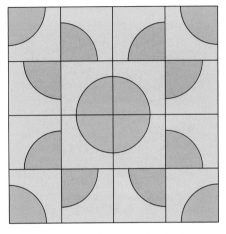

3. If multiple shapes are needed, the fabric can be folded to four thicknesses and then secured with a pin in the center of the marked shape. Use a good pair of fabric scissors to cut out the shapes, cutting just inside the marked lines.

43

PREPARING FABRIC
PREWASHING FABRIC

To wash or not to wash always seems to be one of the first questions asked when working with fabric for a quilt. The answer seems to be divided among quiltmakers. There are those who wouldn't dream of working with a fabric unless it had first been washed; others like to use it as it comes off the bolt. For those who are sensitive to the sizing and chemicals in the fabrics, it is always best to prewash.

If you choose to prewash, it's best to avoid using dryers, at least for the last part of the drying process, as this is when the greatest amount of shrinkage and color loss occurs. Instead, remove the fabric from the dryer while it is still damp and press it dry. Use a spray sizing to restore crispness, if desired.

Quilters may choose to prewash fabrics to preshrink and prevent release of excess dye, also called "bleeding." Release of excess dye can be a problem as you don't want a white fabric to turn pink after the first wash. Fabrics to be especially watchful for are those with deep, rich, jewel-tone colors such as red, royal blue, and purple, as well as batiks. It is always best to test these for colorfastness before using in a quilt. To test, cut small swatches of the fabric and also a swatch of white fabric. Place them in a clear glass with warm water. Let sit for awhile, then check to see if the water or white fabric have changed color. If so, it will be necessary to set the dye by placing the fabric into a sink with fullstrength white vinegar. Let it sit for a few minutes and then remove and rinse thoroughly. Line dry until still damp, then press. Test again with another swatch and if the fabric continues to bleed, choose another fabric.

FABRIC STORAGE

Most quiltmakers are great shoppers and often buy more fabric than required for a particular project. Many buy fabric simply because they like it, with no specific project in mind. These extra fabric pieces go into a collection called a "stash." As you might imagine, after many years of making quilts, the stash can become quite extensive. Depending on your

particular workspace, you may store and display your fabrics on shelves or in bins organized by color. There are a variety of means of organizing and storing fabrics, from individual bins with pieces casually grouped by colors to shelves with neat stacks of folded fabrics organized by color and design. Whatever method you choose, it is always wise to keep the fabrics free from direct sunlight, which will cause fading.

Storing fabric in drawers or on shelves according to color is helpful when planning a quilt.

CUTTING

Before you can begin cutting the fabric, it is helpful to have an understanding of descriptive terms.

SELVAGE: The tightly woven outer edges.

LENGTHWISE GRAIN: Threads that run parallel to the selvage edges. This grain line has the least amount of stretch.

CROSSWISE GRAIN: Threads that run perpendicular to the selvage edges. This grain has more stretch than the lengthwise grain.

STRAIGHT GRAIN: Both lengthwise and crosswise are called straight grains.

BIAS: Any cut that is not made on either the lengthwise grain or crosswise grain is called a bias cut. A true bias is

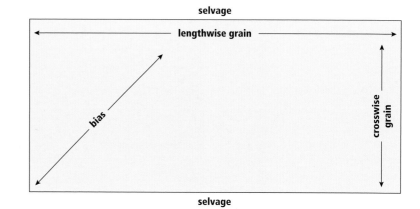

cut at a 45-degree angle from the lengthwise and crosswise grains.

Grain of the fabric is an important consideration when cutting, because whenever possible it is best to position the straight grain of the fabric along the outer edges of a block and quilt. This will prevent the edges of the blocks and overall quilt from stretching and becoming distorted.

Fabric shapes for making pieced quilt blocks can be cut using either a good pair of fabric scissors or a rotary cutter. Using scissors is the traditional way of cutting shapes, but since the rotary cutter was introduced quiltmakers have enjoyed the ease, accuracy, and speed this tool provides.

TRADITIONAL FABRIC CUTTING: USING SCISSORS

1. Place the fabric wrong side up on the sandpaper board. Place the template shape on top. Note any grainline markings on the template corresponding to the straight grain of the fabric. Use a marking pencil to mark around the edge of the shape.

2. The fabric can be folded to four thicknesses before cutting. Secure the layers with pins.

3. Use fabric scissors to accurately cut the shape, cutting just inside the lines.

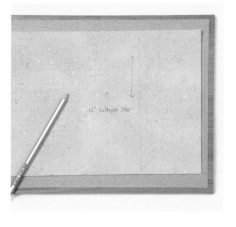

QUICK CUTTING: USING A ROTARY CUTTER

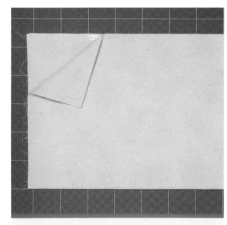

RIGHT-HANDED QUICK CUTTING: Squares and rectangles.

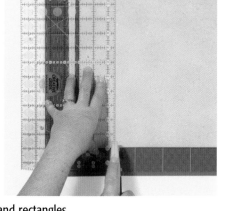

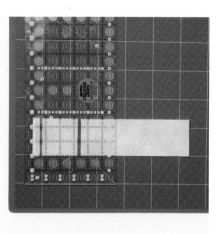

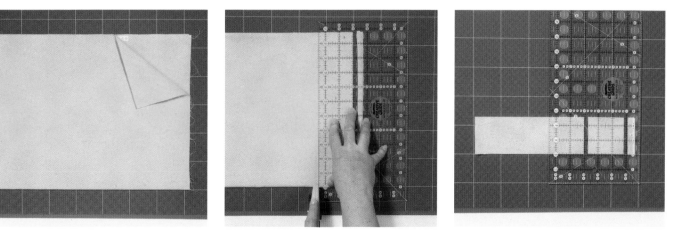

LEFT-HANDED QUICK CUTTING: Squares and rectangles.

QUICK CUTTING: USING A ROTARY CUTTER

1. Fold the fabric in half, matching the selvage edges. If ripples in the fold should occur, slide the selvages in one direction or the other until the fold is smooth (see photos for both right- and left-handed cutting at bottom of page 45).

2. Bring the fold even with the selvage edges. There will now be four layers of fabric. Most likely the side edges will not be even with each other.

3. To square edge of fabric, place ruler at a perfect right angle to the fold and use rotary cutter to cut a strip from the edge.

4. To cut strips, place the ruler over the cut edge of the fabric, aligning desired marking on ruler with cut edge; make cut.

5. When cutting several strips from a single piece of fabric, it is important to make sure that the cuts remain at a perfect right angle to the fold; square fabric edge as described in Step 3 when needed.

6. To remove selvages when cutting lengthwise strips for borders, place the fabric on mat with selvages to your left and squared-up edge at bottom of mat, closest to you. Make a cut the length of the ruler. Move next section to be cut onto mat and make cut. Repeat until you have removed selvages from required length of fabric.

7. To cut lengthwise borders, place ruler over left edge of fabric aligning desired marking on ruler with edge of fabric; make cut. Move the fabric onto mat as in Step 6 and continue making cuts.

QUICK CUTTING FROM STRIPS

Most quick cutting begins by cutting strips with the rotary cutter. Many other fabric shapes (squares, rectangles, triangles, diamonds) can then be cut from the initial strips.

CUTTING TRIANGLES AND DIAMONDS

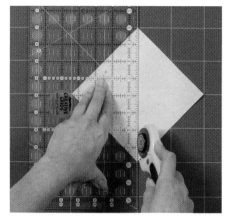
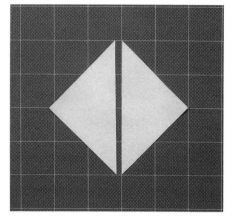

Half-square triangles

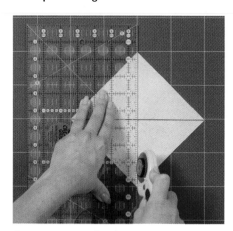
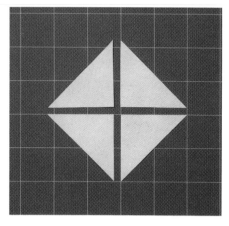

Quarter-square triangles

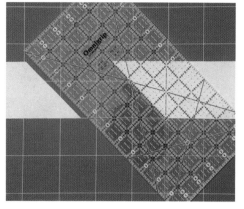

45-degree diamonds

CUTTING HALF-SQUARE AND QUARTER-SQUARE TRIANGLES

1. First cut squares from strips.

2. To make half-square triangles: Position a square on the cutting board, then cut across diagonally to make two triangles.

3. To make quarter-square triangles: Position a square on the cutting board, then cut across diagonally in both directions to make four triangles.

CUTTING 45-DEGREE DIAMONDS

1. Position a strip on the cutting board.

2. Position the 45-degree angle marking on the ruler on the bottom edge of the strip and cut.

3. Keeping the 45-degree angle marking even with the bottom edge of the fabric, slide the ruler to the right so that the marking indicating the width of the strip is in line with the clean cut edge. Cut to make diamonds.

Antique hand pieced quilt block.

SEWING/PIECING

Sewing fabric shapes together in quilt-making is called piecing. Stitches can be made either by hand or by machine.

HAND PIECING

Use small running stitches to sew fabrics together by hand. One of the common sewing terms used in quiltmaking is "with right sides together." This simply means that two pieces of fabric (strips, individual shapes, completed blocks, etc.) are positioned with their right sides facing in preparation for sewing.

1. In order to achieve a straight and accurate ¼" seam allowance, use a small ruler and marking pencil to mark a line ¼" from each raw edge of the shape on the wrong side of the fabric.

2. Place two shapes to be sewn together with right sides facing each other and edges even. Secure with pins.

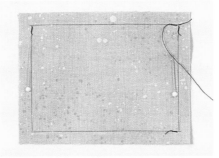

3. Thread a #10 Sharps needle with a neutral colored thread. Begin stitching on the marked line with two small back-stitches to prevent stitches from coming loose. Then pull the needle through the loop to form a knot.

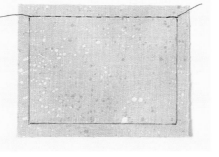

4. Continue stitching across the line with small running stitches, ending ¼" from the end with two small back-stitches.

Note that stitches never extend into the seam allowances. This allows for freedom of stitching order as well as pressing directions.

UNIT CONSTRUCTION FOR HAND PIECING

Join fabric shapes together by sewing to make units; sew units together to make the quilt blocks.

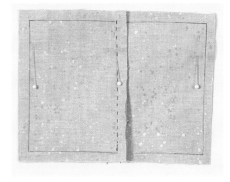

1. To join sewn shapes together, place the right sides facing each other and secure with pins.

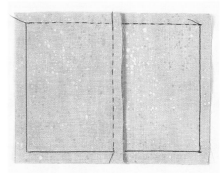

2. Stitch across the marked ¼" stitching line, beginning and ending with two small backstitches. At the intersection of the seams, keep the seam allowances free, without stitching them flat and stitch as close as possible. Then slide the needle through the seam allowances to the other side and continue stitching to ¼" from the end. End with two small backstitches.

3. Press the seam allowance to one side, first on the back and then on the front.

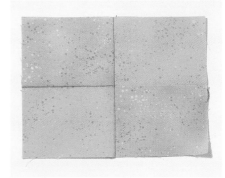

MACHINE PIECING

It is important to be able to sew an accurate ¼" seam allowance before beginning your quilt project.

The seam allowance is the distance from the cut edge of the fabric to the line of stitching. In quiltmaking, ¼" is the usual seam allowance. To maintain accuracy and consistency in piecing, it is important to establish the exact position of the fabric as it runs through the sewing machine.

Follow the steps below to set your machine for an accurate ¼" seam allowance.

1. Place a piece of ¼" graph paper directly under the presser foot of the sewing machine. Lower the needle to insert into the first line from the right hand edge.

2. Temporarily secure the graph paper to the machine with tape.

3. Tape several thicknesses of masking tape or a piece of moleskin in line with the edge of the graph paper.

4. Raise the needle and remove the graph paper. The edge of the masking tape will serve as a guide while stitching to achieve an accurate ¼" seam allowance.

Note: Many machines have a ¼" presser foot or patchwork foot made specifically for this purpose. The edge of the foot is used as a guide. If your machine has this foot, it may not be necessary to apply a tape guide. Also check to see if your machine has the option of moving the needle to position it better in relation to the right edge of the presser foot.

5. To check for accuracy, cut three pieces of fabric, each 1½" x 3½".

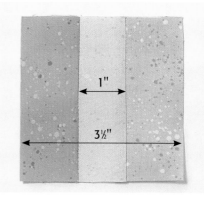

7. Press the seams in one direction. Measure the stitched unit. It should measure 3½" x 3½" and the distance between the seam allowances should be exactly 1".

If this practice piece is accurate, your machine is set up and ready to sew.

6. Sew the three pieces together.

Some quiltmakers enjoy the simplicity of the old Singer Featherweight machines for straight stitching.

STRIP PIECING

Strip piecing is the time-saving technique of sewing multiple fabric strips together to make sets of strips.

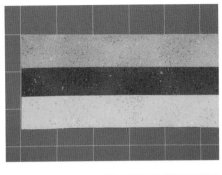

The set of strips can be cut apart to make shorter units.

CHAIN PIECING

Chain piecing will make your work go faster and will usually result in more accurate piecing.

Stack the pieces you will be sewing beside your machine in the order you will need them and in a position that will allow you to easily pick them up. Pick up each pair of pieces, carefully place them together as they will be sewn, and place them into the machine one after the other. Stop between each pair only long enough to pick up the next pair. Don't cut the thread between pieces. After all pieces are sewn, cut threads, press and go on to the next step, chain piecing when possible.

HALF-SQUARE TRIANGLES

The half-square triangle is a common unit in pieced quilt block patterns. It is two right angle triangles joined together to make a square. Whenever possible, with pieced units and blocks, it is best to position the straight grain of the fabric along the outside edge. There are several methods of cutting and constructing these units.

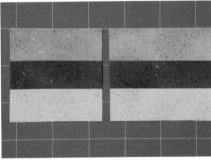

When working with these units, you must first know the desired finished size when sewn into the quilt block. To do this, you must add the seam allowance to determine the cut size of the shapes.

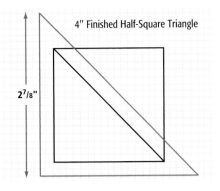
4" Finished Half-Square Triangle
$2\frac{7}{8}"$

A drafted pattern of this shape is helpful in understanding this concept, especially when working with triangles. Look at the diagram of the drafted pattern for a 2" finished half-square triangle unit. The length of each leg of the triangle is 2". A $\frac{1}{4}"$ seam allowance (red marking) is added to the triangle to illustrate the size needed to cut the fabric triangles. The length with seam allowance is $2\frac{7}{8}"$. Therefore the formula for half-square triangles is: finished size + $\frac{7}{8}"$ = cut size. Simply stated, to make 2" finished half-square triangles, you must cut strips $2\frac{7}{8}"$ wide.

Note: Although $\frac{7}{8}"$ is the exact allowance needed for cutting half-square triangles, some quilters find that it leaves no room for error and adjustment. If you prefer, you may add 1" and then trim any extra when straightening the units.

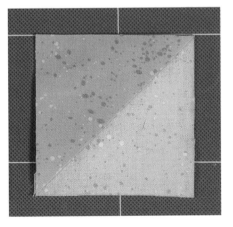

Following are three methods for making 2" finished Half-Square Triangles.

1. Cut a $2\frac{7}{8}"$ wide strip from each of two fabrics (one light and one dark).

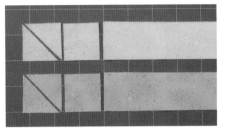

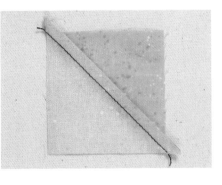

2. Cut the strips into $2\frac{7}{8}"$ squares, then cut the squares in half diagonally to make two triangles.

3. With right sides facing, sew the triangles together in pairs along the longer side. To save time, the units can be chain pieced.

4. Cut the chain of threads between the units and then press the seam in the direction of the darker fabric.

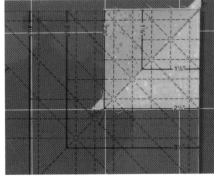

5. Place the unit on the cutting board. Remove the extensions in opposite corners and straighten the edges of the unit. It should accurately measure $2\frac{1}{2}"$ square; trim if needed. It is ready to be incorporated into a quilt block.

49

METHOD TWO

1. Cut a 2⅞" wide strip from each of two fabrics (one light and one dark).

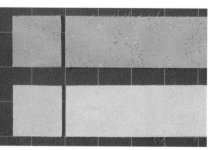

2. Cut the strips into 2⅞" squares.

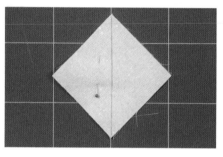

3. Use a marking pencil to draw a diagonal line on the wrong side of the lighter fabric. Place a light and dark square together with right sides facing. Pin to secure.

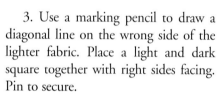

4. Stitch ¼" from both sides of the marked diagonal line.

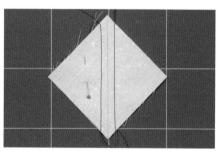

5. Cut along the diagonal line.

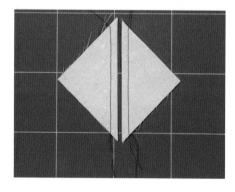

6. Press the seam in the direction of the darker fabric.

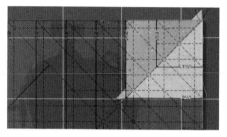

7. Place the unit on the cutting board. Remove the extensions in opposite corners and straighten the edges of the unit. It should accurately measure 2½" square. It is now ready to be incorporated into a quilt block.

METHOD THREE

1. Cut an 18" x 22" piece from each of two fabrics (one light and one dark).

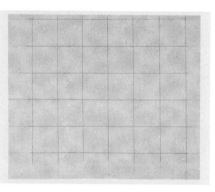

2. On the back side of the lighter fabric, accurately mark a 2⅞" grid of squares.

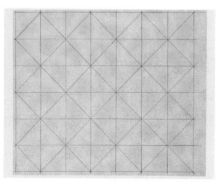

3. Mark diagonal lines in every square.

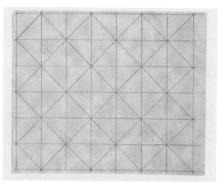

4. With right sides facing, place the light fabric onto the dark fabric and secure with pins.

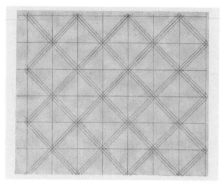

5. Sew around the grid of squares, stitching ¼" from both sides of the marked diagonal lines.

6. To separate the individual units, use the cutting tools to cut on all of the marked lines, both straight and diagonal.

7. Follow Step 7 in Method Two.

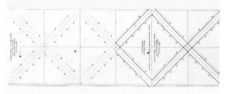

Note: Rolls of paper that are marked in various grid sizes and designed specifically for making these units are available. Many quilters prefer this to marking on the fabric. After stitching around the grid and cutting units apart, the paper is pulled away to complete the unit.

QUARTER-SQUARE TRIANGLES

Similar to the half-square triangle unit, the quarter-square triangle is made by joining four right angle triangles together to form a square. The methods described below place the straight grain of the fabric along the outside edge of the unit to prevent stretching and distortion. There are several methods of cutting and constructing these units; two of the most common are included here.

When working with these units, you must first know the desired finished size when sewn into the quilt block. To do this you must add the seam allowance to determine the cut size of the shapes.

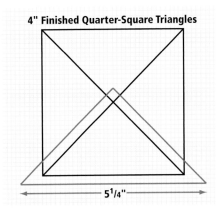

4" Finished Quarter-Square Triangles

5¼"

A drafted pattern of the shape is helpful in understanding this concept, especially when working with triangles. Look at the diagram of the drafted pattern for a 4" finished quarter-square triangle unit. A ¼" seam allowance (red marking) is added to the triangle to illustrate the size needed to cut the fabric triangles. The length with seam allowance is 5¼" which is 1¼" larger than the finished size. Therefore the formula for cutting

quarter-square triangles is: finished size + 1¼" = cut size. Simply stated, to make 4" finished quarter-square triangles, you must cut strips 5¼" wide. Following are two methods for making 4" finished quarter-square triangles

METHOD ONE

1. Cut a 5¼" wide strip from each of two fabrics (one light and one dark).

2. Cut the strips into 5¼" squares, then cut the squares into quarters diagonally to make four triangles.

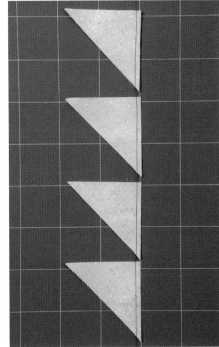

3. With right sides facing, sew the triangles together in pairs along a shorter side. To save time, the units can be chain pieced.

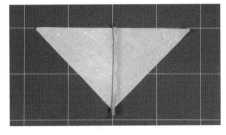

4. Cut the chain of threads between the units and then press the seams in one direction.

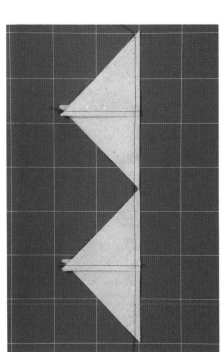

5. Place two of the pressed units together with right sides facing; secure the opposing seam allowances with a pin. Stitch along the longer side. Several units can be chained one after the other.

6. Cut the chain of thread connecting the units then press the new seam allowances to one direction.

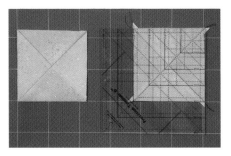

7. Place the unit on the cutting board. Cut to remove the corner extensions and straighten the edges of the unit. It should accurately measure 4½". It is ready to be incorporated into a quilt block.

METHOD TWO

1. Cut an 18" x 22" piece from each of two fabrics (one light and one dark).

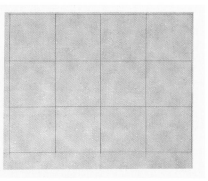

2. On the backside of the lighter fabric, accurately mark a 5¼" grid of squares.

3. Next mark diagonal lines in every square.

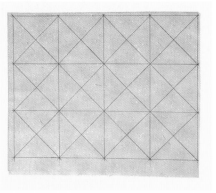

4. With right sides facing, place the light fabric onto the dark fabric and secure with pins.

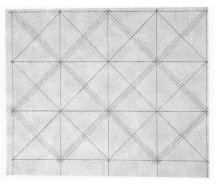

5. Sew around the grid of squares, stitching ¼" from both sides of the marked diagonal lines.

6. To separate the individual units, cut on all of the marked lines, both straight and diagonal.

7. Press the seams in the direction of the darker fabric.

8. Follow Steps 5–7 of Method One to complete the units.

Note: Rolls of paper that are marked in various grid sizes and are designed specifically for making these units are available. Many quilters prefer this to marking on the fabric. After stitching around the grid and cutting units apart, the paper is pulled away to complete the unit.

52

FLYING GEESE UNITS

The flying geese unit is made from one large triangle and two smaller right angle triangles. It is found in many pieced quilt block patterns. The obvious way to construct this unit is to sew the three triangles together. However, if the triangles are not perfectly aligned when sewn, the end result can be a misshapen unit. Following are two quick methods for making a 2" x 4" finished flying geese unit. They involve cutting and sewing only squares and rectangles which provides less opportunity for stretch and distortion. Try some sample units to see what method you prefer.

METHOD ONE: SQUARES AND RECTANGLES

Cut: Two 2½" squares of dark fabric

One 2½" x 4½" rectangle of light fabric

1. With right sides facing each other and edges even, place a square onto a rectangle. Stitch across the square diagonally, from corner to corner, through both layers.

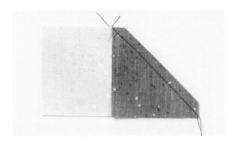

2. Trim, leaving ¼" beyond the stitching line.

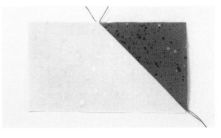

3. Press the triangle over the stitching line.

4. With right sides facing each other, and edges even, place another square onto the rectangle. Stitch across the square diagonally, from corner to corner.

5. Trim, leaving ¼" beyond the stitching line.

6. Press to complete the unit. It should accurately measure 2½" x 4½" and is ready to incorporate into a quilt block.

METHOD TWO: SQUARES

Cut: Four 2⅞" squares of background fabric

One 5¼" square of geese fabric

1. Mark a diagonal line on the backside of each small square.

2. With right sides facing each other and edges even, place two background squares onto the square of geese fabric. Secure with pins.

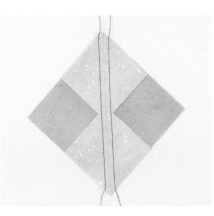

3. Stitch ¼" away from both sides of the marked diagonal line.

4. Cut on the marked diagonal line to make two units.

5. Press the background triangles over the stitching line.

6. With right sides facing, place the two remaining background squares onto the new units. Secure with pins then stitch ¼" away from both sides of the marked diagonal lines.

7. Cut on the marked diagonal lines then press the background triangles over the stitching lines to make four flying geese units.

8. Trim the extensions. Each unit should accurately measure 2½" x 4½" and is ready to incorporate into a quilt block.

VARIABLE SIZE FLYING GEESE UNITS

Flying Geese Units can be made in any size you desire. Follow Steps 1-4, below, to cut the pieces then follow Steps 2-7 of Method Two: Squares, Page 53, to construct the units.

1. To make 4 Flying Geese Units, you will need 1 square A of fabric (geese) for the large center triangle and 4 square B's of a contrasting fabric (background). For example, let's say the project calls for 36 Flying Geese Units. You would need 9 square A's (36 ÷ 4 = 9) and 36 square B's.

2. For cutting sizes for squares A and B, first determine the desired finished size for the Flying Geese Units. A finished Flying Geese Unit is twice as

wide as it is tall. For example, let's use the finished size of 6"w x 3"h.

3. Cutting size for the square A's is the finished width measurement + 1¼". For our example, it would be 6" + 1¼" = 7¼". The cutting size for square A would be 7¼" x 7¼".

4. Cutting size for the square B's is the finished height measurement + ⅞". For our example, it would be 3" + ⅞" = 3⅞". The cutting size for the 4 square B's would be 3⅞"x 3⅞".

UNIT CONSTRUCTION FOR MACHINE PIECING

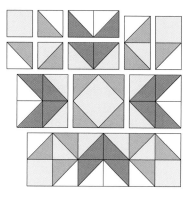

Pieced quilt blocks are much like building blocks. Join small pieces together to make larger units, then sew units together to make the quilt blocks.

APPLIQUÉ

Appliqué is the technique of stitching fabric shapes onto a background fabric either by hand or machine. Hand appliqué has a soft edge and sometimes puffy look, whereas machine appliqué has a sharper edge with a flatter finished look.

Floral Medallion appliqué project, page 130.

HAND APPLIQUÉ

Following are two methods used for preparing shapes for hand appliqué.

METHOD ONE: USING FREEZER PAPER

To make templates from appliqué patterns, trace the shapes onto paper or template plastic and cut out.

1. With the shiny side of the freezer paper facing down, draw around the template with a pencil or permanent pen as many times as called for in your pattern instructions.

2. Use paper scissors to cut out the freezer paper shapes on the drawn lines.

3. Leaving at least ½" between shapes, press the shiny side of the freezer paper shapes onto the backside of the fabric.

4. Use fabric scissors to cut the fabric ¼" beyond the edge of the freezer paper.

5. There are two options for preparing the applique shape for stitching.

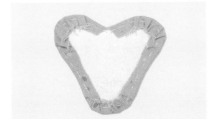

a. Turn the fabric extension to the backside of the shape and hand baste through all layers, approximately ⅛" from the folded edge. For smooth curves, keep the stitches fairly small.

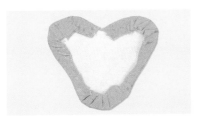

b. Spray some starch into a small jar. Use a small paint brush to apply starch to the fabric extension. Use a mini iron to press and secure the fabric extension over the edge of the paper shape. Allow the shape to dry completely; carefully remove the freezer paper.

6. Use small appliqué pins or Glue-Baste-It™ to hold the shape in place on the background fabric. Sew around the shape using one of the stitches described below. **Note:** If using Step 5a, refer to Removing Freezer Paper before beginning to stitch.

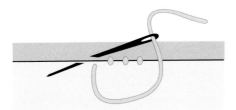

HAND APPLIQUÉ STITCH

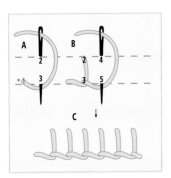

BLANKET STITCH

METHOD TWO
1. Follow Method One Steps 1 and 2.

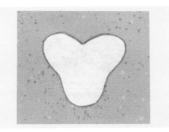

2. Press the shiny side of the freezer paper pattern onto the right side of the fabric. Use a fabric marking pencil or pen to draw around the shape.

3. Remove the freezer paper pattern and use fabric scissors to cut the shape ³⁄₁₆" beyond the edge of the marked line.

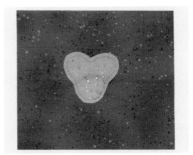

The shape is prepared and ready to be hand stitched onto the background fabric using needle turn appliqué techniques (see page 74). Use small appliqué pins or Glue-Baste-It™ (applied at least ½" from the cut edge) to hold the shape in place for stitching.

REMOVING FREEZER PAPER
If you have used Method One, Step 5a, there are two options for removing the freezer paper.
• After stitching around the edge of the shape, remove all of the basting stitches. Turn the fabric to the backside and make a small cut in the background fabric. Carefully pull the freezer paper through the cut.

• Leaving approximately 1" unsewn (may vary with the size of the shape), stitch around the shape as described in Step 6. Remove the basting stitches. Use tweezers to gently pull the freezer paper through the opening. Stitch the opening closed.

MACHINE APPLIQUÉ
Following are three methods used for preparing shapes to be machine appliquéd.

METHOD ONE: FUSIBLE WEB
1. Trace the shape outlines onto the paper side of the fusible web. Be sure to leave at least ½" between shapes.

2. Cut out the shapes, cutting approximately ¼" beyond the marked lines.

For a softer finish, remove the inside of the paper shape, cutting ¼" inside the marked line.

3. Follow the manufacturer's instructions to press the shape onto the wrong side of the fabric.

Note: The heart on the left has not been cut away on the inside. Either preparation is acceptable.

4. Use fabric scissors to accurately cut the shape on the marked line.

5. Peel off the paper backing, then, with the right side of the fabric shape facing up, press it onto the background fabric.

6. Use a decorative hand or machine stitch around the outside edge of the shape.

METHOD TWO: LIGHTWEIGHT NONFUSIBLE INTERFACING

1. Trace the outline of the individual shapes onto the smooth side of the interfacing.

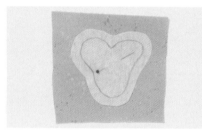

2. Cut out the shapes, cutting approximately ¼" beyond the marked lines.

3. Place the rough side of the interfacing shape on the right side of the fabric and secure with a pin.

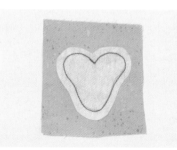

4. Stitch through both layers, exactly on the marked line, as shown.

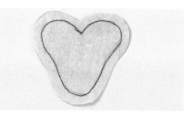

5. Cut the excess fabric ¼" beyond the stitching line. For smoother edges on curved shapes, make clips up to, but not through the stitching.

6. Cut a small slit in the interfacing and carefully turn the shape right side out; press.

7. The prepared shape is ready to be stitched to the background fabric by either hand or machine.

METHOD THREE: FREEZER PAPER WITH SPRAY STARCH OR GLUE

Same as for Hand Appliqué (see page 54).

MACHINE APPLIQUÉ STITCHES

BLANKET: The blanket stitch is often used as a decorative edging around raw-edge machine appliquéd shapes. A variety of threads can be used to give different looks and textures to the outline of the shape.

SATIN STITCH: The satin stitch is a tight zigzag stitch which creates a heavy outline around the shape.

A stabilizer is often used on the backside between the fabric and the feed dogs to keep the fabric flat during stitching. It is torn away when stitching is complete.

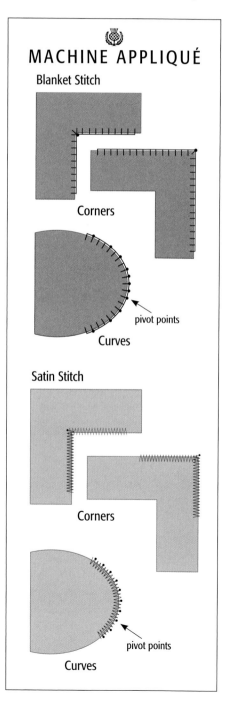

MACHINE APPLIQUÉ
Blanket Stitch

Corners

Curves

pivot points

Satin Stitch

Corners

Curves

pivot points

56

PRESSING

Pressing is one step of the quiltmaking process that you do not want to skip or rush through. Proper pressing techniques (notice the word pressing and not ironing) are critical to the overall success of the finished project. (Pressing involves an "up and down" motion that will set the stitches and flatten the fabric without distortion. Ironing is moving the iron in a random motion that can cause distortion to cut edges of fabric.) It is important to know that cut fabric pieces and blocks are fragile until they are sewn together into a quilt top. They need to be handled with care not only to prevent stretched edges but also to prevent stitches from coming undone. Use a steam iron set on "cotton" for most pressing.

Press as you sew, taking care to prevent small folds along seam lines. Seam allowances are almost always pressed to one side, usually toward the darker fabric. However, to reduce bulk, it may occasionally be necessary to press seam allowances toward the lighter fabric or even to press them open. In order to prevent a dark fabric seam allowance from showing through a light fabric, trim the darker seam allowance slightly narrower than the lighter seam allowance. To press long seams, such as those in long strip sets, without curving or other distortion, lay strips across the length of the ironing board.

1. After the stitching, it is best to first press flat on the wrong side to set the seam. Place the darker fabric on top for this step.

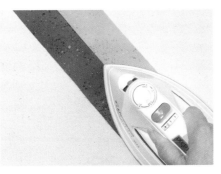

2. Turn the darker fabric over the stitching line and press again, this time on the right side to create a sharp seam.

CONSTRUCTING THE QUILT TOP
SETTINGS, SASHINGS, AND POSTS

A SETTING or set is a term used for the arrangement in which quilt blocks are sewn together to construct the quilt top. For ease in joining the blocks, it is helpful to first give them a final pressing with spray starch. Then use the cutting tools to straighten and clean up the edges, if necessary. Place your completed quilt blocks onto the design wall into the desired arrangement (setting). The two basic and most common settings are straight and diagonal.

STRAIGHT SETTING

A straight setting is made up of blocks sewn together in straight horizontal and vertical rows. The mola quilt shown below is an example of a straight setting.

DESIGN OPTIONS FOR STRAIGHT SETTINGS

Following are several options that are often used when arranging blocks in a straight setting. These are easy to include, add interest to the quilt, provide the opportunity to use another fabric and can give order to blocks that may otherwise be difficult to combine into one quilt. They also help to enlarge the quilt.

EITHER HORIZONTAL OR VERTICAL SASHING STRIPS

Blocks are sewn together in either horizontal or vertical rows. The rows are joined with sashing strips. When adding this element to the quilt, it is important to make sure that the seams joining the individual blocks remain in a straight line. Measure and pin carefully when attaching the sashing strips to keep the line straight.

57

This collection of mola blocks are sewn in a straight setting with horizontal and vertical sashing strips.

BOTH HORIZONTAL AND VERTICAL SASHING STRIPS

Sashing strips can also be added in both directions, giving separation to the individual blocks. The Sampler quilt on page 165 shows an example of using sashing strips to isolate the center appliqué block from the surrounding pieced blocks. It is important to measure and pin carefully when attaching these sashings to keep the short vertical strips in line.

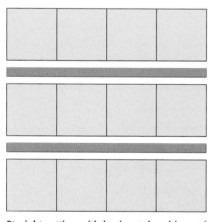
Straight setting

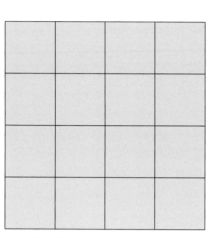
Straight setting with horizontal sashing strips

Straight setting with vertical sashing strips

POSTS

Squares of fabric, called posts can be added at the intersections of the setting with both horizontal and vertical sashing strips. Posts offer an opportunity to introduce another fabric and also act as anchors, keeping all of the sashing strips in line, both vertically and horizontally.

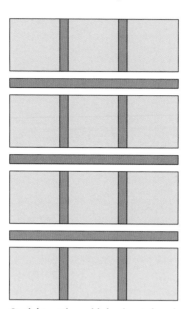
Straight setting with horizontal and vertical sashing strips

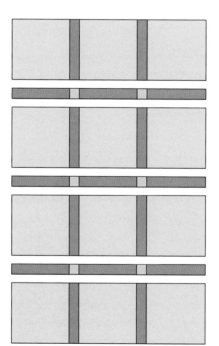
Straight setting with sashing strips and posts

ALTERNATE BLOCK SETTINGS

When blocks are set side-by-side in a traditional setting, the pattern of the blocks sometimes blends together and the eye moves constantly from block to block. Alternating solid squares of print or solid color fabric between the pieced or appliquéd blocks can give a very different look to a quilt top. These alternate blocks allow the pieced or appliquéd blocks to stand out and provide a space for decorative quilting.

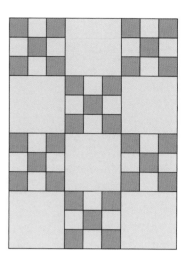

Another setting option for alternating blocks is to combine a busy pieced block, such as a star, with a simple block such as a snowball. This type of alternate block is sometimes referred to as a linking block.

DIAGONAL SETTINGS

A diagonal setting is made up of blocks that are turned (called "on point") and sewn together in diagonal rows. Notice that there are triangles around the edges of a quilt top with a diagonal setting. These are necessary to straighten an otherwise jagged edge. The triangles of fabric along the sides and top and bottom are called side triangles and the four corner triangles are called corner triangles. Just like straight settings, diagonal settings can be constructed using sashings or sashings with posts. The Miniature Bear's Paw quilt on page 122 is a good example of a quilt with a diagonal setting.

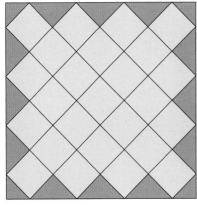

Diagonal setting

Diagonal setting with sashing strips

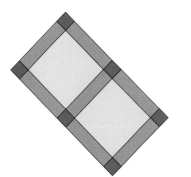

Diagonal setting with sashing strips and posts

SIDE AND CORNER TRIANGLES

To prevent stretching and distortion of the quilt top, it is important to cut the side and corner triangles so that the straight grain of the fabric pieces fall around the outer edges of the quilt top. The following will help with cutting these pieces. The measurements given allow a little extra for trimming and straightening the edges of the quilt top after construction.

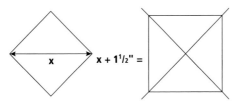

Side triangles: Add $1\frac{1}{2}$" to the diagonal measurement of a block to determine the cut size. Cut the square into quarters diagonally to make four side triangles.

Corner triangles: Add 1" to the measurement of the block to determine the cut size. Cut the square in half diagonally to make two corner triangles.

ADDING BORDERS

Borders are strips of fabric that are sewn around the outer edge of the quilt top. Not all quilts have borders; however, adding them provides an easy solution to making a larger quilt. Borders can also serve as a visual frame to control and contain the blocks.

Quilts can have a single border or more than one border can be added to a quilt.

Borders can be joined at the corners to make either a straight or a mitered seam. Borders can be pieced with a design such as piano keys. For extra interest, add corner posts of a contrasting fabric or pieced blocks to straight borders.

Single straight border

Single mitered border

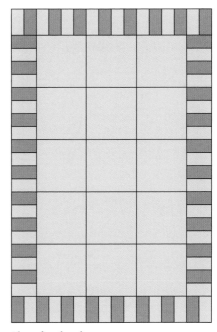

Piano key border

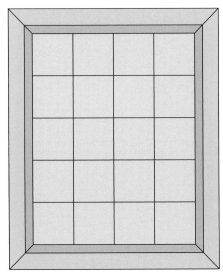

Single straight border with corner posts

Multiple straight borders

Multiple mitered borders

ADDING STRAIGHT BORDERS

1. Mark the center of each edge of the quilt top.

2. Straight borders are usually added to the sides, then the top and bottom edges of the center section of a quilt top. To add side borders, measure through the center of the quilt top to determine the length of the borders. Trim side borders to the determined length.

3. Mark the center of side borders. Matching center marks and raw edges, pin borders to quilt top, easing in any fullness; stitch.

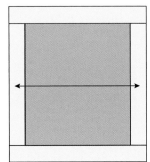

4. Measure the center of the quilt top, including attached borders, to determine the length of top and bottom borders. Trim borders to the determined length. Repeat Step 3 to add top and bottom borders to the quilt top.

5. Attach additional borders in the same sequence.

ADDING STRAIGHT BORDERS WITH CORNER POSTS.

1. Follow Steps 1-3 of Adding Straight Borders.

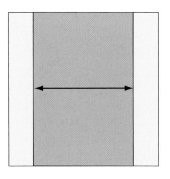

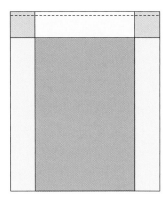

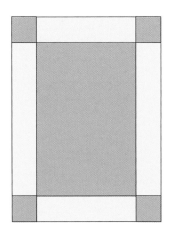

2. Measure through the center of the quilt top (excluding side borders); add $1/2$" for seam allowances. Trim top and bottom borders to this measurement. Sew one corner post to each end of the top and bottom borders. Repeat Step 3 of Adding Straight Borders to sew top and bottom borders to quilt top.

ADDING MITERED BORDERS

1. Mark the center of each edge of the quilt top.

2. Mark the center of one long edge of the top border. Measure across the center of the quilt top.

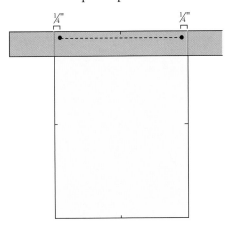

3. Matching center marks and raw edges, pin the border to the center of the quilt top edge. Beginning at the center of the border, measure half the width of the quilt top in both directions and mark. Match marks on the border with the corners of the quilt top and pin. Easing in any fullness, pin the border to the quilt top between the center and corners. Sew the border to the quilt top, beginning and ending the seams exactly ¼" from each corner of the top and backstitching at the beginning and end of the seams.

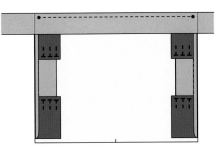

4. Repeat Step 3 to sew the bottom, and then the side borders, to the center section of the quilt top. To temporarily move the first two borders out of the way, fold and pin the ends.

5. Fold one corner of the quilt top diagonally with right sides together and matching edges.

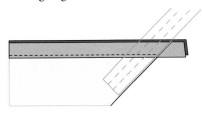

6. Use a ruler to mark a stitching line as shown.

7. Pin the borders together along the drawn line. Sew on the drawn line, backstitching at the beginning and end of the seam.

8. Turn the mitered corner right side up. Check to make sure it will lie flat with no gaps or puckers.

9. Trim the seam allowance to ¼"; press to one side.

10. Repeat Steps 5–9 to miter each remaining corner.

MARKING, LAYERING, AND BASTING
MARKING DESIGNS ONTO THE QUILT TOP

If you haven't already done so, now that the quilt top is complete, it is time to think about the quilting design. There are many wonderful designs available for stitching the layers together. Some require marking the design on the quilt top before joining the three layers together. Fabric marking pencils, various types of chalk markers, and fabric marking pens with inks that disappear when exposed to air or water are readily available and work well for different applications. Lead pencils work well on light-color fabrics, but the marks may be difficult to remove. White pencils work well on dark-color fabrics, and silver pencils show up well on many colors.

When you choose to mark your quilt, whether you mark before or after the layers are basted together is a factor in deciding which marking tool to use. If you mark with chalk or chalk pencil, handling the quilt during basting may rub off the markings. Intricate or ornamental designs may not be practical to mark as you quilt; mark these designs before basting using a more durable marker. Marks should be carefully removed according to the manufacturer's instructions. Press down only as hard as necessary to make a visible line.

When choosing marking tools, take all these factors into consideration and test different markers on scrap fabric until you find the one that gives the desired result.

Some quilters simply use a ruler and marking pencil to draw quilting lines while others use quilting stencils designed for this purpose. A wide variety of precut quilting stencils as well as entire books of quilting patterns are available. Using a stencil makes it easier to mark intricate or repetitive designs on your quilt top.

Precut quilting stencil for marking the design.

BASTING THE LAYERS

The process of joining the three layers of the quilt (top, batting, and backing) is called layering and basting. The method used depends on whether the quilt is being prepared for hand or machine quilting or tying. Use a large utility table for this step. Several may be necessary if you are making a large quilt.

To prepare the quilt for layering and basting you will need the following:

- Quilt top neatly pressed
- Batting—at least 4" larger than the quilt top all the way around. If you are using packaged batting, it is best to take it out of the packaging and allow it to relax to remove all of the folds before layering.
- Backing fabric—at least 4" larger than the quilt top all the way around.

BACKING FABRIC

QUILT SIZE	PIECING DIAGRAM*	YARDAGE: BASED ON 42" WIDE FABRIC
35" X 56"	A	1¾
50" X 65"	B	3
63" X 87"	C	5⅛
63" X 92"	C	5⅜
78" X 87"	C	5⅛
84" X 92"	D	7⅜
88" X 88"	D or E	7¾
90" X 108"	D	8
92" X 100"	D	8⅜
96" X 96"	D or E	8⅜

*Allows for a 4" extension all the way around the edge of the quilt top for layering and basting.

LAYERING AND BASTING FOR HAND QUILTING

This method is appropriate if you are planning to quilt in a hoop. If using a quilting frame, stretch the three layers onto the frame using the instructions that accompany it.

1. Use masking tape to secure the edges of the backing fabric to the table with the wrong side facing up. The backing should be slightly taut, so give a small tug on the tape when pressing it onto the table. If using a directional fabric, keep this in mind when placing the quilt top onto the layers.

2. Place the batting over the backing fabric, smoothing it evenly from the center to the edges.

3. Position the quilt top over the batting.

4. Use straight pins placed approximately 8" apart to hold the layers together for basting.

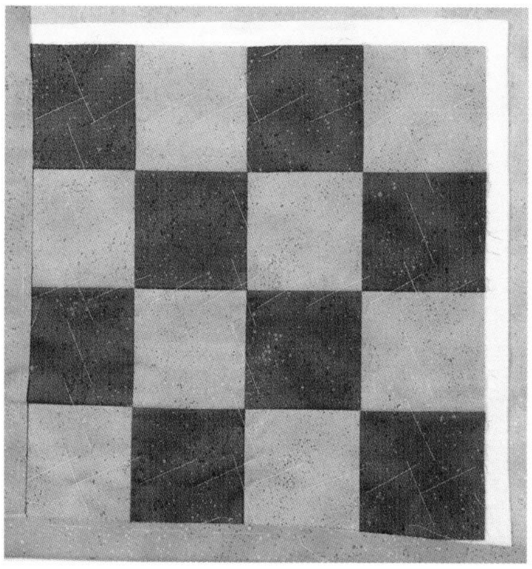

5. Use a light-colored thread and darning needle to secure the layers with a long diagonal basting stitch (see diagram, below). The stitches should start in the center of the quilt and form an overall grid approximately 6" apart.

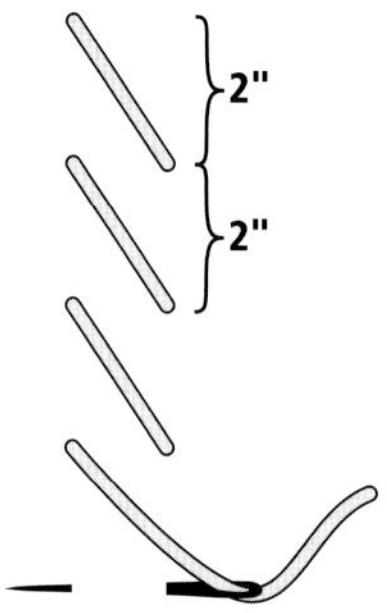

Diagonal basting stitch

6. Remove the straight pins as well as masking tape from around the edges.

Then to protect the edges of the quilt top while quilting, turn and fold the extension of backing fabric over the edge of the quilt top. Use long running basting stitches to hold it in place.

LAYERING AND BASTING FOR MACHINE QUILTING

1. Refer to Steps 1–3 for Layering and Basting for Hand Quilting.

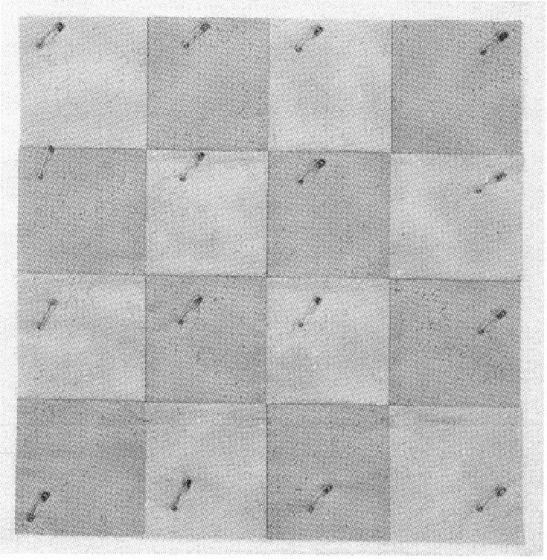

2. Working from the center of the quilt to the edges, use small safety pins to secure the three layers. Pins should be placed approximately 6" apart.

3. Remove the masking tape from around the edges.

LAYERING AND BASTING FOR TYING

1. Refer to Steps 1–4 for Layering and Basting for Hand Quilting.

PIECING DIAGRAMS FOR BACKING

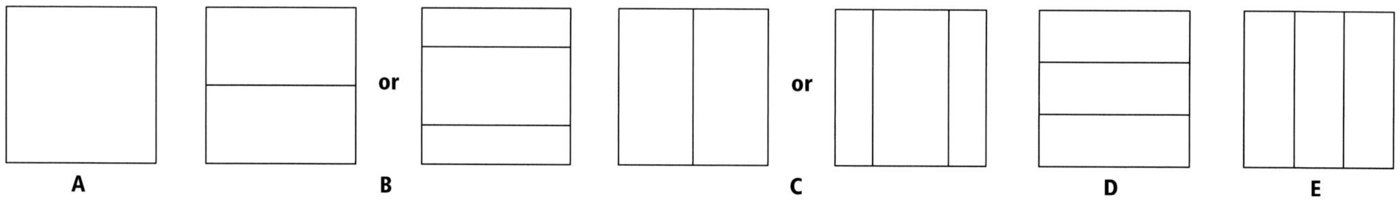

Alex Anderson enjoys hand quilting on the beautiful handcrafted frame made by her father Joe Sladky.

QUILTING
HAND QUILTING

For many quiltmakers, this step is the icing on the cake. They love the rhythm of the rocking motion used to make the small, even quilting stitches that hold the three layers of the quilt together. These stitches also provide an additional texture and design to the quilt. Hand quilting can be done in a hoop or in a quilting frame. Many quilters like the ability to easily transport their quilts and prefer using one of the numerous styles of hoops available to them. The large quilting frames that are associated with quilting bees of the past are the perfect solution for working on a larger quilt.

Although a big enough space is needed to accommodate the frame, it holds the layers of the quilt taut to provide the needed tension for hand quilting.

If using a frame, follow the manufacturer's instructions for properly attaching the quilt to achieve the best tension for quilting. If using a hoop, separate the outer ring from the inner ring and position the center of the quilt in the middle of the hoop. Whether you use a hoop or a frame, it is better to begin stitching in the center of the quilt and work toward the edges.

THE QUILTING STITCH

1. Thread a quilting needle with a short (approximately 20") length of quilting thread in a color to coordinate with your quilt.

2. Tie one end of the thread with a knot.

3. Place a thimble on the middle finger of your quilting hand (right if you are right-handed) and a finger cot on the index finger of the same hand.

4. Beginning approximately ½" away from the starting point of the quilting line, insert the needle into the top layer of the quilt. The needle will glide into the batting layer and not go through to the backside of the quilt. Bring the needle up at the starting point of the quilting line and pull it and the length of the thread all the way through. The knot should be resting on the top of the quilt. Give a gentle tug on the thread to "pop" the knot into the batting layer.

5. To prevent the knot from coming through with the first stitch, the first stitch will be a backstitch. This means that the needle will be inserted behind rather than in front of the thread. This is the first stitch and tends to be the most difficult to make short. Holding the end of the needle with the thimble, position the tip of the needle on the fabric.

6. Position the thumb approximately 2" in front of the needle while turning the needle perpendicular to the quilt. Push slightly on the end of the needle with the thimble while bringing the tip of the needle up and through the quilt to make a stitch. You should feel a slight prick on the finger of your free hand that is on the backside of the quilt. The thumb controls the length of this stitch. Do not push the needle all the way through.

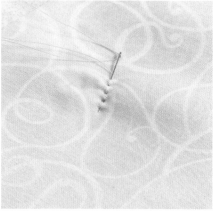

7. Quickly repeat the down and up rocking motion with the thumb and thimble finger to feed approximately four stitches onto the needle.

8. Firmly grasp the tip of the needle with the index finger (the one with the cot) and thumb; pull the needle and thread all the way through.

9. Continue with the quilting stitches to the end of the quilting line.

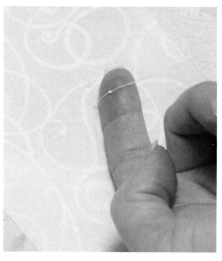

10. To end the stitching, bring the needle and thread to the top of the quilt. Make a small knot on the top by wrapping the thread twice around the needle and pull to create a knot.

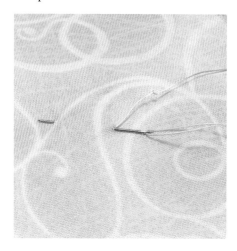

11. Insert the needle into the same hole in which the thread emerged, again just going into the batting layer. Bring it out again approximately ½" away. Give a gentle pull on the thread to "pop" the knot on the top into the batting layer. Cut the excess length of thread.

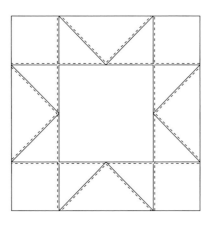

MACHINE QUILTING

Quilting by machine continues to appeal to quilters who enjoy the speed it provides. Most home sewing machines will do the job just fine if used with a walking foot or darning foot. The walking foot allows the three layers of the quilt to feed evenly through the machine at the same rate, preventing pleats and puckering on the backside of the quilt. Some machines made by Brother and Juki have models with longer beds to accommodate the bulk of the quilt. Bernina has a new model with a stitch regulator to control and even the length of the stitches. Achieving even stitch length requires practice for anyone interested in machine quilting.

Large machines, called "longarms" are also very popular among quilters who may not only want to quilt their own quilts but perhaps start a business quilting for others. If you are a quilter who "sends your quilt out to be quilted," this may be the type of machine used by your quilter. It has a large frame to hold the layers of the quilt taut during the quilting process.

Whether you are working on a home machine or a longarm, you will want to start with some simple quilting, such as "in the ditch," outline quilting, straight/diagonal and meandering before attempting some of the more challenging designs.

IN THE DITCH

Stitching that is made right into the seam is called in the ditch or ditch quilting. The purpose is to hold the layers while hiding the thread. Use a thread color to blend with the fabric. Use a bobbin thread in a similar color, rather than high contrast to prevent small dots of color from showing through on either side of the quilt. The clear threads (monofilaments) are used for this purpose as they become invisible after sewing. Some machines have presser feet with guides that run along the seam line while sewing, These are very helpful in keeping stitches right on the seam line.

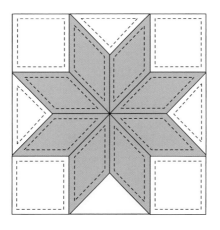

OUTLINE QUILTING

Stitching that follows the outline of the shapes of the pieced or appliquéd designs is called "outline" quilting. Marking is generally not necessary as the side of the shape can be used as a guide for stitching.

STRAIGHT OR DIAGONAL LINE QUILTING

The spacing of straight line or diagonal quilting can vary according to the patchwork design you are using. Choose

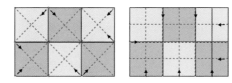

this pattern to add strength and texture to utility quilts and other projects that need stability.

Stitching on the bias of your fabric can cause more "give" than you would experience when you stitch on the straight-grain. Good basting is an important step in diagonal line quilting. Be sure to alternate the direction in which you are quilting. For example, work down, top left to bottom right, then return up, bottom right to top left. This keeps the fabrics from moving in the single direction of the quilt stitches and distorting your finished quilt.

MEANDERING

Think of large puzzle pieces or wiggly lines, and you will have a picture of what meandering looks like. Rather than exactly following any lines or shapes, these curved lines are made randomly to form an all-over pattern either within a confined space or to cover the entire quilt top. The space between the lines depends on the look you want and the type of batting used. Start with big movements to get a feel for the flow of the design and then gradually work to smaller spacing between the curves, if you desire. Very closely spaced meandering is called stippling or stipple quilting.

Longarm machines are popular among some machine quilters who work on large quilts or are interested in turning their skills into a fulltime business.

STITCHING METHOD

The following instructions are for straight-line quilting, which requires a walking foot or even-feed foot. The term "straight-line" is somewhat deceptive, since curves (especially gentle ones) as well as straight lines can be stitched with this technique.

1. Wind your sewing machine bobbin with general-purpose thread that matches the quilt backing. Do not use quilting thread. Thread the needle of your machine with general-purpose or transparent monofilament thread if you want your quilting to blend with your quilt top fabrics. Use decorative thread, such as a metallic or contrasting-color general-purpose thread, when you want the quilting lines to stand out more. Set the stitch length for 6 to 10 stitches per inch and attach the walking foot to the sewing machine.

2. After pin-basting, decide which section of the quilt will have the longest continuous quilting line, oftentimes the area from center top to center bottom. Leaving the area exposed where you will place your first line of quilting, roll up each edge of the quilt to help reduce the bulk, keeping fabrics smooth. Smaller projects may not need to be rolled.

3. Start stitching at the beginning of longest quilting line, using very short stitches for the first ¼" to "lock" the beginning of the quilting line. Stitch across the project, using one hand on each side of the walking foot to slightly spread the fabric and guide it through the machine. Lock stitches at the end of the quilting line.

4. Continue machine quilting, stitching longer quilting lines first to stabilize the quilt before moving on to other areas. Other straight lines and gentle curves can be stitched using the walking foot.

FREE MOTION QUILTING

For more decorative designs such as those shown on pages 227-233, it will be necessary to use a darning foot. This style of machine quilting is called free motion. To practice free motion quilting, lower the feed dogs on the sewing machine to provide a smooth surface while stitching. Use the needle as a pencil to draw the desired designs. It takes practice to achieve even stitches. Start with simple shapes and with time and patience you will improve.

TYING

Holding the layers of a quilt together with ties of yarn or thread is not a new idea. Many old utility quilts were secured with wool yarn. It is a quick and easy method for finishing a quilt. The ties can either be made by hand using a large needle and heavy thread or yarn or by machine with a tacking stitch. A zigzag stitch on the sewing machine is used for this.

TYING BY HAND

1. Thread a needle with a long length of either embroidery floss, perle cotton thread or yarn.

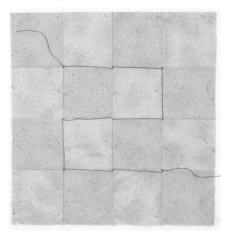

2. Working from the center to the edges, take small stitches approximately 6" apart. This can be done in one continuous line of stitching.

3. Cut the length of thread between stitches then tie the ends into a square knot.

4. Leave approximately a 1" tail, trimming any extra, if necessary.

TYING BY MACHINE

1. Take a few stitches in place to secure the ends of the thread.

2. Set the machine for zigzag and take about four complete stitches.

3. End by taking a few stitches in place to secure the thread and prevent it from coming loose when cut.

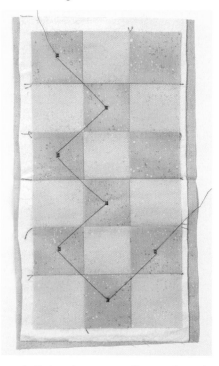

4. Raise the presser foot and, without cutting the chain of thread, move to another section of the quilt. Repeat Steps 1–3.

5. After all the stitches have been made, cut the chain of thread between the stitches on both the front and back of the quilt.

FINISHING

ATTACHING A SLEEVE

A sleeve is a tube of fabric that is attached to the back of the quilt across the entire top. It is used for hanging the quilt.

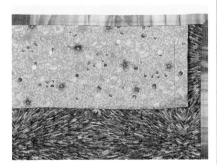

1. Cut a 6" to 8" strip of fabric the width of the quilt plus 1". Turn under ½", press and stitch a hem on each end.

2. With the right side facing out, fold and press the strip in half lengthwise.

3. With raw edges even with each other, stitch the sleeve to the backside of the quilt, along the top edge.

4. Hand slip stitch the folded edge to the backing fabric.

BINDING

Attaching the binding is the last step in the quiltmaking process. The binding is generally a separate piece of fabric that is double-folded and sewn around the outer edges of the quilt to encase the raw edges of the layers. The fabric strips used for the binding are best cut on the straight grain of the fabric and sewn together for the needed length. Bias strips are best used for quilts that have curved edges, as the bias cut will allow the strips to curve nicely around the edges. Some fabrics, such as plaids and stripes look great when cut and stitched on the bias. If using bias cut strips, be careful not to pull the strips while sewing and always use a walking foot to allow the layers to feed evenly. See page 96 for more about bias binding. As a rule, it is always best to use a walking foot, regardless of the cut of the fabric strips. Binding strips can be attached in four separate pieces, one for each side of the quilt, or with one long continuous piece. The difference is the finished look at the corners. The continuous strip creates a small miter on both the front and back of the quilt, while the four separate strips do not.

STRAIGHT BINDING WITH OVERLAPPED CORNERS

This binding is sewn in four separate strips and forms straight seams at the corners.

1. Measure then cut and sew strips together for each side of the quilt top. Add 2" to the measurement for both the top and bottom strips.

YARDAGE FOR BINDING

FINISHED SIZE	EXTENSION	CUT STRIP WIDTH	NO. OF 42" LONG STRIPS	YARDAGE FOR
¼"	none	1⅞"	5	Crib: ⅜
			8	Twin/Long Twin: ½
			9	D/Queen: ½
			10	King/Cal King: ⅝
⅜"	⅛"	2¼"	5	Crib: ⅜
			8	Twin/Long Twin: ½
			9	D/Queen: ⅝
			10	King/Cal King: ⅝
½"	¼"	2¾"	5	Crib: ½
			8	Twin/Long Twin: ⅝
			9	D/Queen: ¾
			10	King/Cal King: ⅞
¾"	½"	3¾"	5	Crib: ⅝
			8	Twin/Long Twin: 1
			9	D/Queen: 1
			10	King/Cal King: 1⅛
1	¾"	4¾"	5	Crib: ¾
			8	Twin/Long Twin: 1⅛
			9	D/Queen: 1¼
			10	King/Cal King: 1⅜

*Note: A ¼" seam allowance is used for the double-fold binding. An extension of batting and backing is needed beyond the edge of the quilt top for all bindings wider than ¼" finished.

67

2. With the right side of the fabric strips facing out, fold and press in half lengthwise.

3. With raw edges even with each other, use a ¼" seam allowance to stitch the side binding strips onto the right side of the quilt.

4. Turn and pin the binding to the backside of the quilt and hand stitch to the backing fabric along the folded edge. Use binding clips to hold in place for stitching.

5. With raw edges even with each other, use a ¼" seam allowance to stitch the top and bottom binding strips onto the right side of the quilt. Allow a 1" extension on each end.

6. Fold the binding strip over the stitching line, then fold the extensions in. Finally, fold the binding to the backside and hand stitch to the backing fabric along the folded edge of the binding.

CONTINUOUS STRAIGHT BINDING WITH MITERED CORNERS

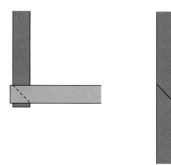

1. Using a diagonal seam, sew binding strips together end to end. Fold in half lengthwise and press.

2. Beginning with one end near center on bottom edge of quilt, lay binding around quilt to make sure that seams in binding will not end up at a corner. Adjust placement if necessary. Matching raw edges of binding to raw edge of quilt top, pin binding to right side of quilt along one edge.

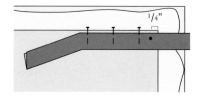

3. When you reach first corner, mark ¼" from corner of quilt top.

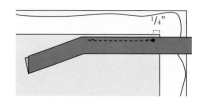

4. Beginning approximately 10" from end of binding and using ¼" seam allowance, sew binding to quilt, backstitching at beginning of stitching and at mark. Lift needle out of fabric and clip thread.

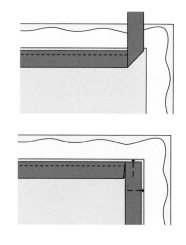

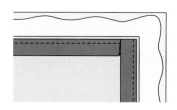

5. Fold binding as shown and pin binding to adjacent side, matching raw edges. When you've reached the next corner, mark ¼" from edge of quilt top.

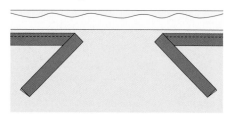

6. Backstitching at edge of quilt top, sew pinned binding to quilt; backstitch at the next mark. Lift needle out of fabric and clip thread.

7. Continue sewing binding to quilt, stopping approximately 10" from starting point.

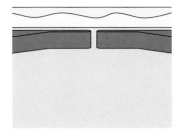

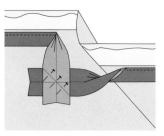

8. Bring beginning and end of binding to center of opening and fold each end back, leaving a ¹/₄" space between folds. Finger press folds.

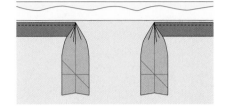

9. Unfold ends of binding and draw a line across wrong side in finger-pressed crease. Draw a line through the lengthwise pressed fold of binding at the same spot to create a cross mark. With edge of ruler at cross mark, line up 45° angle marking on ruler with one long side of binding. Draw a diagonal line from edge to edge. Repeat on remaining end, making sure that the two diagonal lines are angled the same way.

10. Matching right sides and diagonal lines, pin binding ends together at right angles.

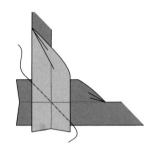

11. Machine stitch along diagonal line, removing pins as you stitch.

12. Lay binding against quilt to double check that it is correct length.

13. Trim binding ends, leaving ¹/₄" seam allowance; press seam open. Stitch binding to quilt.

14. If using 2³/₄"w binding (finished size ¹/₂"), trim backing and batting a ¹/₄" larger than quilt top so that batting and backing will fill the binding when it is folded over to quilt backing. If using narrower binding, trim backing and batting even with edges of quilt top.

15. On one edge of quilt, fold binding over to quilt backing and pin pressed edge in place, covering stitching line. On adjacent side, fold binding over, forming a mitered corner. Repeat to pin remainder of binding in place.

16. Blindstitch binding to backing, taking care not to stitch through to front of quilt.

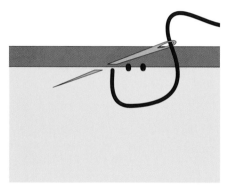

beyond the basics

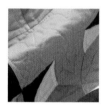

NOW THAT YOU ARE COMFORTABLE with the basic skills, it's time to enter the broader landscape of quiltmaking. Here you will discover many methods of quilting gathered from near and far, each bringing a different appearance to the finished project. Pieced quilts, whole cloth quilts, art quilts and oh so many more! Large or small, intricate or plain, all have a place in the world of quilting. Each and every one of them is unique and all are beautiful.

Since the beauty of quilting is both tactile and visual, it's time to perfect your color skills. When selecting fabrics the choices are unlimited, from sublime silks to rustic denims and everything in between. Recognizing what colors work together and discovering the symmetry of pattern will assist you in creating a muted, subtle, understated quilt or maybe a bold, bright colorful one. Your decisions make the difference.

Think of beyond the basics as an appetizer before the main course. Come along and together we will sample the many styles and techniques.

One of the most important elements of a successful quilt can often be the most challenging. Selecting a color scheme to complement the pattern you have selected for your project takes time and practice.

Choose a project, then choose the fabrics. Color delights the eye and speaks to the heart. But how do you decide among all the wonderful color selections? You might look outdoors to the colors of nature in all the seasons. You will find everything from earth tones to flamingo pink and brilliant turquoise. Butterflies, rocks, trees, and flowers can inspire you. Let nature guide you; then use the information below to help you express yourself.

THE COLOR WHEEL

Use the color wheel as a starting point for creating your own color combinations. Primary colors are red, blue, and yellow. Halfway between the primary colors are the secondary colors: orange, green, and violet. All the colors between the primary and secondary colors are intermediate colors.

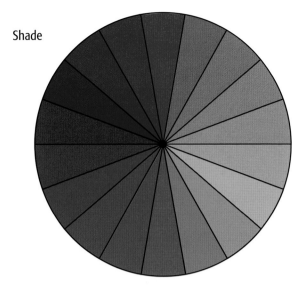
Shade

SHADE is pure color with black added. Shades have depth and richness. They include the warm hues of autumn and the deep blue tones of night.

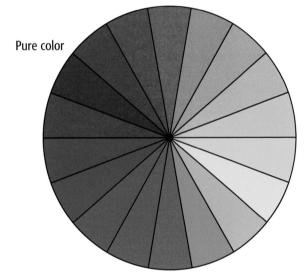
Pure color

COLOR TERMS

PURE COLOR is undiluted, intense, and brilliant. The use of pure color creates excitement and energy.

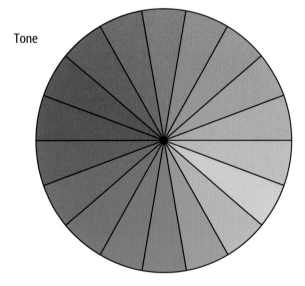
Tone

TONE is pure color, a tint, or a shade that has been grayed. Tones are subdued, subtle colors. Tones enhance the colors around them.

High intensity · Low intensity

INTENSITY refers to the degree to which a pure color has been tinted, shaded, or toned.

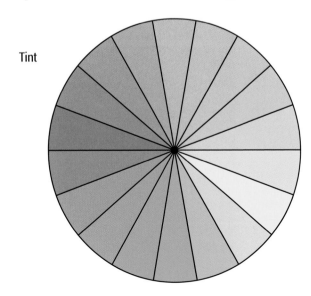
Tint

TINT is pure color with white added. Pastels are tints. A tinted color conveys a feeling of softness and delicacy.

Value

Contrast

VALUE of a color refers to its darkness or lightness. The contrast between the values of colors can be very strong, such as black to white, or very subtle, such as yellow to white.

COLOR SCHEMES

Colors can be combined in endless ways. Certain types of combinations will always produce pleasing results. Deciding on a color scheme depends on your project. Home décor items usually are based on the colors in the home. Wearing apparel often is based on the color preferences of the person who will be wearing it. Choose colors you love and have fun finding new ways of combining them with other colors.

Decide what mood or feeling you want to convey. Warm colors such as red, orange, and yellow suggest heat. They can be fun and exciting to work with. Cool colors convey a wintry mood, relaxing and subtle. Choose the type of color that will enhance the feeling you want: pure color, tints, shades, or tones. Allow one type to dominate. The next consideration is value. How dark and light the colors are in each project affects the feeling of the piece. Strong contrasts in value are dramatic. Low contrasts in value are calming.

The following color schemes will help you explore ways to combine your favorite colors. In all the color schemes below, the colors can range from bright and pure to grayed and subtle. The values can also range from very strong to very soft.

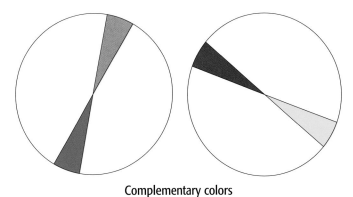

In these two examples, the pure colors green and red (center squares) darken when shaded (at left) and lighten when tinted (at right).

MONOCHROMATIC schemes use colors from the same "family." Choose one color from the color wheel and use different values, tints, tones, and shades to create a color scheme. Monochromatic color schemes are cohesive and sophisticated.

Complementary colors

COMPLEMENTARY colors are opposite each other on the color wheel. Allow one of the colors to dominate. For example, if red is the dominant color, use a touch of green to complement it.

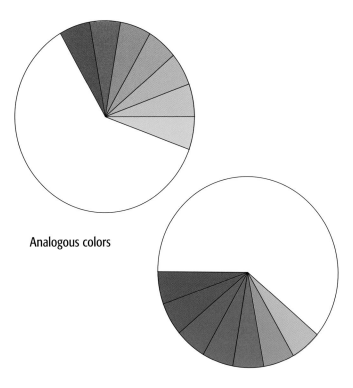

Analogous colors

ANALOGOUS colors are next to each other on the color wheel. Choose three to seven colors that are side by side. Include tints, tones, or shades with intense colors for a dynamic color scheme. Vary the values of the colors you have selected to add interest to your color scheme.

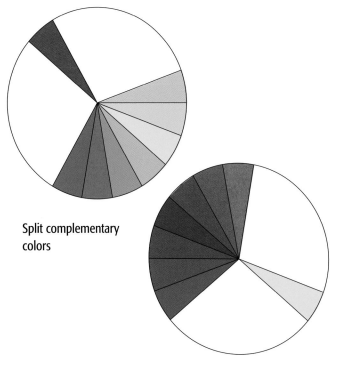

Split complementary colors

SPLIT-COMPLEMENTARY color schemes use an analogous combination of colors with an added twist: a complementary color. The color of your complement will be opposite the middle color of your analogous color group. If the analogous color scheme is made up of red, red orange, and orange, the compliment would be blue-green. Split-complimentary color schemes are among the most beautiful. ✿

73

A pieced heart is revealed when the top layer of yellow fabric is turned under using reverse appliqué techniques. Made by Jan Mullen.

NEEDLE TURN APPLIQUÉ

This traditional method of stitching fabric shapes to a background fabric is used in many of the heirloom quilts, especially the Baltimore Albums. It takes a bit of practice to perfect the technique, especially when working with very small shapes. Unlike some of the other methods described in the Basics section, this one has no fabric or paper guidelines for stitching. Instead, the edges of the shapes are turned under using the needle and then stitched in place to the background fabric using a small hand appliqué stitch. See page 55.

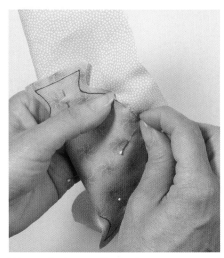

Edges of the appliqué shape are turned under with the needle.

The beautiful, vibrantly-colored and intricately stitched owl in this mola is an example of the reverse appliqué technique. Collection of Dena Canty.

REVERSE APPLIQUÉ

This method differs from other appliqué in that the fabric for the design shapes is below the top layer of fabric, which is usually the background fabric. The top layer of fabric is cut and turned under to expose the underlying layer, creating the design shape. The edges of the cut shape are turned under and stitched in place with an appliqué or embroidery stitch.

The mola is a beautiful example of the use of this technique. Molas are made by the Kuna (or Cuna) Indians who live in the San Blas Islands off the coast of Panama. Mola is the Kuna word for blouse. These intricately stitched, multilayered panels are used for the fronts and backs of the women's loosely fitted blouses. Many of the designs reflect traditional themes from their legends and culture, such as animals, flowers, and historical objects, as well as objects or people from their everyday lives.

A mola is usually made from 100% cotton and can have from two to seven layers of fabric. The dominant colors are red, black, and orange, but every color can be used as an accent. Using a reverse appliqué technique, cuts are made following the outline of marked designs. The cut edges are turned under to reveal layers of color and fabric underneath. The cuts can be made through one or multiple layers to reveal the maker's color of choice. Generally the larger shapes are cut from the top layer with smaller patterns cut from the underlying layers.

The Pa Ndau, or flower cloth, of the Hmong people is similar in style to the mola. The Hmong emigrated from China in the mid-nineteenth century and settled in Laos, Cambodia, and North Vietnam. Their beautifully stitched pictures provide a way of telling stories and keeping their history alive.

Detail of Baby Biscuit quilt. Made by Sherry Hutchens.

BISCUIT

The technique of making small puffy fabric pillows is also called puff quilting. The stuffed pillows join together to make the easy-to-construct and charming biscuit quilt. The look of this quilt is appealing as it is reminiscent of warm biscuits fresh from the oven. A project with instructions for making a baby biscuit quilt is found on page 106.

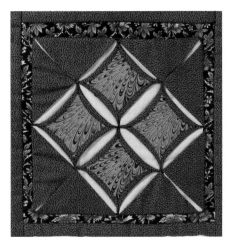

This small cathedral window block illustrates the folding required to reveal the background layer of fabric. Made by Laura Nownes.

REVERSE APPLIQUÉ

Try this technique with a small heart design:

1. Cut two 4" x 4" pieces of fabric, one for the heart shape and one for the background.

2. Use a pencil to trace the heart shape from page 222 onto the background fabric.

3. Use a pair of embroidery scissors to remove the inside of the heart shape, cutting ¼" inside the marked

line. Make small clips, almost to the line, at both the top and bottom of the heart.

4. With both right sides facing up, place the cut-out background fabric over the heart fabric. Secure with basting stitches or small sequin pins.

5. Use the tip of a needle to turn under the raw edge of the heart shape on the background fabric and stitch to the heart fabric with small appliqué stitches. See page 55.

CATHEDRAL WINDOW

This beautiful traditional quilt pattern showcases windows of fabrics in a hand-rolled frame of background fabric. There is no batting or backing in this style quilt as the background forms the backing. The background fabric is folded and stitched to four thicknesses to create a heavy textured framework. Individual units are then sewn together to make the overall quilt. The window pieces are small, and can be made from a variety of fabrics, making it a perfect scrap quilt pattern.

The size of the background square determines the finished size of the window. The most common sizes to cut background squares range from 6"-9". For our example, we will use 6½" x 6½" background squares, which will make 3" folded squares. Each block is made from 4 folded squares for a 6" finished block. **Note:** These instructions are for a two-color background (green and light green) as shown in photo. For a traditional single color background, do not cut any small squares and skip Step 5.

For each block:
Cut 4 background squares 6½" x 6½" from main fabric

Cut 4 small squares 3½" x 3½" of a contrasting fabric.

Cut 4 windowpanes 2" x 2".

1. Press each edge of background square ¹/₄" to the wrong side.

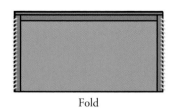

Fold

2. Matching right sides, fold background square in half. Whipstitch each short edge together. Turn right side out.

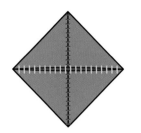

3. Matching seams at center, refold background into a square. Whipstitch open edges together through top layer only. This is the right side of the square.

Fold

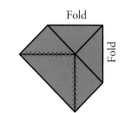

Fold

4. With right side facing up, fold each corner of square to the center and press; unfold.

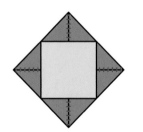

5. Press each edge of a 3¹/₂" x 3¹/₂" small square ¹/₄" to the wrong side. Matching pressed edges of small square with foldlines on right side of square, appliqué small square to background square.

6. Stitching through all layers, tack points of folded corners at center. Edges of folded corners will be loose. This is the right side of the folded square. Make 4 folded squares.

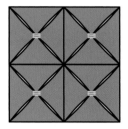

7. Matching right sides, whipstitch 2 folded squares together to make a rectangle. Repeat with remaining squares. Whipstitch 2 rectangles together to make a block.

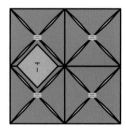

8. With right side facing, pin one windowpane square to the center of the diamond shape formed where two folded squares meet.

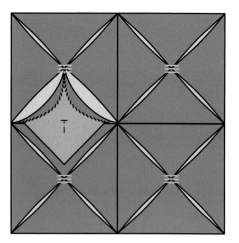

9. Curving as shown, roll and blindstitch each folded edge of the background fabric over each raw edge of the windowpane square. Repeat for remaining 3 windowpane squares to make one Cathedral Window Block.

10. Follow the chart, below, for the number of blocks, blocks in a row, and number of rows you will need to make a bed size quilt, based on a 6¹/₂" background square. Depending on the cut size of your background square, these numbers may vary.

11. Join the suggested number of blocks to make a row. Add windowpane squares to the diamonds formed by adjacent blocks. Join the suggested number of rows to make quilt top. Add windowpane squares to the diamonds formed by adjacent rows.

Size	Total Blocks	Blocks In A Row	Number of Rows
Twin	143	11	13
Double	168	12	14
Queen	224	14	16
King	288	16	18

Fabric folded flowers add an elegant dimension to any project. Pattern from Fantastic Fabric Folding by Rebecca Wat. Made by Laurie Grant.

FABRIC FOLDING

Fabric folding is inspired by the ancient Japanese art of paper-folding called origami. Designs can range from simple to complex. Fabric folding transforms scraps of fabric into elegant and impressive three-dimensional designs such as flowers and leaves.

For years quilters have added prairie points to their quilted projects. These simple folded shapes have been used on pillows and clothing as well as for edgings on quilts. Here are two methods for making simple folded prairie points.

METHOD ONE

1. Cut fabric squares. The cut size of the square is twice the finished height plus ½". For example, if you want the finished triangle to be 2½" high, cut 5½" squares.

2. With the right side of the fabric facing out, fold the square in half diagonally, and then in half again.

3. The folded squares are ready to place, raw edges even with the edge of the quilt and one inside the fold of the next. The amount of overlap can be adjusted to fit the length of the side of the quilt.

METHOD TWO

1. Cut fabric squares. The cut size of the square is twice the finished height plus ½".

2. With the right side of the fabric facing out, fold the square in half.

3. With the fold at the top, fold the upper corners even with the bottom raw edge.

4. The folded squares are ready to place, raw edges even with the edge of the quilt, overlapping as needed to fit the length of the side of the quilt.

FOUNDATION PIECING

The foundation used in this style of piecing can be fabric, paper, or washable paper made specifically for this use. The purpose of using a foundation is to stabilize the fabrics while piecing. Fabric shapes used are often randomly cut, such as in Crazy Quilts. The foundation fabric or paper is completely covered with fabric strips or shapes to create a new fabric or quilt block. The shapes can be very small or have points that may be difficult to sew using traditional piecing methods. Using a foundation makes construction easier. In addition to the Crazy Quilt project on page 139, the Miniature Bear's Paw quilt on page 122 and Ring Around the Rosie on page 144 use foundation piecing techniques.

PAPER FOUNDATION PIECING (MACHINE)

GENERAL TIPS BEFORE STARTING
Sew with the printed side of the paper facing up. The fabric will be underneath the paper, next to the feed dogs on the sewing machine.

- Use an open toe or clear plastic presser foot for better visibility.
- Use a short stitch length, approximately 18 to 20 stitches per inch, when stitching through the paper. The short stitches make more perforations in the paper pattern allowing for easier removal of the paper. Also, stitches are less likely to come loose when the paper is torn away.
- Use a size 90/14 needle.
- Numbers are used on the printed patterns to indicate the stitching order of the individual fabric shapes.
- Keep in mind that the finished quilt block will be a mirror image of the printed paper pattern.

GENERAL INSTRUCTIONS FOR PAPER PIECING WITH FOUNDATION PAPER

1. Cut the fabric pieces using a minimum ⅜" seam allowance. Allow more for larger or odd-shaped pieces.

The small pieces used in Vivienne Moore's 19" x 19" Log Cabin Neighborhood quilt make it a perfect candidate for paper piecing techniques.

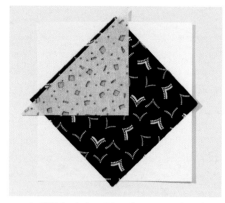

2. With the right side of the first fabric shape facing you, place it into its position (#1 on the unprinted side of the paper pattern). Turn the fabric and paper over so you can see the printed side of the paper and hold it up to a light source to be certain that at least ¼" of fabric extends beyond the printed lines of the shape.

3. Use a pin to secure the fabric shape to the paper pattern, pinning on the printed side of the paper only.

4. With right sides facing each other, place the second fabric shape on top of the first. Be sure that this fabric piece extends into the printed piece #2 shape by ¼" for the seam allowance. If you are unsure that the second fabric shape is in the proper position, pin it along the seam line (the printed line between #1 and #2) then flip it over the seam line to check that the entire printed shape #2 will be covered. This is especially helpful when working with plaid or striped fabrics or shapes with odd angles. When the fabric #2 is in the correct position, secure it with pins placed perpendicular to the sewing line.

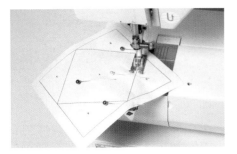

5. Stitch on the printed line between shapes #1 and #2, beginning and ending approximately ¼" before and after the line. It is not necessary to backstitch.

6. Use scissors or a rotary cutter to trim the seam allowance to ¼" (or slightly less for miniature blocks), trimming both fabrics at the same time.

7. Continue adding pieces in the same manner. Trim the edges of the block on the outer dashed lines.

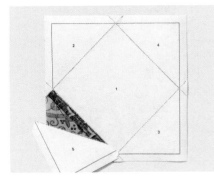

8. Remove the paper pattern to complete the block.

ENGLISH PAPER PIECING is a method of hand piecing using freezer paper, pre-cut paper, or plastic foundation shapes. This is an accurate method for joining shapes that may otherwise be difficult to sew together on the machine. This is often used when making a traditional Grandmother's Flower Garden Quilt. Foundation hexagons can be cut from freezer paper or packages of pre-cut paper or plastic foundation hexagons are available in a variety of sizes.

To cut foundation hexagons from freezer paper, you will first need to make a template. Trace hexagon pattern from project instructions (if given) onto template plastic or draw a hexagon on template plastic or sturdy poster board; cut out on drawn lines. You will need to make a freezer paper foundation for each hexagon in your pattern.

To easily cut multiple freezer paper foundations, cut your freezer paper into sheets (8¹/₂" x 11" is a handy size). With dull side facing up and leaving about ¹/₄" between shapes, trace around the template onto a sheet of freezer paper as many times as will fit on the sheet. With dull side up, stack 5 unmarked sheets together; place traced sheet on top. Touch the tip of a hot iron to the center of each hexagon to fuse the sheets together; cut out on drawn lines. With dull side up and leaving at least ¹/₂" between shapes, press the freezer paper foundations onto the wrong side of your fabric. Cut fabric ¹/₄" larger on all sides than foundation hexagon. Follow Steps 3-6, right, to make fabric hexagons. Freezer paper foundations sometimes can be re-used up to two or three times.

To use pre-cut paper templates or plastic foundations, follow Steps 1-6, below, to cut out and make fabric hexagons. Pre-cut paper foundations can be re-used up to three times by lightly spray starching and dry ironing before each re-use.

1. Place the plastic or pre-cut paper foundation onto the wrong side of the fabric and secure with a pin in the center.

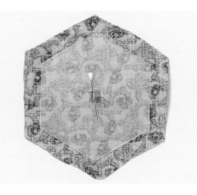

2. Cut fabric ¼" larger than the shape.

3. Turn the fabric extension over the edge of the shape. Working on one corner at a time, overlap the extension and take two small hand stitches to secure. Continue around the shape, making small stitches in each corner. The shape is prepared and ready to be joined to another prepared shape.

4. Place two prepared shapes right sides facing each other. Working on one side at a time, use a thread color to match the fabric to join the shapes together with small hand stitches.

79

5. Continue adding shapes to complete the design. To make the traditional grandmother's flower garden quilt pattern, begin with the centerpiece and work out to the edge of the pattern.

6. Remove foundation after the shapes are completely surrounded by other shapes. Simply snip the small stitches at the corners on the wrong side, and the foundation should come out easily.

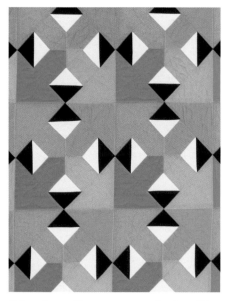

Using the quilt-as-you-go method, quilting is done in sections. Made by Georgia Bonesteel.

QUILT-AS-YOU-GO

Quilt-as-you-go is the popular method of joining three layers together in small sections (a decorative top, batting, and backing) then joining the sections to form an entire quilt. This method, also known as apartment quilting, sectional quilting, and lap quilting, adapts well to today's mobile lifestyle since the sections are easy to carry along wherever you go.

The important part of lap quilting begins at the initial design stage before any appliqué or patchwork piecing begins. One must take into account the bed size and final quilt size, then make divisions according to sections that are easily handled. Having this sketch or master plan on paper is crucial. Once the master plan and sections are established, make a paper code system to label each separate basted layer. These sections can all be about the same dimension, or they can be rows that are joined once the quilting is complete.

Just about any block setting can be lap quilted. Sometimes borders are sewn around blocks or blocks are sewn together as a unit. Outside decorative borders can be added to the perimeter blocks so that they are inclusive to the quilt.

RAG

Unlike traditional quilts with seam allowances hidden from view, these quilts have exposed seam allowances. The frayed edges of the shapes create the ragged look. Fabrics that fray such as flannel and denim work well for this type of quilt. Instead of a batting layer, there is a lining fabric, also made from a fabric that frays easily. Fabric pieces are sewn, wrong sides together, with a 1" seam allowance. Cuts are made into the seam allowances as well as the outer edges of the quilt, every ½" to ¾" apart. To fray the edges for the rag look, wash the quilt and tumble dry.

SLASHING

Similar to the rag quilt, slashed quilts also have exposed and ragged edges. Several layers of fabric are sandwiched together with narrow rows of stitching to create a pattern. The outer layers of the fabric are then "slashed" between the rows. After the fabric is washed and dried it becomes very soft and fluffy, just like chenille. This method works well with soft and loosely woven fabrics such as flannel and rayon. The Chenille Scarf on page 100 is an easy project that makes use of this technique.

Brightly colored squares of flannel fabrics make a lively crib quilt. Exposed seams create the rag look after washing. Made by Donna Heppler.

The soft cozy look of chenille was created using slashing techniques on both the baby blanket and scarf. Blanket by Priscilla Timm, scarf by Cheryl Simpson.

STENCILING AND STAMPING

Early in the 19th century, quilters used paint to stencil and stamp designs onto fabric for their quilts and bedspreads. This method provided a quick alternative by producing a similar look to the labor-intensive Baltimore Album Quilts of the same time. Early stencilers used oil-based paints.

The look of appliqué is shown in this Stenciled Heart Wreath designed by Adele Ingraham, adapted and stenciled by Ren Brown.

TRAPUNTO

Trapunto, or stuffed work, has been used to add decoration and texture to fabric from as early as 1400 A.D. Designs such as vines, leaves, and flowers are outlined with rows of stitches and then stuffed between the stitching lines to create a raised finish to the pattern. The stuffing is added to the underside of the piece, which is a lighter weight lining fabric. Traditionally, this technique was worked by hand with small running stitches, however, with practice, many quiltmakers today who are skilled in using their sewing machines can achieve the same look in a fraction of the time. The Trapunto Pillow on page 149 is a simple project using this technique by machine.

Machine trapunto designs add a textured elegance to the background and borders of this Spring Daisy quilt made by Lynne Todoroff. The Daisy Ballet trapunto pattern was designed by Hari Walner.

Detail of a hand trapunto quilt illustrates the beauty of this stuffed work. Collection of Laura Nownes.

TRAPUNTO BY HAND

Try this technique by hand for stuffing stems and flowers.

Front fabric: 100% cotton, solid color

Lining fabric: Batiste in a color to match front fabric.

Needles: No. 10 Betweens and long tapestry needle

Thread: 100% polyester (for strength) in a color to match front fabric

Yarn: worsted-weight to match fabric

Polyester fiberfill

Note: In photos dark thread is used for clarity. It is best to use thread in a color to match the fabric.

1. Trace the pattern onto the lining fabric. One section of the Old Tulips pattern on page 164 will work well for this practice piece, enlarging it to desired size.

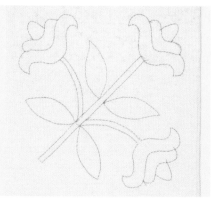

2. With wrong sides facing, use long stitches to baste the front and lining fabrics together.

3. Thread the betweens needle with a single strand of thread and add a knot in one end. Make small, even running stitches on all of the marked lines. Keep all of the knots on the lining side.

4. Thread the long tapestry needle with a double strand of yarn. To fill the stems, insert the needle at one end between the lining and front fabrics and run it to the opposite end.

5. Cut the excess length of yarn on each end.

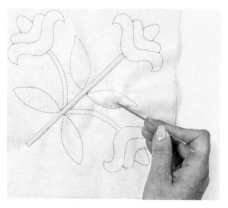

6. To fill the flowers and leaves, make a small slit in the center of each shape on the lining side.

Carefully insert fiberfill, using the blunt end of the needle to work it into the points.

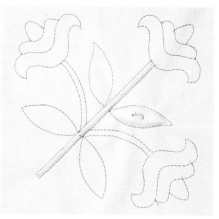

7. Use a small hand stitch to close the slits and the design is ready to be incorporated into the quilt.

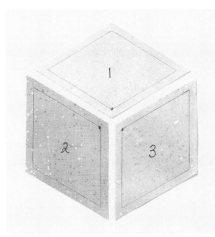

Y-SEAM CONSTRUCTION

This method of construction is used for patterns that fall into the eight-pointed star design category. Other patterns such as the traditional tumbling or baby blocks also require this construction. Think of the letter "Y." The point at which the three lines meet is the focus of this construction. Stitches never extend into the seam allowances at that point. Look at the three diamonds to be sewn together using this construction. For clarity, pieces have been numbered 1, 2, and 3 and seam allowance lines have been marked onto the wrong side of each piece. Dots are marked at the points where the three will meet.

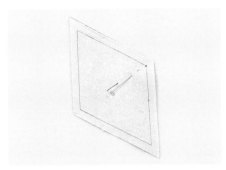

1. With right sides together, use a pin to anchor shapes 1 and 2 together at the dots.

2. With shape 1 on top, insert the needle into the dot and take a few stitches. Then take a few backstitches. This is necessary, since seams never cross each other at the dots. Continue the stitching line to the end of the shapes.

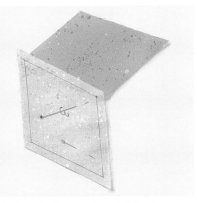

3. Attach shapes 1 and 3 in the same manner. With right sides together, place shape 3 on top and secure with a pin.

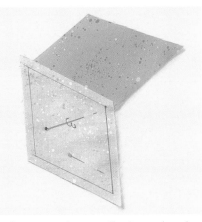

4. Insert the needle into the dot, take a few stitches forward and then in reverse. Then continue stitching to the end of the shapes.

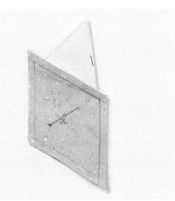

5. To complete the construction, join shapes 2 and 3. With right sides together and a pin to secure the dots, begin with a few stitches forward and then in reverse and continue stitching to the end of the shapes.

6. Turn the shapes to the backside. Press the seams in the directions shown in the photo. Note that the seam between shapes 2 and 3 is pressed open. This is one of the few cases in quiltmaking when this occurs. It is done to prevent excess bulk when these units are joined together with more of the same.

7. Turn and press the unit on the right side. The seams should meet perfectly at the "Y," with no puckers. Puckers will occur if any of the stitching lines extend beyond the dots into the seam allowance.

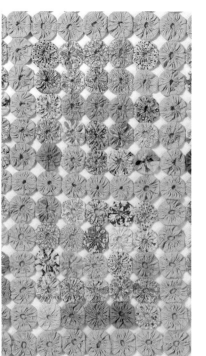

It is clear to see why this pattern was named the yo-yo. Gathered circles of fabric are stitched together to form the overall design. Collection of Dena Canty.

This handy yo-yo maker comes in various sized round, heart, flower, shamrock, and butterfly shapes.

YO-YO QUILT

Since it doesn't have batting or backing, the yo-yo quilt might instead be considered a decorative coverlet. Circles of fabric are gathered into puffy rounds called yo-yos. Individual yo-yos are joined together with hand stitches to make the overall coverlet. Yo-yo quilts were popular from the 1920s to the 1940s. Their popularity may be attributed to the fact that yo-yos are small, easy to hand sew, and portable. The small gathered circles were also used to make craft items such as clown dolls.

Used individually or in clusters, today's quilters also like to use yo-yos as appliqués for clothing, pillows, tote bags, and wall hangings. Their popularity has grown so quickly that there is a whole line of "yo-yo makers" designed specifically for making yo-yos.

TO MAKE TRADITIONAL YO-YOS

1. Cut fabric circles. A circle with a 4½" diameter makes a yo-yo that's approximately 2" wide when finished. The size can be adjusted to the look you desire. A small plate or saucer is helpful for tracing circles on your fabric.

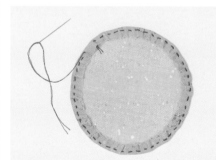

2. Use a double strand of thread with a knot in the end. Turning ¼" of the fabric edge to the backside as you go, sew small running stitches all the way around the circle.

3. Pull the thread to gather the edge. Be careful not to break the thread. There will be a small hole in the center of the gathered circle. The size of the hole will vary with the size of the yo-yo. The side with the hole is the right side of the yo-yo.

4. Keep the hole in the center and flatten the yo-yo. Make a few small backstitches, knot and cut the thread.

Make several more yo-yos.

5. To join, place two yo-yos with right sides facing. Use a small hand stitch to sew them together just where they touch when opened flat.

6. Continue sewing yo-yos together for the size coverlet you desire. It is complete when all of the yo-yos are stitched together; no batting or backing are needed.

quilt styles

Baltimore Album quilt designed and made by Patricia West. Read details of this outstanding work of art on page 86.

ALBUM AND SIGNATURE

These terms are used to describe a variety of different quilts. One of the most familiar of these is the Baltimore Album Quilt. Elly Sienkiewicz, leading expert and author of many books on the subject, defines the Baltimore Album Quilt as "an historic quilt style (ca. 1843–1855) characterized by a collection of different blocks set together in a grid design. The blocks are appliquéd (punctuated, though rarely, by a pieced star) and are comprised of botanical blocks, picture blocks of people, places, and things, and an intentional symbolism. Their iconography underscores the impassioned nature of great numbers of these quilts, having been made within a circumscribed period in the neighborhood of Baltimore City, Maryland."

This quilt style became popular at a time in history when young people had autograph books and albums and collected signatures from friends and family members. The invention of indelible ink encouraged the writing of messages on fabric.

Friendship, raffle, and presentation are other names for album and signature quilts. Although not all album quilts contain signatures, enough of them do to place them into this category. These quilts were made by groups of quilters, often friends and family members, and given to a special recipient to commemorate an event. Others were used as raffle prizes to raise funds for a particular organization or cause.

The Baltimore album quilt shown on page 85, was made by Patricia West of Centreville, Virginia, and was completed in 2001. The quilt measures approximately 96" square and is made of 100% cotton fabrics and batting. The appliqué is stitched with silk thread. The quilt includes all the traditional elements of a Baltimore album quilt, including appliqué, embroidery, and inked lettering. The layout of the blocks in the center uses traditional symmetry.

The patterns used include many traditional blocks from Elly Sienkiewicz's books as well as adaptations and original designs. The designs for the borders are entirely original. The armature of the borders is adapted from the enameled and etched designs on a pair of family heirloom buckle bracelets that date from about 1850—coincidentally close to the height of the era of the Baltimore album quilts. The bracelets were a gift from Patricia's grandmother on her 100th birthday.

The inking includes quotes from Thomas Jefferson, which appear around the border and inside the center medallion grape wreath. The drawing in the center medallion is the garden house at Monticello, his home in Charlottesville, Virginia. The silhouette is based on one done at Disneyland when Patricia was five years old. The quilt label on the back (see page 97) is a book about the quilt that tells of the artist's inspiration—both in life and in quilting.

The Diamond in the Square quilt made by Alex Anderson is typical of the simplistic pieced style made by the Amish.

AMISH

The Amish and their quilts are justly famous for their distinctive designs and use of color. The most recognizable quilts, the ones that built their reputation, came from Lancaster County, Pennsylvania. The classic period was from 1890 to 1940.

Amish quilts utilize large fields of geometric shapes (blocks and stripes in solid colors).

The fabrics used are deep, rich jewel-tone colors of darker hues. Black is used as an accent color. The quilting was renowned for its small stitches and the intricate designs set on the large solid color fields.

These quilts were made to be given as gifts. They were unsigned, as everyone in the community knew who created the quilts. This is why when you see an Amish quilt from the classic period the name of the quilter will often be listed as "anonymous."

Amish quilts reflect the everyday values of the Amish community—simple and powerful abstract designs and colors made with careful attention to excellence in workmanship.

ART QUILTS

During the 1960s and 1970s some quilters redefined the norms of quiltmaking by bringing a more artistic sensibility to their work. Prior to this time, quilts in this category were called contemporary or nontraditional. The desire was to incorporate artistic principles and experiences into the quilts. Quiltmakers used innovative designs with nontraditional fabrics and techniques. The goal was to expand the realm of the quilt from the home and family into public viewing in art galleries.

Royal Rags by Sandi Cummings. The richness of the fabrics set the mood for this art quilt. Sandi felt it would be fun to take the warm, creamy yellows and combine them with dark rich tones to make a cloth fit for a king. Private corporate collection. Photo by Sharon Risedorph.

BARGELLO

The designs for this style quilt are based on needlepoint tapestry techniques. Squares and rectangles of fabric are sewn together in waves of color to create intricate and complex patterns. Quilt design software is available for designing these beautiful quilts quickly and easily.

Ormen Lange (Long Serpent), 61" x 77", made by Eldrid Royset Forde of Norway. The title is inspired by a Norwegian counting rhyme.

BRODERIE PERSE

Fabrics made in France with large floral designs as well as imported chintz from India were originally used for these elaborately appliquéd quilts. Designs and motifs were cut out from the printed fabrics and appliquéd or embroidered to a background fabric using a tiny buttonhole stitch. Large printed motifs were used for the center medallions of these quilts. Some of the patterns included tree of life medallions, as well as all-over designs.

Tree of Life, by Judy Severson is a beautiful example of using a large chintz print for the broderie perse appliqué quilt.

CELTIC

Traditional Celtic patterns fool the eye into thinking that they are constructed from cords that interweave throughout a design. Celtic design can be found in many cultures today from Scandinavia to New Zealand. A more accurate name for this art style is "knotwork or interlace." Usually cords are continuous, having no apparent beginning or end. This was thought to represent "infinity, continuity, or eternity." (The Celts, having no concept of a beginning of humanity, thought all life was a continuum.) Complexity depends on the number of times cords cross each other, not from the number of cords used. This can vary from one upward. The cords are made from narrow strips of fabric cut on the bias. The cords are stitched onto a background fabric following a design pattern of "overs" and "unders." Spaces between the cords can be left open to expose the background fabric or an additional fabric can be inserted for more design interest.

The simplicity of Celtic Rose Window, (c. 1999) 41" x 58", made by Philomena Durcan, shows the continuous knotwork designs of the Celtic quilts.

Hold Your Heads Up High by Patricia Magaret is a beautiful example of watercolor/colorwash quilts. Photo by Mark LaMoreaux, Moscow, ID.

Detail of beautifully stitched and embellished crazy quilt. Designed and made by Judith Baker Montano.

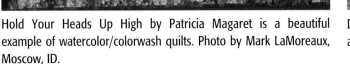

The simple shape of the Tumbler pattern is used in this antique charm quilt. Collection of Dena Canty.

CHARM

"Someday my Prince (Charming) will come." Such is the dream of many a young girl. During the Victorian era however, this dream became somewhat of a game. Girls would collect 999 scrap pieces of fabrics, no two being the same, and sew them into a quilt. (This was also done with buttons.) The belief was that if she were successful with her collection,

her true love would bring her the 1000th piece. Since most girls did not have an extensive stash of fabrics, they needed to be resourceful in trading or begging for pieces. For this reason, the charm quilt was also known as a "beggar's quilt." Simple, one-patch quilts, which use one pattern such as the Tumbler shown in the photo, are typical of this style. The charm quilt is the ultimate scrap quilt.

A variation on the "charm" game is the scrap quilt that contains one duplicate. The challenge is for the viewer to hunt for the duplicate pieces of scraps. This could keep many young family members entertained for hours.

COLORWASH OR WATERCOLOR

Quilts made in this style are constructed of many small squares of fabric, usually measuring about 1" or 2". Together the squares create the illusion of an impressionistic painting. Sometimes an overall colorwash look is desired while other quilts in this style "paint" an entire scene in fabric.

CRAZY

Crazy quilt author and teacher Judith Baker Montano states that by definition, crazy quilts are not really quilts at all. The fancy pieces of fabrics used are appliquéd to a square or rectangular piece of muslin fabric. The pieces are then sewn together to form the top. Every seam is then carefully covered with combinations of embroidery stitches. Once the top is embroidered it is sewn in pillowcase fashion to a fancy backing fabric. There is no batting in a crazy quilt. The two layers (top and backing) are tied together with invisible threads or fancy threads, with the ties visible on the back. To try your hand at crazy quilting using an updated method developed by Judith, see her project on page 139.

Love Thy Neighbor pillow by Alex Anderson combines redwork with shadow embroidery. The hidden message of "Love Thy Neighbor" is embroidered on top of the redwork design.

New machine-embroidered redwork quilt, made by Sandy Klop, designer of American Jane patterns.

90

EMBROIDERED

Many quilters also enjoy the fine art of hand embroidery and incorporate embroidered designs into their quilts. One of the most popular and highly recognizable embroidery styles is seen in redwork quilts. Outlines of charming little designs including animals, flowers, children, and toys are stitched primarily with either red or blue cotton embroidery floss on pieces of muslin fabric. In the past these colors were the most commonly used because they were the first to be colorfast. Any plain outline stitch, including the backstitch, and outline and stem stitches, is used on these simple designs, which were at one time given away by magazine publishers in an effort to promote new subscriptions. Later 6" squares of stamped designs were sold at dry good stores for one penny, giving them the name of "penny squares." These are often found in old redwork tea towels, bedspreads, pillows, and petticoats.

Today many computerized sewing machines have software available to create fantastic embroidered designs. With a few simple commands you can program the machine to work the designs in your desired thread colors. While you attend to other activities, the machine will stitch a beautiful design for you to incorporate into your next quilting project.

FEEDSACKS

In the early 1800s fabric was used to pack food such as sugar and grains. Thrifty women could not bear to throw away the precious cloth. Even though the original sacks were made of plain white cloth with just the contents and manufacturer's name printed on the outside, they were often recycled into tea towels, toys, diapers, nightgowns, and various other useful items. Later manufacturers began printing designs onto the fabric in an effort to increase sales, as multiple bags were often needed for larger projects such as clothing. Quilting was not far down the list of uses for these charming pieces of fabric. Today authentic feedsacks are a collectible among quilters.

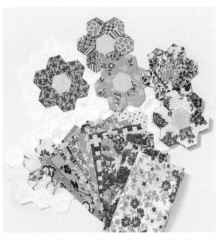

Old feedsacks are still available and collected by quiltmakers for new projects. Collection of Faith O'Hara.

Detail of family friendship quilt dated 1896. Each block is signed with small, ¼" cross-stitched letters. Collection of Laura Nownes.

This full bed size quilt exemplifies the large cut-out designs used in Hawaiian quilts. Hand appliquéd by Dena Canty.

FRIENDSHIP

Friendships are important to any sewing or quilting group. Members regularly make quilts to give to other members for various reasons such as mementos for someone who is moving. These "friendship" album quilts (see also page 85) contain signatures and other information such as dates and love sentiments, either written with permanent ink or embroidered onto the quilt blocks. The quilts are often made from scraps of fabric or old clothing donated by the makers. The purpose was and is always the same—to give the recipient a record of her dear friends and family members.

HAWAIIAN

Prior to the introduction of fabric to the Hawaiian Islands, the Hawaiian women prepared their own fabric called tapa. They would gather on the sides of streams and spend long hours pounding away the bark of the wauke to make the tapa. It was here in these tapa circles that the Hawaiian women created family designs and insignias that were then incorporated into their unique quilts. Hawaiian women created their own style of cutting the appliqué design all at once from a whole piece of fabric. The fabric piece was folded into fourths or eighths from which the design was cut. Quilts were made using repeated design motifs based on beautiful floral surroundings, old gods, legends, and the quiltmakers' innermost feelings of love.

Often the use of only two colors make these designs unique—one color for the design appliqué and a contrasting color for the background. Intricate quilting, often echo or outline quilting is used on these quilts. A project for making a Hawaiian quilted pillow is shown on page 157.

JACOBEAN APPLIQUÉ

The reign of James I of England from 1603 to 1625 marked the development of exotic design in English embroidery, which came to be known as Jacobean embroidery. Jacobean designs often consist of large leaves and flowers springing from a tree trunk, generally with small hills at the base on which might be stags, rabbits, squirrels, etc. The vibrantly colored shapes of flowers, leaves, vines, and animals create striking designs for quilters who have adapted them for appliqué. Quilt maker Patricia B. Campbell is well known for her Jacobean appliqué designs.

Detail of Jacobean Rhapsody 1 quilt. See full quilt photo, page 92.

Jacobean Rhapsody 1 quilt designed and made by Patricia B. Campbell.

Floral Medallion by Verna Mosquera.

LANDSCAPES

This style of quilt is a fabric "painting" of a natural landscape. Inspiration for the quilt is often a photograph or a memory of a scene from nature. The challenge and excitement for the quilt maker is translating the image into fabric. Quilters often use a variety of techniques including piecing, appliqué, painting, thread work, and embroidery.

MEDALLION

Any quilt with a central design motif surrounded by rows of blocks or borders is called a medallion quilt. Many early American quilts are made in this style with large pieces of printed cloth around a center medallion. The center design can be pieced, appliquéd, stenciled, or any combination. The Baltimore Album quilt on page 85 and Floral Medallion, above, are both beautiful examples of this style of quilt. Instructions for making the Floral Medallion quilt begin on page 130.

Yosemite Falls designed and made by Linda Schmidt. The falls were hand painted then appliquéd with silk organza, opalescent organdy, tulle, and sparkle organza. All of the edges were carefully burnt with a candle.

MEMORY

Quilters love making quilts for other people. Any occasion provides an opportunity to make a new quilt. A marriage, new baby, college enrollment, or move to a new city can be the inspiration for a memory quilt. These quilts generally contain fabrics personal to the recipient: old baby clothes, scraps from dresses, bits of uniforms, t-shirts, and often photos become a visual reminder of special times shared between the maker(s) and the loved one. These quilts often incorporate photo transfers, which today are easy to make using computer software programs and specially treated fabric sheets for home printers. The crazy quilt on page 139 has numerous photo transfers incorporated into the design.

MOSAIC

Quilts of this style were constructed from small fabric pieces, usually the same repeated shape such as a hexagon. The shapes are sewn together to form overall designs similar to a tile mosaic. The hexagon mosaic quilt became what we commonly refer to as Grandmother's Flower Garden.

PIECED QUILTS

Some call it piecework, while others call it patchwork. This style of block design was first seen in the early 1800s with the simple pinwheel and nine-patch patterns. Individual, geometric shapes were cut and sewn together to make an isolated block. Soon all-over pieced designs such as the Irish Chain were introduced. Today there are thousands of pieced quilt block patterns. Barbara Brackman's *Encyclopedia of Pieced Quilt Patterns* is not only a valuable reference for anyone wanting to identify old patterns but inspiration for those looking for more designs.

Memory quilt by Alex Anderson made for her daughter Adair's high school graduation.

Detail of Grandmother's Flower Garden quilt by Laurie Grant is an example of a mosaic style quilt.

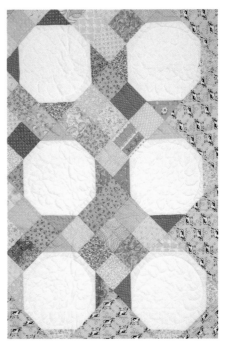

Snowball quilt pattern by Nancy Wong Spindler is an example of a pieced quilt.

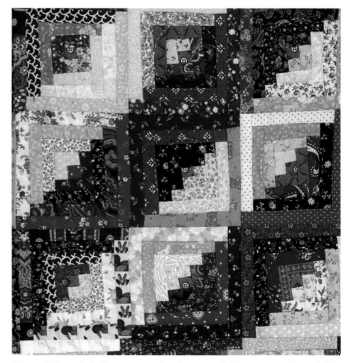

The simplicity of the design is typical of the sashiko style of quilting. Made by Laurie Grant.

Nancy Wong Spindler appropriately named this scrappy Log Cabin quilt Silk Purse From a Sow's Ear.

SAMPLER QUILT

This style of quilt incorporates several different quilt blocks and possibly multiple techniques. A sampler quilt is often the first quilt made by novice quilt makers. It is the perfect format for learning a variety of patterns. Much like the old cross-stitched samplers of the past, the sampler quilt can be a record of one's first quilt blocks and stitches. The Kaleidoscope Sampler on page 165 is a lively example of how several different quilt patterns can work together in one quilt.

SASHIKO

Sashiko quilting is a style originally used by the Chinese and Japanese.

Simple running stitches, larger than the traditional quilting stitches are sewn in repeating or interlocking patterns. Traditionally, white thread such as perle cotton was used on indigo blue fabric.

SCRAP QUILTS

This style of quilt uses an abundance of fabrics. Many quilts fall into this category, such as the charm and string quilts. During times when fabric was scarce, this style was a means to use whatever fabric was available and left over.

SEMINOLE PATCHWORK

This style of patchwork is distinctive to the Seminole Indians. Bands of brightly colored squares, rectangles, and diamonds are pieced together in strips, cut apart, and resewn to create patterns. The patterns often reflected elements of everyday life such as rain, fire, mountains, trees, and lightening bolts. These beautifully pieced designs, first made of necessity from scraps of fabric, became a form of decoration used on clothing. Quilt makers, inspired by these designs,

incorporate this same style of patchwork into jackets, vests, and other quilted projects.

SHADOWWORK APPLIQUÉ

Thin, transparent fabrics such as silk organza and netting are used as overlays to create a shadow effect for underlying colors of fabrics. The technique can be done either by hand or machine to give a soft look to the appliqué design.

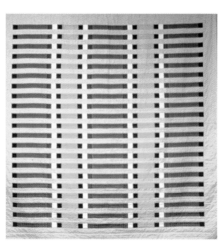

Beaded Strip quilt by Margaret Wood made of colorful horizontal strips alternating with tan strips was inspired by a beaded hide robe.

An example of shadowwork appliqué by Hetty van Boven of Australia taken from her quilt called From My Garden, with Love.

Stained glass wall hanging Kala Lily 1 designed and made by Eldrid Royset Forde of Norway.

String Strippy, 74" x 93", c. 1910-20. Collected in Shipshewana, Indiana. Quilted in all-over fans. Backing made of feed sacks, all of which read from top to bottom, "100 lbs. Net, Master Mix, 40%, Hog Concentrate, McMillen Feed Mills, Inc., Fort Wayne, Indiana."

STAINED GLASS

This style of quilt is made to resemble a stained glass window. The dark black lines around the colored shapes that form the "leading" are stitched either with reverse appliqué techniques or narrow bias strips similar to those used in Celtic quilts.

STRING QUILTS

String quilts are another example of the scrap quilt, made of strips of leftover fabrics deemed unsuitable for anything else. These humble string quilts were made by people of few means without formal commercial patterns, and they were made to be used. While found in most parts of the country, string quilts were as common as cornbread in the South. Often these quilts rose artistically far beyond their unpretentious beginnings. Though lacking in refined technique, they more than made up for it in their powerful visual impact.

The recent attention focused on the quilts made by the women from Gee's Bend, Alabama, has awakened a new appreciation for this style of work in both the quilt and art world.

WHOLE CLOTH

The whole cloth was the most widely used quilt style during colonial times as it was one of the first brought to America by the immigrants. It differs from other traditional quilts in that there is no piecework or appliqué. A solid piece of fabric (white or bold in color, floral printed calicos, or glazed chintz) became the background to showcase intricate quilting designs. The whole cloth quilt was the perfect style for skilled quilters, providing a large space for design. The heavily quilted designs often included trapunto (stuffed work) to produce a formal and elegant look of textures and shadows.

The Linsey-Woolsey quilts were some of the earliest whole cloth quilts. They were dyed with natural indigo dyes and made from a blend of linen and wool fibers.

Lace #1 whole cloth quilt by Tracey Browning was inspired by a photo in the book The History of Lace. Photo by Andrew Cadd, Moonta, South Australia.

finishing touches

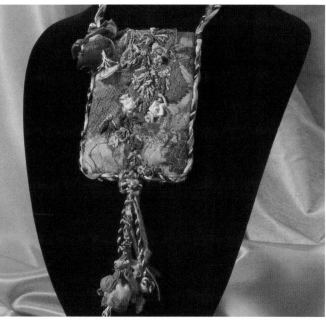

Designed and made by artist Judith Baker Montano. This lovely little neck pouch (3¹/₄" x 4¹/₄") holds a room key, credit card, or a lipstick, yet it looks like a piece of soft sculptured jewelry. It uses machine embroidery, fabric collage, silk ribbon embroidery, bead and ribbon work, traditional embroidery, and tassel embellishments.

Designed and made by quilt artist Karen Boutté. This project uses raw edge machine appliqué techniques on Ultrasuede®. The mask is sewn to a whole cloth background. The features on the mask are created using decorative machine stitches with embellishments of beads, threads, and quilting stitches.

EMBELLISHMENTS

Many quilters enjoy adding embellishments to their quilts and quilted projects. It began with art quilts, as well as the crazy quilt style of adding embroidery, ribbons, lace, yarn, buttons, charms, and beads to decorate and add interest to quilts. The embellishments can be attached by hand or machine. One machine technique, called couching, uses zig-zag stitches to attach fibers or rows of beads onto the fabric.

BIAS BINDING

The best time to use bias strips for binding is when finishing a quilt with curved edges. The bias cut pieces will work smoothly around the curves without creating puckers and ripples. Refer to the chart for binding yardage on page 67 and cut as many strips as needed to extend around the entire edge of the quilt; stitching them together to make one continuous strip.

To help stabilize the edge of the quilt and prevent stretching while sewing, mark the curves, attach the binding and then remove the excess border, batting, and backing fabric. This is only possible when starting with a straight edge.

Striped and other geometric fabrics look wonderful when cut on the bias and used for the binding. It is an acceptable way to finish a quilt, but be very careful when sewing, using the walking foot to prevent stretching and distortion along the edges. Refer to page 44 for help with cutting strips on the bias.

For added interest, consider adding covered cording in a contrasting color to the edge of the quilt top before attaching the binding.

BLOCKING

Occasionally a quilt becomes distorted after being quilted, especially if it has been heavily quilted. The best way to correct this is by blocking it into shape. Do this if the fabrics have been prewashed or you are sure they are colorfast. You don't want any surprises. This is done after everything is done, including binding.

1. With the right side facing up, lay the quilt on a carpeted floor that has been covered with an old light-colored flannel sheet.

2. Fill a spray bottle (approximately 12 oz.) with cool water. Lightly spray the quilt until the top is wet. The backing will not be wet.

3. Manipulate the edges to straighten. A board or straightedge may be helpful for this step. The water soaks through the top layer into the batting, setting the shape as it dries.

4. Allow the quilt to dry completely. This may take up to two days, depending on the weather.

QUILT CARE AND STORAGE

To keep your quilt in good condition, keep it clean and air it regularly so dust and soil don't work into the fibers. Wash with a mild soap only when necessary. Dry cleaning is not recommended because it leaves a chemical residue. Never display a quilt in direct sunlight. Even indirect light through windows can fade the colors over time.

If you wish to store your quilt, you'll want to investigate safe storage methods. Attics and basements aren't a good choice because of extremes in temperature and moisture. Never store quilts in plastic, as it traps moisture and encourages the growth of mildew. If you have the space, roll the quilt around a tube covered in cotton fabric. Folding is potentially damaging to stored quilts, so layering crumpled acid-free tissue inside the folds helps support the fibers and protect them from long-term hazards. Fold it differently every time you replace the quilt after use. Wrap the whole quilt in a cotton sheet or pillowcase.

Personalized quilt labels with names, dates, and other important information can be made using computer programs, printed fabric, embroidery, or calligraphy.

SIGNING AND DATING YOUR QUILT

Your completed quilt is a work of art and it is important to document the date of completion and quiltmaker's name. A purchased or self-made decorative label will keep a record of your work for generations to come. You may want to include the occasion for which the quilt was made along with your name and the date. Following are some ideas for labeling your quilt:

- Embroider your name, the date, and any additional information on the quilt top or backing. You may choose embroidery floss colors that closely match the fabric you are working on, such as white floss on a white border, or contrasting colors.

- Make a label from muslin and use a permanent marker to write your information. Your label may be as plain or as fancy as you wish. Stitch the label to the back of the quilt.

- Chart a cross-stitch label design that includes the information you wish then stitch it in colors that complement the quilt. Stitch the finished label to the quilt backing.

quilting projects

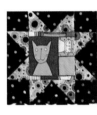

CONGRATULATIONS, YOU HAVE MADE IT through the basics and beyond. Now it's time to try your hand at your newfound skills. Each of these wonderfully diverse quilting projects is designed by one of our enormously talented designers. They have graciously gathered together here to share their expertise with you.

Discover quilting projects that are perfect for every skill level from beginner to advanced quiltmakers. You will find that a simple faux chenille scarf, a trio of wool appliqué pillows, or a string quilt are all quite doable for beginners. Intermediate quilters will find the challenge of the Floral Medallion Quilt, miniature wall hanging, or paper-piecing quilts perfect for their skills. Curved piecing, crazy quilting, trapunto or Hawaiian pillows will entice those who want something different. If you fancy trying several block patterns at one time, the exciting sampler quilt is the perfect vehicle for everyone. Each and every project is beautiful and will increase your quilting repertoire.

The art of quiltmaking is in the unique union of colors, patterns, and workmanship. Your expertise and enjoyment will increase with each quilt. From the first selection of fabric to the last beautiful stitch, you will be honing your new skills while creating heirloom keepsakes for friends and family.

chenille scarf

In just a few hours you can easily make this warm and cozy scarf. Take some flannel, a little straight stitching, an ingenious little slashing tool, and voilà! You have created a handmade chenille scarf. You will be amazed at the finished project, and just that simply, you're quilting!

MADE BY CHERYL SIMPSON
Skill level: Beginner
Finished scarf size: 5" x 72"
Technique: Slashing

MATERIALS

Pink flannel: 2 yards 40" to 45" wide. Do NOT prewash. It's best to use a yarn-dyed flannel that is the same color on both sides.

Thread to match fabric

Slashing cutter, small, sharp scissors, or electric scissors

Safety pins or quilt basting spray

Ruler: at least 5" x 24"

Rotary cutter and large mat

Walking foot

CUTTING

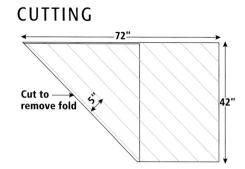

Fold the fabric at a 45-degree angle. Cut along the fold then use the cutting tools to cut five 5"-wide strips on the bias.

PREPARATION

1. Sew two strips together to measure 74" long. Trim and straighten the ends. This will be the center piece. If using basting spray, apply a small amount on the top layer of this strip.

2. Place the strip on a flat surface. Leaving a 1" extension on both ends, place another strip of fabric, right side facing up, on top of the center strip.

Butt two pieces together, if necessary to extend the entire length. Press firmly to hold the layers together or secure with pins.

3. Repeat with another strip of fabric, also placing it right side facing up to make a third layer. It is best not to have any butted ends in the same place, but rather stagger them along the length of the strip.

4. Turn the layered strips over and add two more layers of strips, right sides facing up, to the opposite side of the center piece, always remembering to begin and end 1" from the end and to stagger any butted strips.

5. On one side of the layered strips, use a ruler and marking pencil to mark a line down the center from end to end.

CONSTRUCTION

Note: A walking foot will prevent the layers from slipping while you're sewing.

1. Stitch along the marked line.

2. Sew rows of stitching lines on both sides of the stitched centerline. The distance between the lines of stitching is $3/8$" to $1/2$". If using a large walking foot, you may be able to use the edge of the foot as a guide for this distance.

3. After stitching all lines, trim any excess fabric beyond the outermost lines to measure half the distance between the stitching lines. For example, if the distance between the lines of stitching is $1/2$", trim the lengthwise edges to $1/4$" beyond the stitching lines.

SLASHING

1. Working on one side of the scarf at a time, slash through just the top two layers of fabric. Use your tool of choice to cut between all of the rows

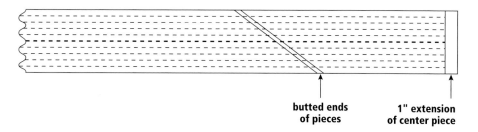

butted ends of pieces

1" extension of center piece

of stitching, cutting down the entire length of the layered strips. Do NOT cut through the center piece of fabric. The 1" extension of the center piece is helpful for placing the tool for cutting.

2. Turn the fabric over and repeat on the opposite side again cutting through the top two layers only.

3. Trim to remove the 1" extensions of fabric on both ends.

4. To create fringe, measure 6" from each end and cut through the center piece between stitching lines.

FINISHING

1. To create the soft, fluffy chenille look, wash the scarf in either hot or warm water with a little detergent and fabric softener.

2. Place in dryer on regular setting and tumble until completely dry.

3. Remove and *violà!* You have a chenille scarf complete with curly fringe.

For as long as she can remember, Cheryl Simpson has loved quilts. She says that fabric is her "candy" and enjoys playing with color and fabric to create quilts, garments, and totebags. She is especially drawn to the texture and color options that chenille provides.

wool appliqué pillows

Decorate for the season with quick and easy felted wool pillows. The simple appliqué embroidered shapes will add holiday cheer to any home. Create modern pillows reminiscent of the penny rugs popular in the 1800s. These charming home accents also make great handmade gifts.

DESIGNED AND MADE BY ANNE SUTTON
Skill level: Beginner
Finished pillow sizes: Heart – 9" x 8", Ornaments – 14" x 7", Star – 11" x 11"
Technique: Hand blanket stitch appliqué and embroidery

MATERIALS
Felted wool–specific amounts given with each project
Freezer paper
Pencil
Fabric and paper scissors
Chalk pencil or water soluble pen
DMC embroidery floss or fine-weight wool embroidery thread – white, red, green, gold, and black
Embroidery needle, #5, 6, or 7
Polyester fiberfill

GENERAL INSTRUCTIONS
Felted wool is used for these projects. It is the preferred material as felting prevents the edges of the fabric from fraying and raveling. To felt wool, wash it first in hot water, rinse in cold, and then tumble dry in a hot dryer. Wool fabric that has been hand dyed has already been felted.

All of the cut measurements for each pillow are given for felted wool. If you need to treat your fabric to felt it, be sure to purchase at least 3" extra to allow for shrinkage before cutting.

1. Use a pencil to trace the needed pattern pieces onto the paper side (not plastic side) of a piece of freezer paper. Be sure to trace all embroidery details.

2. Use paper scissors to cut the shapes, approximately $1/4$" beyond the marked lines.

3. Use a dry iron to press the plastic side of the pattern onto the right side of the wool.

4. Use fabric scissors to cut the shape, cutting directly on the marked line. Do not remove the pattern from the wool.

5. Mark the placement of the embroidery details onto the wool by placing straight pins through the markings on the paper pattern and into the wool.

6. Carefully lift the paper pattern and use the chalk marker or water soluble pen to mark dots on the wool where the pins are inserted.

7. Remove the pins and paper pattern. Then connect the dots to indicate the entire embroidery pattern.

Note: All embroidery is done with two strands of embroidery floss or one strand of fine-weight wool embroidery thread.

HEART PILLOW
MATERIALS
Red wool: 11" x 16" piece
White wool: 7" x 8" piece
Green wool: 3" x 3" piece
Scrap of gold wool
Ribbon: 8" of $1/4$" wide light green
Buttons: Three $3/8$" mother-of-pearl
Beads: Ten small red

ASSEMBLY
1. Referring to the General Instructions, enlarge pattern 200%, then trace and cut the following fabric shapes: two hearts, one dove (including beak and two wings) and two holly leaves.

2. Embroider flowers on the dove's wing, using a lazy daisy stitch.

3. Use a blanket stitch to attach the dove, beak, wings, and holly to the pillow front piece.

4. Attach three buttons, referring to the photo for placement.

5. Embroider a French knot for the dove's eye.

6. With wrong sides facing, place the front and back pillow pieces together. Use a blanket stitch and red floss to stitch around the edges, leaving an opening between the marks for stuffing.

7. Add polyester fiberfill to lightly stuff the pillow.

EMBROIDERY STITCHES

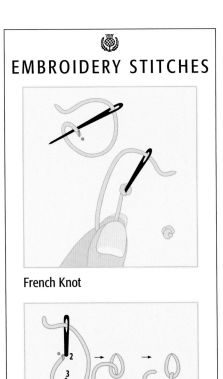

French Knot

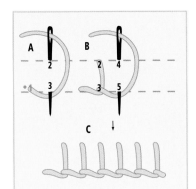

Lazy Daisy

Running Stitch

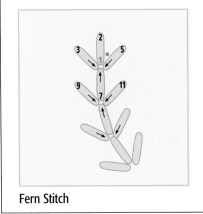

Blanket Stitch

Fern Stitch

8. Continue the blanket stitch around the edge of the pillow to close the opening.

9. Tie the ribbon into a small bow and attach to the top of the heart.

10. String the 10 beads (two sets of five) and then secure them in the center of the bow.

ORNAMENT PILLOW
MATERIALS
Black felted wool: Two 14" x 7" pieces
White wool (snowman): 4" x 4" piece
Light Green wool (star): 4" x 5" piece
Red wool (tree): 4" x 4" piece
Light Gold wool (star): 3" x 3" piece
Green wool (tree): 3" x 3" piece
Brown wool (trunk): Scrap
Orange wool (nose) : Scrap
Gold wool (ornament tops): 3" x 3"
Ribbon: 21" of 1/4" wide
Two 3/16" buttons

ASSEMBLY
1. Referring to the General Instructions on page 102, enlarge pattern 200%, then trace and cut all of the ornament shapes.

2. SNOWMAN ORNAMENT: sew two buttons onto the white wool ornament for the eyes. Attach the nose shape with small running stitches.

3. STAR ORNAMENT: Pin the gold star to the green ornament and use a blanket stitch to secure around the edges.

4. TREE ORNAMENT: Pin the green tree and brown trunk to the red ornament and use a blanket stitch to secure around the edges.

5. Position and stitch the three ornaments to the front pillow piece. Use a blanket stitch to secure around the edges of each ornament.

6. Use a blanket stitch to attach the tops to each ornament.

7. Use an outline stitch and gold floss for the hangers and red floss for the strings.

8. Make three bows from the ribbon and attach to the ornaments' strings.

9. With wrong sides facing each other, place the front and back pillow pieces together. Use a blanket stitch and black floss to stitch around the edges, leaving an opening for stuffing.

10. Add polyester fiberfill to lightly stuff the pillow.

11. Continue the blanket stitch around the edge of the pillow to close the opening.

STAR PILLOW
MATERIALS
White wool: Two 11" squares
Dark gold wool: 10" x 11" piece
Light gold wool: 12" x 12" piece
Green wool: 3" x 5" piece

ASSEMBLY
1. Referring to the General Instructions on page 102, enlarge pattern 200%, then trace and cut the stars, letters "j" and "y", and the circle wreath. **Note:** Cut only the shape for the wreath from freezer paper.

2. Press the paper wreath circle onto the center of the large light gold star. Use a chalk pencil or water soluble pen to mark the placement around the edge of the circle.

3. Embroider the outline of the wreath circle using an outline stitch and green floss. Use a feather stitch around the outlined wreath shape. Then add French knots and a thread bow using red floss to complete the wreath.

4. Attach the letters "j" and "y" to the front with blanket stitches around the edges.

5. Use a blanket stitch to attach the large light gold star to the large dark gold star. Then attach this unit to the pillow front with blanket stitches.

6. Use a blanket stitch to attach the three small stars to the pillow front, referring to the photo for placement.

7. With wrong sides facing, place the front and back pieces together. Use a blanket stitch around the edges, leaving an opening for stuffing.

8. Add polyester fiberfill to lightly stuff the pillow.

9. Continue the blanket stitch around the edge of the pillow to close the opening.

Anne Sutton designs under the name of Bunny Hill Designs. She is the coauthor of *Country Quilts for Friends*, and her work has been featured in *American Patchwork and Quilting*. Anne started sewing at a very young age. By taking every sewing class available from home economics to apparel design, she fine-tuned her sewing skills. Eight years ago she discovered her passion for quilting. Her love of fabric became her obsession. She loves the relaxation that comes from stitching by hand. Embroidering a little wool pillow or appliquéing a quilt, the joy comes from watching it come to life.

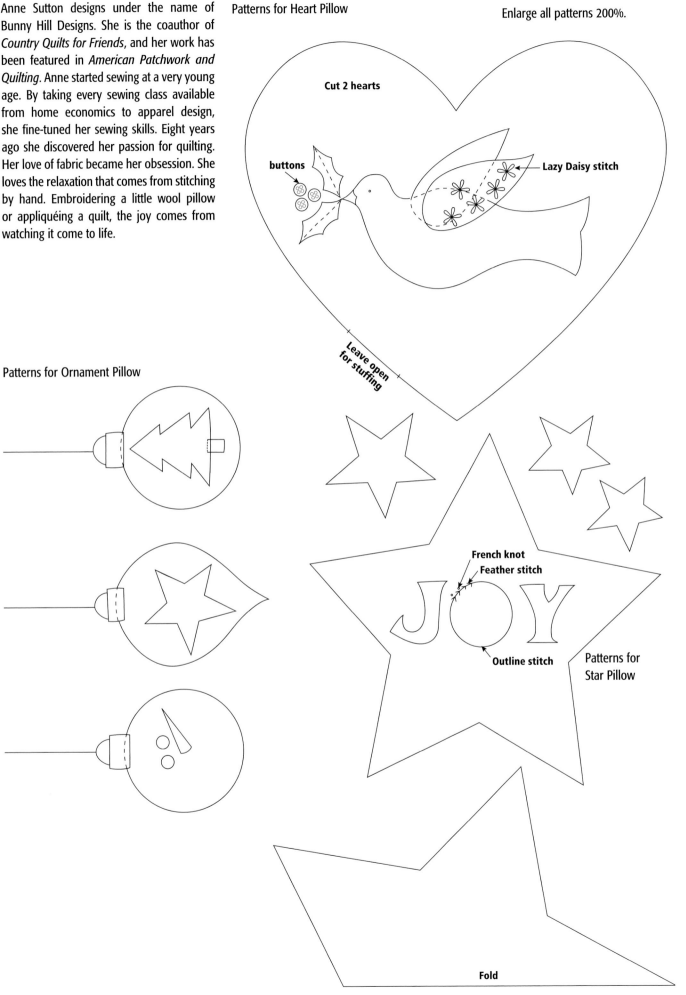

Patterns for Heart Pillow

Enlarge all patterns 200%.

Cut 2 hearts

buttons

Lazy Daisy stitch

Leave open for stuffing

Patterns for Ornament Pillow

French knot
Feather stitch

JOY

Outline stitch

Patterns for Star Pillow

Fold

Do not use buttons on quilts intended for young children.

baby biscuit

Young and old alike will enjoy this charming quilt made with individually stuffed pillow-like blocks called "biscuits." Once you have mastered the technique, you'll be making puffs by the dozen. Babies love the feel of this quilt, and so will you.

DESIGNED AND MADE BY SHERRY HUTCHENS
Skill level: Beginner
Finished quilt size: 45" x 60", excluding ruffle
Techniques: Quick cutting, machine piecing, and tying

MATERIALS

Yardage: Based on 42" fabric, selvage to selvage
White fabric: 1¼ yards
Yellow fabric: ⅛ yard each of eight fabrics
Pink fabric: ⅛ yard each of ten fabrics
Blue fabric: ⅛ yard each of 16 fabrics
Lining fabric (lightweight): 2¾ yards
Pink inner piping fabric: ⅜ yard
Blue outer ruffle fabric: 1⅜ yards
Backing fabric: 3⅝ yards
Batting (lightweight): 49" x 69" or larger
Binding fabric: ⅜ yard
Perle cotton
Polyester fiberfill: 12 oz. bag

CUTTING

Cut crosswise from selvage to selvage.
White: Eight 3½" strips. Cut the strips into 3½" squares (need 96)
Yellow: Eight 3½" strips. Cut the strips into 3½" squares (need 52)
Pink: Ten 3½" strips. Cut the strips into 3½" squares (need 96)
Blue: Sixteen 3½" strips. Cut the strips into 3½" squares (need 188)
Lining fabric: Thirty-one 3" strips. Cut the strips into 3" squares (need 432)
Pink inner piping: Six 1½" strips
Blue outer ruffle: Eleven 4" strips
Backing: Cut or piece together enough fabric to measure 2" larger all around than the quilt top
Binding: Six 1½" strips

CONSTRUCTION

To make each "biscuit," the top layer fabric squares are sewn together with the lining fabric squares and individually stuffed. The stuffed biscuits are then sewn together in the desired design arrangement to complete the quilt top. The squares of lining fabric are cut ½" smaller than the top layer fabric squares. To make the two pieces the same size for joining together, it is necessary to make small pleats along the edges of the top layer squares before sewing. This will create fullness and allow for stuffing.

1. With wrong sides facing, place an outer fabric square on top of a lining square. Place pins at the four corners to secure.

2. To work in the fullness on the top layer, fold small pleats at the center point of three sides. Secure with pins.

3. With a ½" seam allowance, stitch around three sides of the square, removing pins as you sew.

With a little practice you will be able to hold the pleats with your fingers as you sew to save time in pinning each piece.

4. Place a small handful of stuffing into each biscuit. Use enough stuffing to make the biscuits puffy but not so much that they are difficult to sew. Practice with a few to find the correct amount.

5. Fold a small pleat in the last side and stitch to close.

ASSEMBLY

Note: It is helpful to place all biscuits into paper bags according to color. Construct the quilt in four sections. The biscuits can become bulky and difficult to work with, so working in sections makes it easier. Seams cannot be pressed or the biscuits will become flat. Chain piecing will speed the sewing process. After a little practice you should be able to sew without pinning each side.

1. Referring to the diagram for color placement, lay out three or four horizontal rows of one section at a time. Check to be sure that fabric prints are randomly distributed.

2. With right sides facing, sew the biscuits together in rows, matching biscuit seams and using a $1/4"$ seam allowance.

3. Join the rows together, alternating the direction of the seams at the intersections.

4. Sew the four sections together, referring to the diagram to complete the quilt top.

FINISHING

Finish this quilt in the same way as for a conventional quilt. Use a lightweight batting to prevent the seams from showing through the backing fabric.

1. Layer the backing, batting, and quilt top, being careful not to stretch the biscuits during this process.

2. Secure the layers with pins in every other set of four biscuits.

3. Use buttons, ties, or ribbons to hold the three layers together.

4. Remove the pins.

5. Machine baste close to the edge, stitching through all layers.

6. Trim the excess batting and backing fabric even with the edge of the quilt top.

7. Sew all of the strips for the pink piping together, end to end. With the right side of the fabric facing out, fold and press the pink strip in half lengthwise. Then pin and stitch to the edge of the quilt, allowing extra fullness in the corners. Trim the excess length as needed.

8. To make the outer blue ruffle, sew enough strips together to extend around the outside of the quilt two times.

Section 1 ... **Section 2**

Section 3 ... **Section 4**

9. With the right side facing out, press the ruffle strip in half lengthwise. To gather the strip, zigzag over a piece of perle cotton close to the edge, then pull to form gathers. To allow the cord to pull smoothly, it is important not to stitch directly onto the perle cotton. Pin the ruffle to the edge of the quilt, evenly distributing the gathers; stitch around.

10. Prepare the binding by sewing strips together, then folding and pressing in half lengthwise. Sew around the quilt edge, using a $1/4"$ seam allowance. Fold and turn it to the backside to cover raw edges. Pin to secure. Then stitch it in place by hand to the backing fabric.

As an option for young children, eliminate the buttons and tie with perle cotton or ribbon instead. See tying on page 66.

When Sherry Hutchens isn't busy with her successful real estate career, she loves to spend time with her quilt group, "The Fabulous Thursday Night Quilters." Her love of color and design started in high school, when she made a very simple patchwork quilt for her little brother. Years later, a picture of a Crazy Log Cabin quilt on a magazine cover inspired her to get serious about quilting, and she's been doing it ever since.

tote
bag

Machine piecing is not only much faster than hand piecing, it also yields a sturdier seam due to the interlocking threads of the spool and bobbin. Fusible appliqué is another technique that makes great use of the sewing machine. This tote bag is an excellent design for mastering both techniques.

DESIGNED AND MADE BY LINDA TIANO

Skill level: Intermediate
Finished tote bag size: approximately
18$\frac{1}{2}$" x 17$\frac{3}{4}$"
Techniques: Machine piecing
and fusible appliqué

MATERIALS

Yardage: Based on 40" wide fabric (excluding selvages)

Brown tone-on-tone fabric:
   10¹/₂" x 11" (appliqué background)
Brown check fabric: ¹/₈ yard
   (inner border)
Brown print fabric: ¹/₄ yard (outer border
   and binding)
Assorted print fabric scraps: ³/₈ yard total
   (pieced border and appliqués)
Heavyweight upholstery fabric:
   1 yard (back and handles)
Lining fabric: ⁵/₈ yard
Fusible fleece: 19" x 18¹/₄"
Chenille yarn: approximately 2 yards
Paper-backed fusible web
Stabilizer (optional)
Embroidery floss
6 white E-beads
³/₄" dia. magnetic snap
Chalk pencil

CUTTING

Cut crosswise, from selvage to selvage. All measurements include ¹/₄" seam allowances.

BROWN CHECK FABRIC

Two top/bottom inner borders
   9" x 1³/₄".
Two side inner borders 12" x 1³/₄".

BROWN PRINT FABRIC

One binding strip 2¹/₂" wide.
One bottom outer border
   16¹/₂" x 1³/₄".
Two side outer borders 18¹/₄" x 1³/₄".
Two tabs 3¹/₂" x 3".

ASSORTED PRINT FABRIC SCRAPS

20 rectangles 3¹/₂" x 3".

HEAVYWEIGHT UPHOLSTERY FABRIC

One back 19" x 18¹/₄".
Two straps 5" x 25".

LINING FABRIC

One lining front and one lining back
   19" x 18¹/₄".

APPLIQUÉ

Fusible Appliqué patterns, page 113, are printed in reverse and do not include seam allowances.

1. Refer to Machine Appliqué, Method One: Fusible Appliqué, page 55, to prepare and cut out shapes listed below from assorted print fabrics.

One of each flower petal.
One of each calyx.
One of each flower accent.
One of each stem.
One of each leaf.
One of each leaf accent.

2. Working from the background up, center, layer, and fuse shapes to appliqué background.

3. Follow Machine Appliqué Stitches, page 56, to satin stitch around shapes.

4. Keeping top of flower approximately 1¹/₄" below edge of fabric, trim appliquéd rectangle to 9" x 9¹/₂".

PIECING THE TOTE FRONT

Match right sides and use ¹/₄" seam allowances unless otherwise noted.

1. To make tote center, sew top/bottom and then side inner borders to appliquéd rectangle.

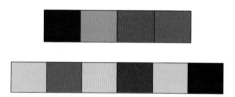

2. Matching short edges, sew 4 rectangles together to make top pieced border. Repeat to make bottom pieced border. Sew 6 rectangles together to make side pieced border. Make 2 side pieced borders.

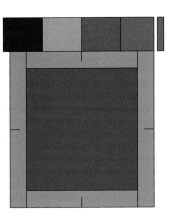

3. Mark the center of each edge of the tote center. Matching center marks with center seam of top pieced border, sew top border to tote center; press. Trim excess pieced border even with edges of tote center.

4. Repeat Step 3 to sew bottom and then side pieced borders to tote center.

HAND STITCHES
Couching

Bring yarn to be couched up at 1 and hold in place with non-sewing hand. Bring thread up at 2, go down at 3, up at 4, down at 5. Continue coming up at even numbers and going down at odd numbers until reaching end of drawn line. Take yarn and thread to the back and secure.

Stem Stitch

Come up at 1. Keeping thread below the stitching line, go down at 2 and come up at 3. Continue until reaching end of drawn line.

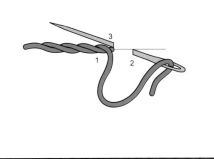

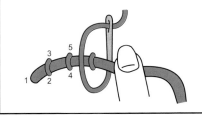

5. Sew bottom and then side outer borders to tote center.

6. Fuse fleece rectangle to wrong side of tote front. Machine quilt as desired. Our tote front is echo quilted around the appliqué shapes and quilted in-the-ditch between the inner and pieced borders.

7. Use chalk pencil to freehand draw a wavy placement line for chenille yarn in the inner border and 2 stamens for each flower. Follow Hand Stitches, above, to Couch the chenille yarn to the tote front using thread. Use 3 strands of floss to Stem Stitch the stamens. Sew a bead to the tote front at the end of each stamen.

CONSTRUCTION

1. Matching wrong sides, sew tote front and back together. Repeat to sew lining front and back together.

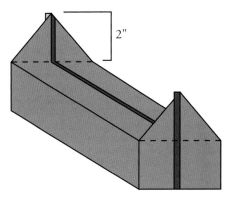

2. To box bottom of tote, work from the wrong side to align tote side seam with bottom seam. Sew across point 2" from tip. Repeat for remaining side. Leaving a $^1/_2$" seam allowance, trim points. Repeat to box bottom of lining.

111

3. Turn tote right side out. Matching wrong sides and side seams, slip lining into tote. Baste top raw edges together.

4. To make tab, sew long edges together. Turn tab right side out. Press tab with seam at center back. Repeat with remaining tab. Matching raw edges, fold each tab in half with seam on inside; press and then unfold.

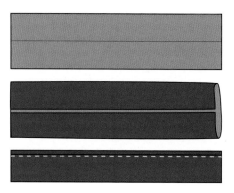

5. Attach one side of the magnetic snap to each tab, slightly above crease line. Baste raw edges of tabs together.

6. Mark top center of front and back lining. With snaps facing, match raw edges and baste one tab to tote front and back lining at marks.

7. Matching wrong sides and raw edges, press binding strip in half lengthwise. Press one end of binding strip diagonally.

8. Beginning with pressed end of binding on right side of tote near one side seam, match raw edges and pin binding to tote.

9. Using a $1/2$" seam allowance, sew binding to tote until binding overlaps beginning end by about 2". Trim excess binding.

10. Fold binding to lining side of tote, covering stitching line; pin in place.

11. Working from right side of tote, stitch in-the-ditch between binding and tote, catching folded edge of binding in stitching on lining side.

12. Matching wrong sides and raw edges, press strap in half lengthwise; unfold. Fold each long edge to center crease; press. Fold in half again lengthwise; topstitch along double-folded edge. Repeat for remaining strap. Zigzag or serge across strap ends.

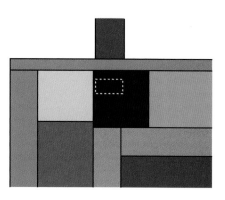

13. For strap placement, mark $3 1/2$" from side seam and 2" from top edge on each side of lining front and back. Aligning ends with marks, pin strap ends to lining. Topstitch a rectangle through all layers just above strap end.

112

Petal

Flower accent

Calyx

Flower accent

Petal

Calyx

Stem

Stem

Flower accent

Petal

Calyx

Stem

Leaf

Leaf

Leaf accent

Leaf accent

113

joseph's coat

String quilts originated in the 1860s but came back into popularity around 1930 when every little scrap of fabric was precious. Today, by combining string foundation quilting with the saturated colors associated with Amish quilts, you can achieve a strikingly dramatic quilt.

DESIGNED AND MADE BY GWEN MARSTON
MACHINE QUILTED BY JAMIE SCHANTZ

Skill Level: Beginner
Finished quilt size: 54" x 63"
Techniques: Quick cutting

Traditionally string quilts were foundation pieced as a way to control both the odd-shaped scraps and the finished size of the block. Gwen has developed a new technique to achieve the old-fashioned string look.

Although instructions are given for this quilt, remember that early string quilts were made without directions. Feel free to use the directions loosely as a guide to making your own original string quilt.

MATERIALS

Note: The individual pieces are referred to as strings, and the vertical rows as bars.

Approximately 26 different fabrics, using scraps up to $^1/8$ yard pieces, were used for the strings.

Traditionally, string quilts were made of available scraps rather than fabrics purchased for a specific quilt. This practice contributed greatly to the unpredictable and spontaneous look that is so characteristic of antique string quilts. Most were made with prints and a few solids mixed in. Amish quiltmakers made string quilts in their characteristic solids. Joseph's Coat is made with a variety of strong solid color fabrics.

Yardage: Based on 42" fabric, from selvage to selvage.
Border strips:
  Lavender: $^1/8$ yard
  Medium Violet: $^1/8$ yard
  Red Violet: $^1/4$ yard
  Red: 1¼ yards (includes binding)
  Blue Violet: $^1/4$ yard
  Navy: $^5/8$ yard
  Dark Navy: $^1/8$ yard
  Black: $^1/8$ yard
Batting: 72" x 90" (prepackaged) or 1½ yards at least 70" wide, sold by the yard
Backing: 3¼ yard (one fabric, pieced horizontally) or enough pieces sewn together to measure at least 1½" larger than the quilt top all the way around.

CUTTING

Cut crosswise from selvage to selvage.

Cut all of the fabrics for the strings into strips, varying in width from 1¼" to 3". Then cut the strips into shorter pieces. The length of the pieces will be the width of the vertical bars plus 1". For example, for Row A (see Construction, Step 3) strips should be 5½" long. The extra width allows for straightening and squaring up the bars after they are sewn.

BORDERS: Refer to the diagram on page 116 for the placement of the border strips.
#1 Lavender: 3$^1/2$" x 21$^1/2$"
    Medium Violet: 3$^1/2$" x 16$^1/2$"
#2 Blue Violet: 3$^1/2$" x 17$^1/2$"
    Red Violet: 3$^1/2$" x 37$^1/2$"
#3 Red: 3$^1/2$" x 27$^1/2$"
    Red Violet: 3$^1/2$" x 6$^1/2$"
    Medium Violet: 3$^1/2$" x 21$^1/2$"
#4 Navy: 3$^1/2$" x 7$^1/2$"
    Black: 3$^1/2$" x 16$^1/2$"
    Navy: 3$^1/2$" x 31$^1/2$"
#5 Blue Violet: 3$^1/2$" x 28$^1/2$"
    Red: 3$^1/2$" x 18$^1/2$"
#6 Navy: 4$^1/2$" x 46$^1/2$"
#7 Navy: 3$^1/2$" x 21$^1/2$"
    Dark Navy: 3$^1/2$" x 40$^1/2$"
#8 Navy: 3$^1/2$" x 61$^1/2$"

BINDING: Cut seven 4$^3/4$" strips of red fabric.

CONSTRUCTION
SEWING THE ROWS OF BARS

1. Sew one bar of strings together at a time. Working quickly and *intuitively*, sew the fabric strings together in pairs, chaining one pair directly behind the next one.

Step 1

Use a variety of colors and widths of fabric strings. For added interest, sew the strings at an angle, then cut and join the new pieces together, as shown.

2. Join the pairs together to make fours, then eights, etc. until the bars measure 51¹/₂" long.

3. Carefully cut the bars to the needed width, referring to the following chart and the layout diagram for the bar you are working on.

A: 4¹/₂" wide
B: 3¹/₂" wide
C: 5¹/₂" wide
D: 4¹/₂" wide
E: 7¹/₂" wide
F: 5¹/₂" wide
G: 4¹/₂" wide
H: 5¹/₂" wide

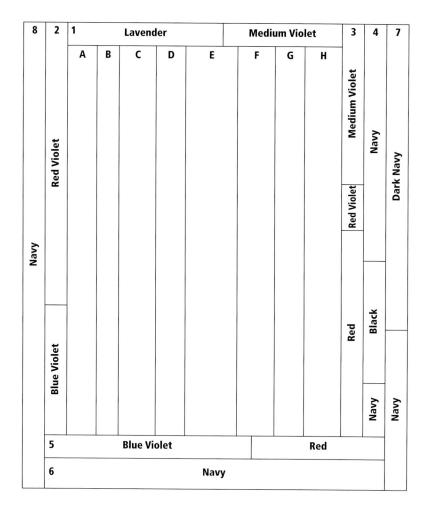

ASSEMBLY

1. Carefully pin and then sew the bars together lengthwise. Press after the addition of each new bar. **Note:** Joining the pieced bars is like attaching borders but more complicated due to the numerous seams. It is important to take your time, press well, measure carefully, pin thoroughly. Pin both ends and the middle. Continue pinning every 3 to 4 inches then sew carefully to prevent stretching.

2. Attach the border strips (1–8) referring to the diagram for the exact placement. Join shorter pieces together first before attaching to the quilt top.

3. Layer and baste the quilt top in preparation for quilting. Refer to pages 61-62 for help.

4. This quilt was quilted by machine. Some of the designs used are shown on page 233.

5. Prepare and attach a straight binding, referring to page 68 for help. Do not trim the excess backing and batting even with the edge of the quilt top, but instead leave a ³/₄" extension of both to fill in the extra-wide binding.

Gwen Marston is an avid quiltmaker, teacher, and author. She has written 18 books, including *Liberated String Quilts*; *Mary Schafer: American Quilt*; and, her latest, *Classic Four-Block Appliqué Quilts: A Back-to-Basics Approach*. She has also been a regular columnist for *Ladies Circle Patchwork Quilts* and has appeared on the television show *Simply Quilts*. Gwen has had 19 solo exhibits, participated in many group shows, and teaches both nationally and internationally. Her annual quilt retreat on Beaver Island, Michigan, is in its 21st year.

owl and honey bee quilt

If you admire the look of hand appliqué but want fast results, mock hand appliqué is an excellent option. Your sewing machine makes it possible to secure the appliqué piece to the background fabric with tiny, almost invisible, stitches!

DESIGNED AND MADE BY PAT SLOAN

Skill level: Intermediate
Finished quilt size: 42" x 44½"
Techniques: mock hand appliqué

MATERIALS

Yardage: Based on 40" wide fabric (excluding selvages)
Green print No. 1: ³/8 yard
Green print No. 2: ½ yard
Green floral: ³/8 yard
Green stripe: ¼ yard
Blue print No. 1: 1⅝ yards (includes binding)
Blue print No. 2: ³/8 yard
Blue print No. 3: ¼ yard
Tan print No. 1: ⅛ yard
Tan prints No. 2 and No. 3: ¼ yard each
Cream print: 8" x 15"
Orange print: 6" x 6"
Backing fabric: 2¾ yards
Batting: 46" x 48½"
Heat-resistant template plastic
Spray starch
Small craft paintbrush
Small cup
Basting glue
Size 70 multi-purpose sewing machine needles
60 weight 100% cotton thread in colors to match appliqués
Open toe presser foot
Green 1" diameter buttons: 10

CUTTING

Cut crosswise, from selvage to selvage. All measurements include ¼" seam allowances.

GREEN PRINT NO. 1
Two 8½" x 11" rectangles.

GREEN PRINT NO. 2
One 3½" strip. Cut the strip into 8 small rectangles 5" x 3½".
One 11" strip. Cut the strip into 4 medium rectangles 3½" x 11" and 4 large rectangles 4¾" x 11".

GREEN FLORAL
Three 8½" x 11" rectangles.

GREEN STRIPE
Two top/bottom middle borders 1½" x 31½".
Two side middle borders 1½" x 36".

BLUE PRINT NO. 1
Two lengthwise top/bottom inner borders 1½" x 29½".
Two lengthwise side inner borders 1½" x 34".
Two lengthwise top/bottom outer borders 4½" x 33½".
Two lengthwise side outer borders 4½" x 44".
Five binding strips 1½" wide.

BLUE PRINT NO. 2
Two 2" strips. Cut strips into 2 long strips 2" x 20" and 1 short strip 2" x 10".

FROM TAN PRINT NO. 1
One 2" strip. Cut strip into 1 long strip 2" x 20" and 2 short strips 2" x 10".

MAKING THE HONEY BEE BLOCKS

Use ¼" seam allowances throughout.

1. Sew 2 blue print No. 2 long strips and 1 tan print No. 1 long strip together to make Strip Set A. Cut across Strip Set A at 2" intervals to make 8 Unit 1's.

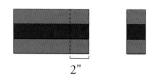

2"

2. Sew 2 tan print No. 1 short strips and 1 blue print No. 2 short strip together to make Strip Set B. Cut across Strip Set B at 2" intervals to make 4 Unit 2's.

3. Sew 2 Units 1 and 1 Unit 2 together to make Nine-Patch Unit. Make 4 Nine-Patch Units.

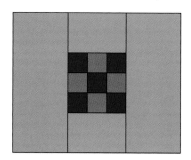

4. Sew green print No. 2 small rectangles to opposite sides of a Nine-Patch Unit. Sew 1 green print No. 2 large rectangle to each remaining side to make Honey Bee Block A. Make 2 Honey Bee Block A's.

5. Sew 2 green print No. 2 small rectangles to opposite sides of a Nine-Patch Unit. Sew 1 green print No. 2 medium rectangle to each remaining side to make Honey Bee Block B. Make 2 Honey Bee Block B's.

APPLIQUÉ PREPARATION

Mock Hand Appliqué patterns, page 121, are printed in reverse and do not include seam allowances.

1. Use a fine-point permanent marker or ink pen to trace patterns onto template plastic. Cut out shapes on traced lines.

Tip: Because the starched fabric will need to dry completely before removing the template for re-use, cutting multiple templates of the same shape will help speed the pressing process when preparing the shapes in Steps 5-9, below.

Tip: Keeping in mind that you will be drawing around the templates onto the fabric with the reverse side facing up, just as you traced the pattern, it might be helpful to mark that side with a "this side up" or even just a WS for wrong side.

2. Place the template, marked side up, on the wrong side of your fabric. Using a washout fabric marker, chalk pencil or fabric marking pencil, draw around the shape. Leaving at least $1/2$" between shapes, draw the number of shapes listed below.
Blue print No. 2: 36 bees.
Blue print No. 3: 12 bees, 5 wings, 5 wings reversed, 5 topknots.
Tan print No. 2: 3 owls.
Tan print No. 3: 2 owls.
Cream print: 10 eyes.
Orange print: 5 beaks.

3. Leaving about a $1/4$" seam allowance, cut out the shapes. Do not cut too closely to the drawn line. The seam allowance can be trimmed later if needed.

4. Set iron to "cotton". Do not use steam. Pour or spray a small amount of starch in the cup. **Note:** Aerosol starch will foam up when sprayed.

5. With the wrong side of the fabric facing up, center the template, marked side up, inside the marked lines of the fabric shape. Using the paintbrush, apply a heavy coat of starch in the seam allowance around the entire shape. Work on one shape at a time and really saturate the seam allowance.

6. Hold the template firmly in place with your fingertips. Starting on the longest flat side, use the tip of the iron to turn and press the seam allowance over the edge of the template.

7. When you reach an outward point, stop turning and pressing about 1" before the point. Fold the point of the fabric perpendicular to the point of the template and press in place. Go back and finish pressing the original side.

8. Fold the second side over the template to give the shape a sharp point and press.

9. Continue turning and pressing until the entire seam allowance is pressed in place. Allow to shape to dry completely. Carefully remove template. Repress seam allowances if needed.

10. Repeat Steps 5-7 to prepare each shape in the project.

APPLIQUÉING SHAPES TO BLOCKS

Refer to photo, page 117, for placement.

1. Thread sewing machine and bobbin with a color of thread that matches the appliqué shape. Attach the open toe presser foot.

2. Set machine to Blind Hem Stitch. This stitch looks like this ⋀⋀⋀ with a tiny bite (∧) and several small straight stitches between the bites. **Note:** If your machine does not have a Blind Hem Stitch, select another decorative stitch such as a blanket or zigzag.

3. Stitch a test sample. Adjust the length and width of the stitch until you are pleased with the look. You will want a tiny bite and small even straight stitches between the bites.

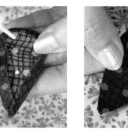

4. Arrange 12 bees on each Honey Bee Block. Use a drop or two of basting glue to hold the shapes in place.

5. Position one Honey Bee Block under the presser foot so, that when stitching, the bite of the stitch will just catch the edge of the shape and the straight stitches will fall on the background fabric.

6. Bring the bobbin thread to the top of the fabric by lowering and raising the needle, bringing up the bobbin loop. Pull the loop to the surface

7. Begin by stitching 5 or 6 stitches in place or use a locking stitch. Return to selected decorative stitch. Referring to Mock Hand Appliqué Stitch as needed, appliqué around each shape on the each Honey Bee Block.

8. To make the 5 Owl Blocks, appliqué 1 owl, 1 wing, 1 wing reversed, 1 topknot, 2 eyes, and 1 beak to each green print No. 1 and green floral rectangle.

MOCK HAND APPLIQUÉ STITCH

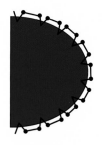

1. (**Note:** Dots on diagrams indicate where to leave needle in fabric when pivoting.) Always stopping with needle down in background fabric, as shown, to stitch outside points, like the tips of leaves. Stop one stitch short of point. Raise presser foot. Pivot project slightly, lower presser foot, and make one angled Stitch 1. Take next stitch, stop at point, and pivot so Stitch 2 will be perpendicular to point. Pivot slightly to make Stitch 3. Continue stitching

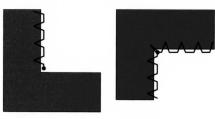

2. For outside corners, stitch to corner, stopping with needle in background fabric. Raise presser foot. Pivot project, lower presser foot, and take an angled stitch. Raise presser foot. Pivot project, lower presser foot and stitch adjacent side.

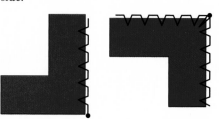

3. For inside corners, stitch to the corner, taking the last bite at corner and stopping with the needle down in background fabric. Raise presser foot. Pivot project, lower presser foot, and take an angled stitch. Raise presser foot. Pivot project, lower presser foot and stitch adjacent side.

4. When stitching outside curves, stop with needle down in background fabric. Raise presser foot and pivot project as needed. Lower presser foot and continue stitching, pivoting as often as necessary to follow curve. Small circles may require pivoting between each stitch.

5. When stitching inside curves, stop with needle down in background fabric. Raise presser foot and pivot project as needed. Lower presser foot and continue stitching, pivoting as often as necessary to follow curve.

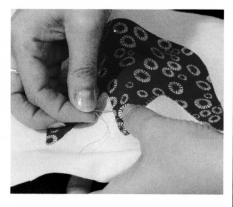

6. When stopping stitching, sew 5 or 6 stitches in place or use a needle to pull threads to wrong side of background fabric; knot, then trim ends.

ASSEMBLY

1. Sew 1 Honey Bee Block A and 2 Owl Blocks together to make Row A. Make 2 Row A's.

2. Sew 1 Owl and 2 Honey Bee Block B's together to make Row B. Make 1 Row B.

3. Alternating A and B Rows, sew rows together to make quilt top center.

4. Sew top, bottom, and then side inner borders to quilt top center.

5. Sew top, bottom, and then side middle borders to quilt top center.

6. Sew top, bottom, and then side outer borders to quilt top center.

FINISHING

1. Refer to Marking, Layering, And Basting, pages 61-62, to mark, layer, and baste quilt top for machine quilting. Refer to Machine Quilting, pages 65-66, for machine quilting instructions. Our quilt is outline quilted around the appliqué shapes and middle border. There is an X through the center of the Nine-Patch Units. The block backgrounds are quilted with an allover loop design. There is a wavy line through the center of the inner border and loops in the outer border.

2. Refer to Attaching a Sleeve, page 67, to make and attach a hanging sleeve, if desired.

3. Use binding strips and follow Binding, page 68, to bind quilt.

4. Sew one button to the center of each eye.

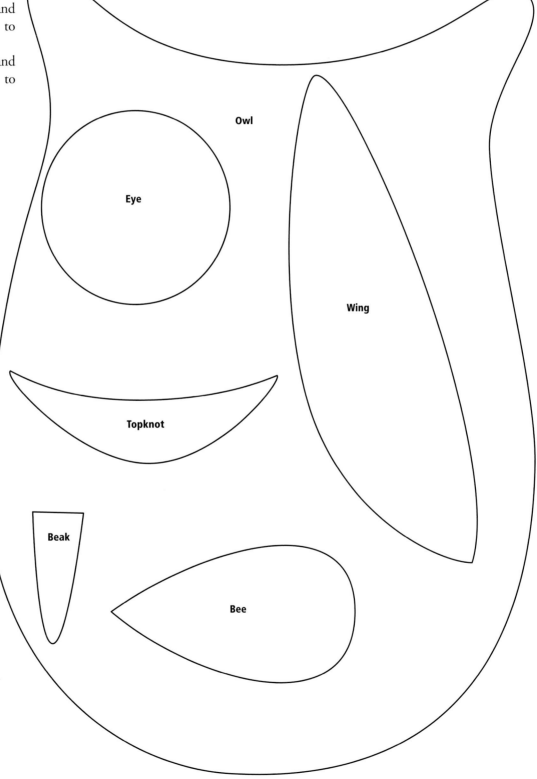

Owl

Eye

Wing

Topknot

Beak

Bee

miniature bear's paw quilt

If you are looking for a stunning miniature wall hanging, try this version of the traditional bear's paw quilt. When using the paper foundation piecing technique, you will be delighted with how easy it is to make precise and perfect tiny points. The timeless design of this quilt makes it worthy of becoming a family heirloom.

DESIGNED AND MADE BY VIVIENNE MOORE

Skill level: Intermediate
Finished quilt size: $20^1/_2$" x $25^1/_2$"
Technique: Paper piecing

MATERIALS

Yardage: Based on 42" fabric, selvage to selvage

Main color (blocks, inner border): $^5/_8$ yard

Background fabric (blocks): $^1/_2$ yard

Alternate squares (side and corner triangles, border, binding): 1 yard

Batting, thin: 24" x 29" piece

Backing: 24" x 29" piece

Sewing machine needle, size 90/14

Scissors for cutting paper

CUTTING

Cut crosswise, from selvage to selvage.

Note: Blocks are constructed using paper foundation piecing techniques; following pieces do not need to be cut precisely (except where noted). See diagram to the right for placement of the pieces.

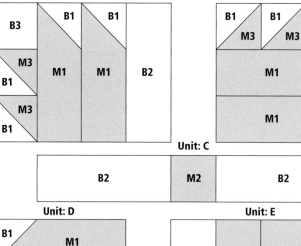

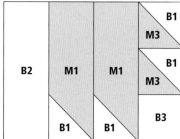

MAIN COLOR FABRIC

M1: Three $2^1/_4$" strips. Cut the strips into 96 $2^1/_4$" x $1^1/_4$" pieces.

M2: One $1^1/_4$" strip. Cut the strip into 12 $1^1/_4$" squares.

M3: Two $1^3/_4$" strips. Cut the strips into 48 $1^3/_4$" squares. Then cut the squares in half diagonally to make 96 triangles.

BACKGROUND FABRIC

B1: Four $1^3/_4$" strips. Cut the strips into 96 $1^3/_4$" squares. Then cut the squares in half diagonally to make 192 triangles.

B2: Two $2^1/_4$" strips. Cut the strips into 48 $2^1/_4$" x $1^1/_4$" pieces.

B3: Two $1^1/_4$" strips. Cut the strips into 48 $1^1/_4$" squares.

ALTERNATE SQUARES, SIDE AND CORNER TRIANGLES

(Cut all pieces precisely):

Alternate squares: One 4" strip. Cut the strip into six 4" squares.

Side triangles: One $6^1/_2$" strip. Cut the strip into three $6^1/_2$" squares. Then cut each square into quarters diagonally to make 12 triangles (only 10 will be used).

Corner triangles: Two 3³/₄" squares. Cut the squares in half diagonally to make four triangles.

Border strips: Cut after the completed blocks are sewn together.

Binding: Cut four 1⁷/₈"-wide strips

CONSTRUCTION

1. Trace or use a photocopy machine to make 12 copies each of units A–E (see page 126).

2. Use the cutting tools to carefully cut the five units apart from each sheet of paper, accurately cutting on the dashed lines. Note that each shape in the units is numbered. The numbers indicate the order in which fabric shapes are sewn onto the paper pattern.

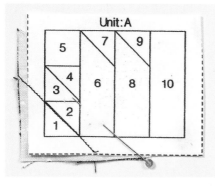

3. **TO MAKE UNIT A:** With right sides together, place a B1 and M3 triangle onto the back (unprinted) side of the paper pattern. Using a larger sewing machine needle (90/14) and a shorter stitch length (8–10 per inch), stitch through the paper pattern and the fabric triangles exactly on the printed lines between triangles 1 and 2.

Vivienne Moore learned how to make quilts in the early 1980s and quilting immediately became her passion. She discovered paper foundation piecing about 10 years later. The ability to achieve precise results on a miniature scale appealed to her. Her work has appeared in *Miniature Quilts* and *Country Living* magazines as well as several books. She loves teaching paper piecing and sharing her enthusiasm for this technique.

4. Turn the unit to the back side and use a pair of scissors to trim the seam allowance to ¹/₄". Then press the #2 fabric triangle over the stitching line.

5. Position the #3 fabric shape (a background B1 triangle) onto the backside of the unit as shown in the photo.

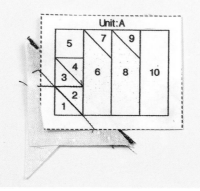

6. Turn the paper pattern to the front side and stitch on the printed line between triangles 2 and 3.

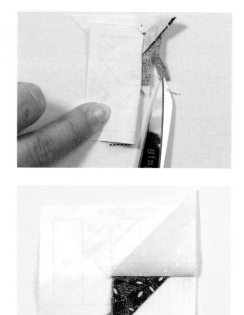

7. Trim the seam allowance to ¹/₄" and then turn and press the light background triangle over the stitching line.

8. Position another M3 triangle (#4) onto the backside, as shown.

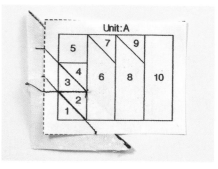

9. Turn to the printed side of the paper pattern and stitch along the line between shapes #3 and #4.

10. Trim the seam allowance on the backside and then press the dark fabric triangle over the stitching line.

11. Position a #5 square onto the backside, as shown.

12. Stitch on the printed side of the paper pattern exactly on the line between shapes #4 and #5. Trim the seam allowance to $1/4$" and then press the background square over the seam allowance, as shown.

13. Position a #6 piece onto the backside, as shown.

14. Stitch on the printed side of the paper pattern exactly on the line. Trim the seam allowance to $1/4$" and press the fabric over the seam allowance, as shown.

15. Position a #7 piece onto the backside, as shown.

16. Stitch on the printed side of the paper pattern exactly on the line. Trim the seam allowance to $1/4$" and then press the fabric over the seam allowance, as shown.

17. Continue in this manner with shapes #8 through #10 to complete Unit A.

18. Use the same sequence of sewing to make Units B, C, D, and E.

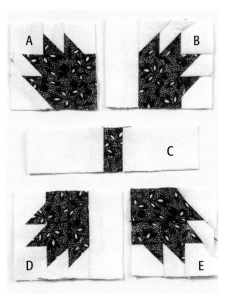

19. Trim the block to size using a rotary cutter. Trim on the dotted line to add an accurate $1/4$" seam allowance.

20. Remove the paper foundations from all of the units. Sew the units together in the following order to complete each block:

(1) Sew Unit A to Unit B. Press the seam toward Unit A.

(2) Sew the A/B Unit to Unit C. Press the seam toward Unit C.

(3) Sew Unit D to unit E, Press the seam toward Unit E.

(4) Sew the D/E Unit to the A/B/C Unit. Press the seam toward Unit C.

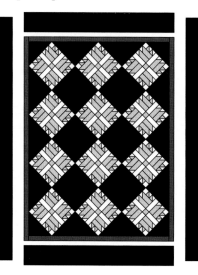

ASSEMBLY

1. Arrange all of the Bear's Paw blocks, alternate blocks and setting triangles, referring to the diagram for the exact placement.

2. Sew all of the pieces together in diagonal rows.

3. Press all seams in the direction of the alternate blocks and setting triangles.

4. Join all rows together, pinning at the intersections of the seams. Press all seams in one direction.

5. Use the cutting tools to trim and straighten the edges of the quilt top to within $1/4$" of the corners of the Bear's Paw blocks.

6. Measure through the center of the quilt top from side to side to determine the length of the top and bottom inner border strips, then cut two strips 1" wide by this measurement.

7. Sew the inner border strips to the top and bottom edges of the quilt.

8. Measure through the center of the quilt from top to bottom to determine the length of the side border strips, then cut two strips 1" wide by this measurement.

9. Sew the side inner border strips to the quilt top.

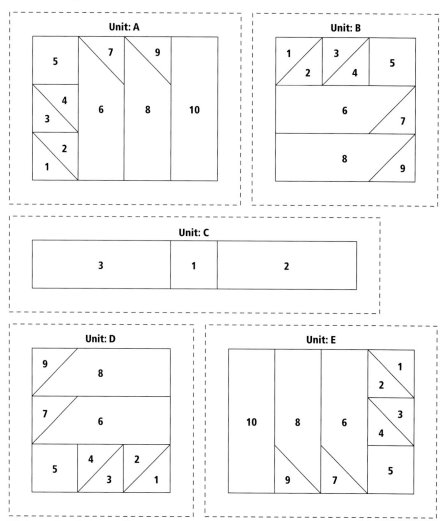

10. Repeat steps 6 through 9 for the outer border, cutting strips $2^3/4$" wide by the needed lengths.

FINISHING

1. Layer the quilt top, backing, and batting in preparation for quilting. See suggestions below.

2. Attach the binding to complete the quilt (see page 68).

BATTING SUGGESTIONS: Mountain Mist® Quilt-Light® or Quilter's Dream Cotton Request Loft.

QUILTING SUGGESTIONS: This quilt can be hand or machine quilted or a combination of the two. Since the seam allowances are close together, hand quilting can be difficult. Quilt in the ditch around the blocks and inner border and around the "paws" to secure the layers. The alternate blocks provide a nice space to showcase hand quilting designs. The quilting design for this quilt is shown on page 232. ❀

Miniature Bear's Paw Quilt master pattern. Actual size; Make 12 copies.

126

under the sea quilt

We all love to save time! Pre-cut fabrics are a great shortcut for busy quilters, and they are available in a wide range of sizes. The Neptune Quilt uses "honey bun" and "charm pack" pre-cuts to help you move from the cutting table to the sewing machine in a hurry.

DESIGNED AND MADE BY PAT SLOAN
Skill level: Beginner
Finished Quilt Size: 43¹/₂" x 54¹/₈"
Technique: Using Pre-cut fabrics

This quilt is made from a combination of pre-cut fabrics and yardage. Pre-cut fabric bundles are composed of one fabric collection or fabrics specifically selected to be used together. They are a real time saver and offer a lot of variety for quilters who want a scrappy look. See page 28 to learn more about pre-cuts.

MATERIALS
Yardage: Based on 40" wide fabric (excluding selvages)
One Honey Bun or 40 strips 1¹/₂" x 40"
One Charm Pack or 32 squares 5" x 5"
White tone-one tone print: 1¹/₂ yards
Green print: ¹/₂ yard (binding)
Backing fabric: 3¹/₂ yards
Batting: 51¹/₂" x 61¹/₈"

CUTTING
Cut crosswise, from selvage to selvage. All measurements include ¹/₄" seam allowances.

WHITE TONE-ON-TONE PRINT
Eight 2" strips. Cut the strips into 24 small rectangles 2" x 5" and 24 large rectangles 2" x 8".
Two 11⁷/₈" strips. Cut the strips into 4 squares 11⁷/₈" x 11⁷/₈". Cut each square twice diagonally to make 16 setting triangles. Discard two setting triangles.
One 6¹/₄" strip. Cut the strip into 2 squares 6¹/₄" x 6¹/₄". Cut each square once diagonally to make 4 corner triangles.
GREEN PRINT
Six binding strips 2¹/₂" wide.

PREPARATION
From Charm Pack, choose 20 assorted light and dark squares for the Log Cabin block centers. Choose 12 assorted light and dark squares for the Floating Square block centers. Separate the Honey Bun strips into lights and darks.

MAKING THE LOG CABIN BLOCKS
Use ¹/₄" seam allowances throughout. **Note:** When using dark center squares, choose light strips for logs 1 and 2. When using light center squares, choose dark strips for logs 1 and 2.

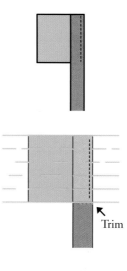

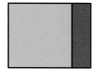

1. Place strip for log 1 on 1 center square with right sides together and matching raw edges. Stitch as shown. Trim strip even with center square where indicated; press open.

2. Turn center square ¹/₄ turn to the right. Using the strip for log 2, repeat Step 1.

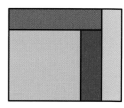

3. Turn center square ¹/₄ turn back to the left (the original starting position). Using a different strip, repeat Step 1 to add log 3.

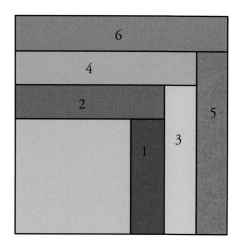

4. Continue adding logs in the same manner until there are 3 logs on each of the 2 sides of the center square to make Log Cabin Block. Block should measure 8" x 8" including seam allowances. Make 20 blocks.

MAKING THE FLOATING SQUARE BLOCKS

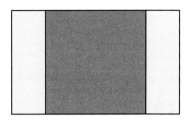
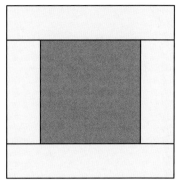

1. Sew 1 small rectangle to opposite sides of a center square. Sew 1 large rectangle to each remaining side of the center square to make Floating Square Block. Block should measure 8" x 8" including seam allowances. Make 12 blocks.

ASSEMBLY

1. Refering to the Assembly Diagram below, sew blocks and setting triangles together into diagonal rows to make quilt top.

2. Sew 1 corner triangle to each corner of the quilt top.

FINISHING

1. Refer to Marking, Layering, And Basting, pages 61-62, to mark, layer, and baste quilt top for machine quilting. Refer to Machine Quilting, pages 65-66, for machine quilting instructions. Our quilt is quilted with a Baptist Fan pattern.

2. Refer to Attaching a Sleeve, page 67, to make and attach a hanging sleeve, if desired.

3. Use binding strips and follow Binding, page 68, to bind quilt using the Continuous Binding Method.

Pat Sloan used to be a computer programmer. It took a big career change to put her where she wanted to be, professionally and creatively. She says, "Since becoming a fulltime quilt designer and teacher a decade ago, I'm more excited about life now." Pat develops patterns, writes quilt books, and designs fabric.

floral medallion

*If you are looking for elegance, this quilt is sure to please, since it
allows you to try out both your hand appliqué and machine piecing skills.
Composed of a delicate hand appliquéd medallion surrounded with simple pieced
blocks, this subtly colored quilt resembles a well-loved vintage heirloom.*

DESIGNED AND MADE BY VERNA MOSQUERA

Quilted by Lynne Todoroff
Skill level: Intermediate
Finished quilt size: 64" x 64"
Techniques: Quick cutting, machine piecing and hand appliqué

MATERIALS

Yardage: Based on 42" fabric, from selvage to selvage

Light pink (background for appliqué and stars): 3/4 yard

Tan (urn): 1/4 yard

Pink, blue, gold, green, and tan (appliqué shapes): scraps and 1/8 yard pieces

Blue floral (large triangles and stars): 3/4 yard

Coral stripe (dark half-square triangles): 5/8 yard

Cream print (light half-square triangles): 1/2 yard

Cream floral (center of square-in-a-square and outer border): 2 1/3 yards

Blue check (triangles in square-in-a-square): 3/8 yard

Cream ribbon stripe (alternate blocks): 1/2 yard

Tan print (inner border): 3/8 yard

Backing: 3 7/8 yards

Blue dot (binding, 1/2" finished): 3/4 yard

Machine embroidery thread in colors to match appliqué shapes

Freezer paper

Black ultra-fine permanent pen (Sharpie)

#10 straw needles

3/4" appliqué pins or Glue-Baste-it

CUTTING

Cut crosswise, from selvage to selvage. Refer to diagram on page 133 for help with placement.

LIGHT PINK BACKGROUND:
One 17" x 17" square
(H) One 2 1/2" strip. Cut the strip into 16 2 1/2" squares
(I) One 5 1/4" strip. Cut the strip into four 5 1/4" squares. Then cut the squares into quarters diagonally to make 16 triangles.

BLUE FLORAL:
(A) One 12 1/4" strip. Cut the strip into two 12 1/4" squares. Then cut the squares in half diagonally to make four triangles.
(G) One 4 1/2" strip. Cut the strip into four 4 1/2" squares
(J) Two 2 7/8" strips. Cut the strips into 16 2 7/8" squares. Then cut the squares in half diagonally to make 32 triangles.

CORAL STRIPE:
(B) Four 4 7/8" strips. Cut the strips into 28 4 7/8" squares. Then cut the squares in half diagonally to make 56 triangles.

CREAM PRINT:
(C) Three 4 7/8" strips. Cut the strips into 20 4 7/8" squares. Then cut the squares in half diagonally to make 40 triangles.

CREAM FLORAL:
Outer border: (cut lengthwise) four 6 1/2" x 70" strips
(D) Three 3 3/8" strips. Cut the strips into 24 3 3/8" squares.

BLUE CHECK:
(E) Four 3" strips. Cut the strips into 48 3" squares. Then cut the squares in half diagonally to make 96 triangles.

CREAM RIBBON STRIPE:
(F) Three 4 1/2" strips. Cut the strips into 24 4 1/2" squares

TAN PRINT: Five 2 1/2" strips. Cut one of the strips into four 2 1/2" x 10" pieces. These short pieces are used to add needed length to the four longer strips.

BLUE DOT: Eight 2 1/4" strips (binding)

PREPARATION
CENTER APPLIQUÉ BLOCK

1. Use the permanent marking pen to trace a full size appliqué design pattern (see page 134) onto a plain piece of paper. This is the master pattern and will be used for placement of the shapes.

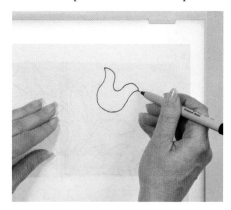

2. With the paper side (not shiny) facing up, position the freezer paper over the master pattern. Use the Sharpie pen to trace the individual pattern shapes onto the freezer paper, leaving approximately 1/4" between shapes.

3. Use paper scissors to accurately cut the individual shapes on the marked lines.

4. Place the plastic-coated (shiny) side of the freezer paper shapes onto the right side of the corresponding fabrics. Press to secure with a steam iron.

5. Use a chalk pencil or Sharpie permanent pen to carefully mark around the outline of the paper shapes onto the right side of the fabrics.

6. Use fabric scissors to cut the shapes a scant 1/4" beyond the marked lines. Remove the paper pattern.

7. With the right side facing up, position the light pink background fabric directly over the full size appliqué design pattern. Tape around the edges to secure. Use a pencil to lightly mark the placement of the shapes onto the fabric. A light box or daylight window may be helpful for this step.

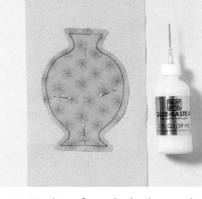

8. Working from the background to the foreground, position and then stitch the fabric shapes onto the background fabric. Use either appliqué pins or glue to hold the shapes in place for stitching.

CONSTRUCTION
CENTER APPLIQUÉ BLOCK

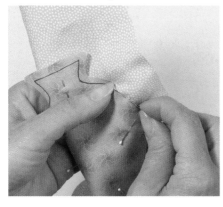

1. Use needle turn appliqué techniques to stitch the shapes to the background fabric. With the straw needle and machine embroidery thread, hand stitch the shapes around the edges, turning under to cover the marked lines. It is not necessary to turn under the edges of those shapes that will be overlapped by another shape.

2. When all of the shapes have been stitched, carefully press the completed block on the back. Trim and straighten the edges to measure 16½" x 16½".

PIECED BLOCKS

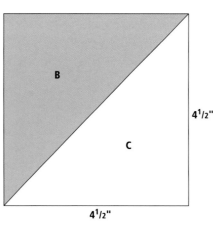

1. Join (B) and (C) triangles together in pairs to make 56 half-square triangle units, as shown. Press the seams toward the darker fabric. They should each measure 4½" x 4½".

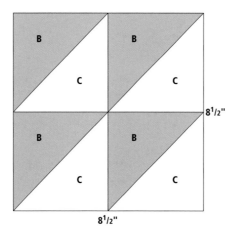

2. Join four half-square triangle units together to make eight units, as shown. They should each measure 8½" x 8½".

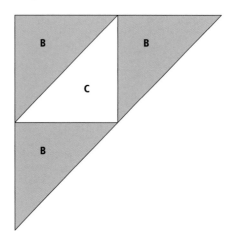

3. Use the remaining half-square triangle units and (B) triangles to make eight units, as shown.

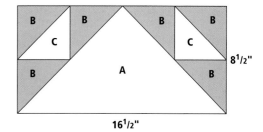

4. Sew two of the units made in step 3 to an (A) triangle to make four units, as shown. They should each measure 8½" x 16½".

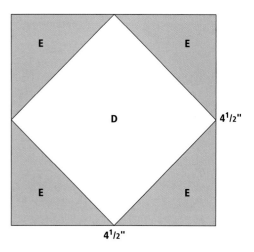

5. Sew four (E) triangles to a (D) square to make 24 square-in-a-square units, as shown. They should each measure 4½" x 4½".

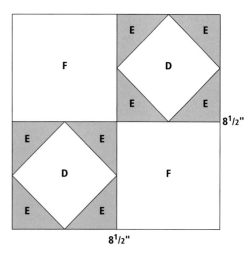

6. Sew two units made in step 5 to two (F) squares to make twelve units, as shown. They should each measure 8½" x 8½".

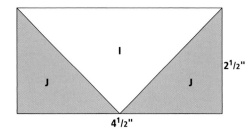

2¹/₂"

4¹/₂"

7. Sew two (J) triangles to each (I) triangle to make 16 units, as shown. They should each measure 2¹/₂" x 4¹/₂".

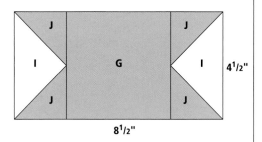

4¹/₂"

8¹/₂"

8. Sew two units made in step 7 to opposite sides of a (G) square to make four units, as shown. Press the seams toward the (G) square. They should each measure 4¹/₂" x 8¹/₂".

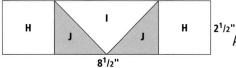

2¹/₂"

8¹/₂"

9. Sew the eight remaining units made in step 7 to the (H) squares to make eight units, as shown. Press the seams toward the (H) squares. They should each measure 2¹/₂" x 8¹/₂".

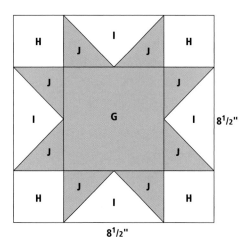

8¹/₂"

8¹/₂"

10. Sew the units together to complete the four star blocks, as shown. Press the final seams toward the center (G) square. They should each measure 8¹/₂"x 8¹/₂".

ASSEMBLY

1. Sew all of the units together with the center appliqué block, referring to the layout diagram for the exact placement.

2. Using a diagonal seam, join each short inner border strip to a long inner border strip.

3. Measure the quilt top through the middle, from top to bottom. Then cut two border strips this length. Sew these to opposite sides of the quilt.

4. Measure the quilt top through the middle, from side to side. Then cut two border strips this length. Sew these strips to the top and bottom edges of the quilt.

5. Repeat steps 3 and 4 for the outer border strips to complete the quilt top.

FINISHING

1. Layer and baste the quilt top with batting and backing in preparation for quilting.

2. This quilt was machine quilted.

3. Sew the binding strips together with a diagonal seam to form one long strip. Press the seams open, then trim the seam allowance to ¹/₄".

4. Attach the binding to complete the quilt. Refer to page 68 for help with a continuous binding. ✤

Verna Mosquera enjoys spending time with her husband and sons, traveling, and doing anything creative. She started quilting as a New Year's resolution and was hooked from day one. She now devotes endless hours to quilting and is constantly on the hunt for new ideas. Verna teaches quiltmaking and designs patterns for her company, The Vintage Spool. She gets a great deal of satisfaction from seeing people learn as well as sharing in their creative endeavors. Her favorite quilts combine both piecing and appliqué, and she considers her strengths to be color and fabric combinations.

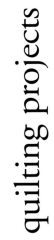

Patterns for Floral Medallion.
Enlarge patterns 133%. Photo on page 130.

spinner

*Color, color, color, what a statement this quilt makes! Repeat a single
fabric pattern in an array of yummy colors and hues to achieve the look
of gentle breezes on a warm, sunny day. Conquer your fear of curved
piecing while making this dramatic quilt.*

DESIGNED AND MADE BY CARA GULATI

Skill level: Intermediate
Finished quilt size: 44" x 44"
Technique: Curved piecing

MATERIALS

Yardage: Based on 42" fabric, from selvage to selvage. Note that extra fabric is allowed for design purposes.

Brightly colored center blocks: Choose four combinations of three fabrics each, for a total of 12 fabrics, $1/4$ yard each.

Pastel colored outside blocks: Choose four combinations of three fabrics each (lighter shades of the center blocks); for a total of 12 fabrics, $3/8$ yard each.

Backing: 48" x 48" square piece*

Batting : 48" x 48" square piece

Binding: ($1/4$" wide finished) $3/8$ yard

Four sheets of heavy duty see-through template plastic

Fine-line permanent marking pen

*You may want to wait until the quilt top is complete to determine the exact size needed.

MAKING TEMPLATES

1. To make full size master patterns, enlarge the templates 300% (see page 138) on a photocopy machine.

2. Use the permanent marking pen to transfer all of the lines, letters, and markings to the template plastic.

3. Use scissors to accurately cut the plastic template patterns apart.

CUTTING

Place arrows on straight grain of the fabric.

The letters refer to the template shapes. Always place the plastic templates face up on the right side of the fabric for marking and cutting.

BRIGHTLY COLORED CENTER BLOCKS:

From each of the four combinations of fabrics, cut four A, four B, and four C

PASTEL COLORED OUTSIDE BLOCKS:

From each of the four combinations of fabrics, cut one each D through L

Binding: Five 2" strips

ARRANGING THE CUT PIECES

1. Arrange all of the fabric pieces onto a design wall, referring to the layout diagram for the exact placement of each shape and the photo of the quilt for color placement. Make any changes in color placement at this point if you desire.

2. Working one block at a time, sew the three shapes together using the curved piecing techniques that follow to complete the block. To avoid turning blocks in the wrong direction, always place them back onto the design wall after sewing.

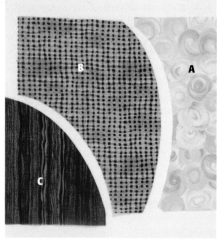

CONSTRUCTION
CURVED PIECING TECHNIQUES

It is a good idea to make a practice block before starting your actual project. Begin by cutting pieces for templates A, B, and C.

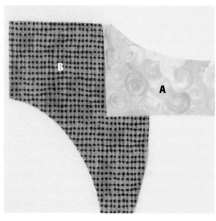

1. To sew a curved seam without pinning, place two shapes right sides together with the convex curved piece (B) on the bottom and the concave curved piece (A) on top, as shown.

2. If your sewing machine has the option of stopping with the needle down it is helpful to use it for the block construction.

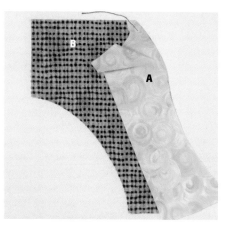

3. Place the two pieces to be sewn (A) and (B) under the presser foot and begin sewing with the usual $1/4$" seam allowance.

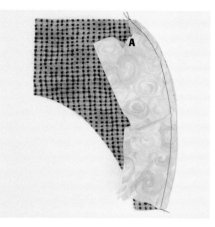

4. Continue stitching until the seam allowances no longer line up, then stop. Raise the presser foot and adjust the edges so the seam allowances are even again. Continue sewing and stopping to readjust the edges as often as needed until you have sewn to the end. It may be necessary to stop every inch or so along the length of the stitching line.

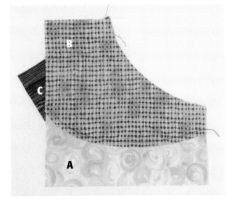

5. With right sides facing each other, position the A/B unit onto the (C) piece. Align the seam allowances as in the previous steps noticing that the beginning of the seams do not line up. When this occurs it is necessary to offset the points while continuing to line up the edges of the seam allowance. To do this, you must move the top piece until a notch is created and both fabrics intersect ¹/₄" away from the seam allowance. This small adjustment will allow you to begin stitching on both fabrics at the same time. Now you can sew the two pieces together, stopping to realign the edges as needed along the length of the stitching line.

6. Turn the block to the backside and press both seams in the direction of the A piece. Then turn and press on the right side to complete the block.

7. Repeat this process for constructing the remaining blocks, working one at a time and returning completed blocks to the design wall for proper placement.

Note that the border blocks as well as the corner blocks are constructed using the same method. They are basically the same block design that has been stretched in different directions.

ASSEMBLY

Before sewing all of the blocks together, check to see that they are all in the correct position and facing in the correct direction. Refer to the diagram for help. This is also a good time to straighten any uneven edges and trim the blocks to a consistent size for ease of construction.

1. Sew the blocks in the center of the quilt first. These are the A/B/C blocks. Join together in rows. Either alternate the pressing direction of the straight seams in each row or press seams open to keep the fullness of the seams even.

2. Join the rows of blocks together. Place pins at the intersections of the blocks to help align the seams.

3. Sew all of the side border blocks together, pressing as above. Then join them to opposite sides of the center blocks.

4. Join the top and bottom rows of border blocks (including the corner blocks) together. Then join them to the center blocks to complete the quilt top.

FINISHING

1. Layer, baste, and quilt as desired.
2. Attach the binding to complete your quilt. Refer to page 68 for help.

Cara Gulati has spent her life around fabric. She has sold fabric and clothes, designed them both, and developed her own company where she designed and manufactured children's wear. Fiber art and quilting in particular grabbed her heart and led her to things of a flatter nature. Cara makes very large art quilts and is currently working on a series called 3-D Explosion. She writes books and teaches workshops on this technique. Her quilt 3-D Party Explosion won Viewer's Choice at the 2003 Houston International Quilt Festival.

Layout diagram

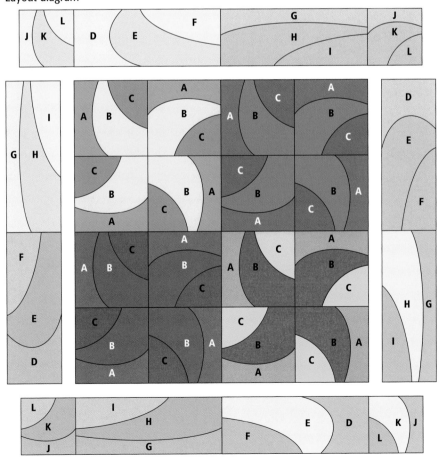

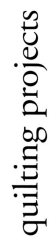

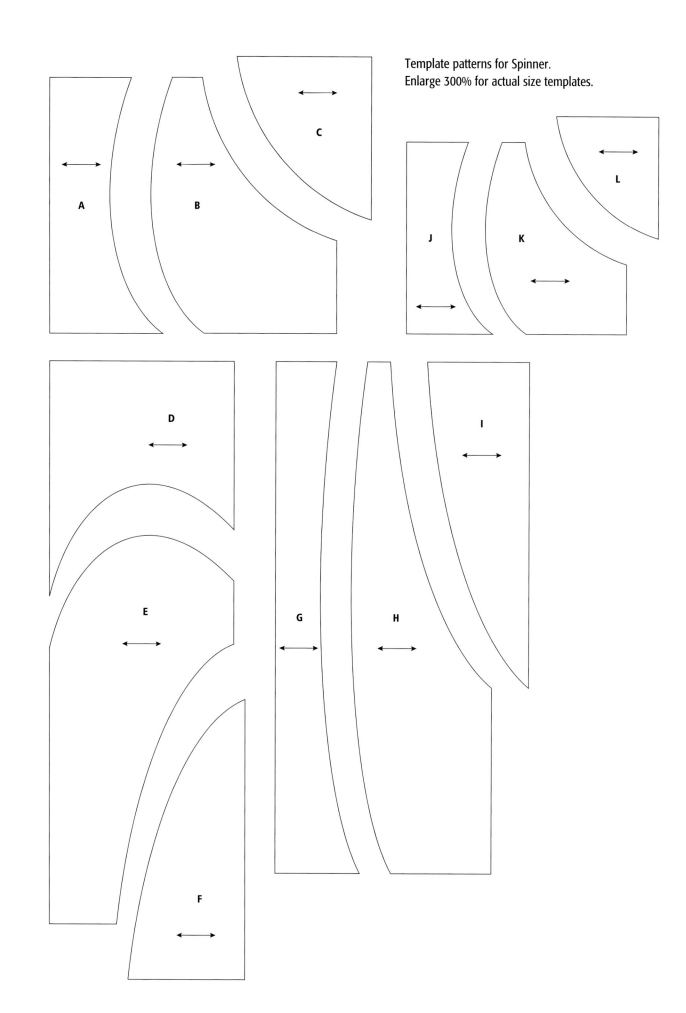

Template patterns for Spinner.
Enlarge 300% for actual size templates.

crazy quilt

The challenge of crazy quilting is the lack of a pattern, which makes you rely upon your own sense of design to lay out the fabric pieces. A good way to meet this challenge is to think like a painter. The muslin base is the canvas. The collaged fabrics are the first color and the embroidery and embellishments are the ongoing layers, which add depth and texture.

DESIGNED AND MADE BY JUDITH BAKER MONTANO

Skill level: Intermediate
Finished quilt size: 54" x 54"
Techniques: Crazy quilting and embroidery

The hardest decision is in choosing your colors and materials. Remember to always use complementary colors in a selected tone of pastels, dusties, or jewel tones. Strive for a pleasing mix of textures, patterns, and solids. As you sew make sure the pieces complement each other in color and fabric type. Above all, remember to never put pattern against pattern to make sure your beautiful embroidery stitches will show up! Always bounce a solid fabric against a patterned fabric.

For a crazy quilt, large or small, you should work on a square or rectangle of muslin or plain fabric. Working 12" or smaller is recommended so that the piecing is easier to handle.

First decide on the finished foundation (muslin) size for each block and cut the muslin 1/2" larger than the desired finished size. This allows for any puckering or tight tension variations that could draw up the size. You can always cut the finished piece down to the proper size later.

MATERIALS

Yardage: Based on 42" fabric, from selvage to selvage
Foundation fabric (muslin): 1¹/₂ yards
Crazy quilt fabrics: Abundance of fancy fabrics, both solids and prints with different textures (silk, rayon, velvet, taffeta, organza, etc.)
Embellishments: Abundance of silk ribbon, trims, lace, buttons, etc.
Embroidery floss: Variety of colors and threads (cotton, silk, metallics)
Embroidery needle
Small embroidery scissors
Water soluble marking pen
Fabric glue stick
Border, velvet (cut lengthwise): 1⁵/₈ yards
Backing fabric: 3¹/₄ yards
Beaded edging: 6³/₄ yards

CUTTING

Cut crosswise, from selvage to selvage.
Muslin foundation fabric: Cut four 12¹/₂" strips, then cut the strips into 12¹/₂" squares (need 12).
CRAZY QUILT FABRICS:
Centers: Cut 12 five-sided pieces, one for each block. Keep the size of this shape in proportion to the size of the foundation piece, neither too large nor too small.
Additional fabrics: Cut into strips, varying from 2" to 3" wide, then cut the strips into rectangles of various lengths.
Border: Cut two 3¹/₂" x 48¹/₂" strips and two 3¹/₂" x 54¹/₂" strips.

CONSTRUCTION

1. Place the five-sided center shape on a square of foundation fabric. Position it right side up and off-center. It is best if none of the five edges are parallel to the edges of the foundation piece.

2. With right sides facing, and raw edges even, place a patterned fabric rectangle on top of the longest side of the center piece, aligning the edges with the longest side. Stitch 1/4" from the aligned edges.

Note: Right-handed quilters will be more comfortable working clockwise around the center piece and left-handers working counter clockwise.

3. Use a steam iron (and pressing cloth, if using delicate fabrics) to turn and press the rectangle over the seam allowance, pressing away from the center piece. Trim the seam allowance close to the stitching line.

4. With right sides facing each other, place a rectangle of solid fabric over the first rectangle and edges even with side 2 of the center piece. Always cover the previous piece (in this case the first rectangle). Sew from the edge of the previous rectangle to the edge of side 2.

5. Turn and press this rectangle over the seam allowance, again pressing away from the center piece. Trim the seam allowance close to the stitching line.

6. Continue sewing additional fabric rectangles to sides 3, 4, and 5 of the

Continued on page 142.

PIECED RECTANGLES

Here's a quick and easy method of piecing rectangles to create any angle.

(a) Using two rectangles of the same width, cut one at an angle on one end. Sew together as shown.

(b) Sew the pieced rectangle to the block.

PIECED AND CURVED SHAPES

One or two pieces of fabric can be joined together. Press seam open. Turn outer edges under, and appliqué in place when the block is complete.

(a) Cut the desired curved shape(s) from the fabric.

(b) Make small clips in the curved edge of the fabric.

(c) Finger press the clipped edge to the wrong side then use a fabric glue stick to hold secure.

(d) Position the curved piece in place on the block.

(e) Trim any fabric extending into this area, leaving a $1/4$" seam allowance where necessary.

(f) Apply fabric glue to the backside of the curved piece. Then position and press in place with a steam iron. The curved edge will need to be appliquéd in place when the block is complete.

PIECED FAN

Many beginners create a "V" angle that can be difficult to fill in with rectangles. A pieced fan shape is a good solution for this space as it uses several pieces of fabric and maintains the desired collage look of the block.

(a) Use a water soluble pen to mark the "pivot" point and the number of "pie wedge" shapes needed to fill in the space (see blue lines in photo).

(b) Sew several different pieces of fabrics together, sewing from the top of the fan shape to the pivot point. Make sure that each time a new fabric rectangle is added that the end extends beyond the previous pivot point by one or two stitches.

(c) Trim the seam allowance very close to the stitching line after the addition of each new piece.

(d) The last rectangle of the pieced fan folds under either in a curve or straight line. Press the edge with a steam iron and then trim any excess fabric from behind the piece.

(e) Turn the seam allowance of the last piece to the wrong side and secure with the glue stick. This edge will be appliquéd in place when the block is complete.

Continued from page 140.

center piece. Note that new angles can be created as you go, and excess length can be cut off, as shown in second photo. Trim any rectangles that extend beyond the foundation fabric even with the edge of the foundation fabric.

Note: The rectangle that will cover side 5 will be long, as it must extend beyond the fabrics on both angles 1 and 4. To add interest and create a more collaged look, consider the following options: Pieced rectangles, pieced and curved shapes, and pieced fans. See page 141 for instructions.

7. Now that you have completed the first go-around and shapes have been sewn to all five sides of the center piece, it is necessary to cut more angles from the pieces you have sewn down. Be brutal in cutting back, cutting from seam edge to seam edge, trying to achieve at least five more angles. Work toward a variety of shapes and sizes.

8. Notice that the first angle of the second go-around in the upper left corner is covered with a curve. Three more angles have been covered and the last angle is ready to be covered with either a pieced rectangle, a curved piece or a fan shape.

9. For the third go-around it will be necessary to piece more toward the outside edges of the block to keep all of the shapes in proportion and to create a collaged look. Always remember:

(a) press each piece over the seam allowance as you go

(b) use rectangular pieces and cut back for more shapes and sizes after each go-around.

10. After the foundation piece has been completely filled with fabric strips, trim the block to the desired size. Press the block on both the front and back. Be sure to appliqué any curved and loose pieces to the foundation piece.

11. Add embellishments of ribbons, trims and laces, stitching them from edge to edge of the foundation piece so that the ends will be included in the seam allowances. It is best not to attach these embellishments parallel and too close to the edges of the block as these spaces will be covered with embroidery stitches.

FINISHING

1. Sew the completed blocks together.

2. Add embroidery stitches over the seam lines joining the blocks. Some suggested stitches are shown opposite.

3. Sew the two shorter border strips to opposite sides of the quilt top.

4. Attach the two remaining border strips to complete the quilt top.

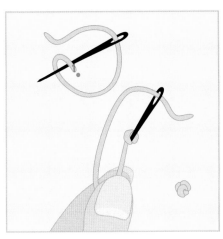

French Knot

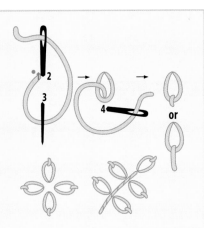

Lazy Daisy

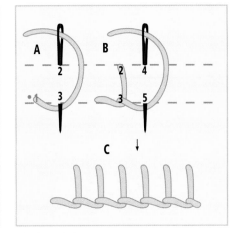

Blanket Stitch

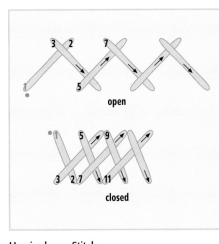

open

closed

Herringbone Stitch

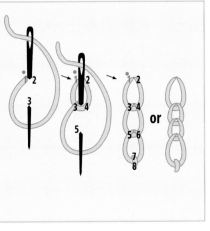

or

Chain Stitch

Feather Stitch

5. Piece the backing fabric to measure 54½" square.

6. With right sides facing, sew the quilt top to the backing fabric. Leave a section unsewn to allow for turning the quilt right side out.

7. Hand stitch the unsewn section closed.

8. A beaded trim was hand stitched around the outer edge of this quilt for an elegant decorative finish. ☙

Judith Baker Montano, the world's leading crazy quilt artist created a machine-pieced method for constructing crazy quilts called "The Montano Centerpiece Method" which hastened the piecing time and allowed the crazy quilter more time for embellishments. Today the Montano method is so popular that it is thought by many to be the original method of crazy quilting; however, Victorian crazy quilters also appliquéd every fabric piece down by hand. Judith's method is a bit like string quilting, overlapping the previous piece sewn down, but she strives for a collaged look with curves and angles. She has written many books on the subject (including *The Crazy Quilt Handbook*) and has won numerous awards for her quilts and garments.

ring around the rosie

Show off your piecing expertise with perfect points at every inter-section. Paper piecing, using the Make It Simpler™ technique, is the secret to success. Rings of Teeter Totter blocks provide the colorful pattern for this playful design.

DESIGN BY ANITA GROSSMAN SOLOMON

Teeter Totter block ©Anita Grossman
Solomon, 2005
Machine pieced by John Willcox
Machine quilted by Janice E. Petre
Skill level: Intermediate
Finished quilt size: 66" x 66"

As you assemble the top, note how few points need to be matched and how little piecing is required. Only 60% of the blocks are pieced, the rest are strips of background fabric.

Paper piecing uses a printed pattern as a guide for stitching. Instead of following a quarter inch mark on a fabric patch, or relying on the width of a sewing machine's presser foot to guide the needle, the paper piecer sews through a printed guideline. This practically assures perfect piecing especially when working with sharply angled patches. With Anita's Make It Simpler™ technique, points and intersections are perfectly matched as well because the block is pieced entirely on one foundation sheet. Since the subunits are never separated, they don't have to be put back together.

MATERIALS

Yardage: Based on 42" fabric, from selvage to selvage
Background: 4 yards
Red print: 1¼ yards
Border: 1⅞ yards
Backing: 4 yards
Batting: 70" x 70"
Binding (¼" wide finished): ¼ yard
No. 14 sewing machine needle
Collins fabric glue stick (water soluble basting adhesive)
Letter opener (optional)
60 sheets of Simple Foundations translucent vellum paper (thin vellum made specifically for paper piecing)
Pressing cloth
6½" square ruler
6½" x 24" ruler
3½" square ruler (optional)

CUTTING

Cut crosswise, from selvage to selvage. See cutting diagram on page 148.

It is advised to cut fabric shapes for one block and make a mock-up before cutting all of the fabric. If you are pleased with the result, proceed to cutting all of the fabric.

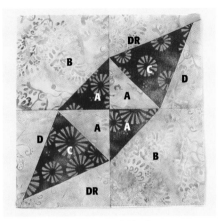

Teeter Totter–6" finished block

BACKGROUND:
Cut a 54" length from the entire fabric. Refer to the diagram on page 148 for cutting the following:
B1: Two 6½" x 12½" strips
B2: Two 6½" x 24½" strips
B3: Two 6½" x 36½" strips
B4: Two 6½" x 48½" strips

Make a photocopy of each of the template patterns (A, B, C, D, and DR) on plain paper (see page 148). To reinforce the templates, cover them with a strip of clear packaging tape before accurately cutting them out. These templates are used as guides for cutting the following shapes.

From the remaining background fabric, cut:
A : Four 2⅝" wide strips. Cut the strips into 60 2⅝" squares. Then cut the squares in half diagonally.
B: Ten 3½" wide strips. Cut the strips into 120 3½" squares. Then use the template to trim to size.
D: Ten 1¾" wide strips. Cut the strips into 120 1¾" x 3½" rectangles. Then use the template to trim to size.
DR*: Ten 1¾" wide strips. Cut the strips into 120 1¾" x 3½" rectangles. Then use the template to trim to size.
*R: Reverse template on fabric.

RED PRINT:
A: Four 2⅝" wide strips. Cut the strips into 60 2⅝" squares. Then cut the squares in half diagonally.
C: Ten 3" wide strips. Cut the strips into 120 3" x 3½" rectangles. Then use the template to trim to size.
BORDER: Four 3½" x 67" strips (cut lengthwise).
BINDING: Cut seven 2½" wide strips.

PREPARATION

1. Make a photocopy of the overall pattern on a piece of the translucent vellum paper (see page 148). This is the foundation paper pattern.

2. Trim the foundation paper patterns, cutting ½" beyond the outside dashed lines, making each one 8¼" square.

3. Fold and crease all of the paper patterns into quarters as indicated by the dotted lines.

CONSTRUCTION

Make 60 blocks.

PAPER PIECING TECHNIQUE

Note: With paper piecing, letters refer to the fabric shapes and numbers indicate the order in which the shapes are sewn onto the paper pattern.

1. With the right side of the fabric shapes facing up, use the fabric glue to secure the B and C pieces to the un-printed side of the paper pattern. Make sure that the creased center lines are free of fabric. Remember it is always best to use a fresh glue stick that is not gummy.

2. With right sides facing each other, place the A and D/DR pieces over the B and C pieces. Lightly apply glue within the seam allowances to secure. No pins are necessary.

3. Position the paper pattern into the machine with the printed side facing you, and the fabric shapes underneath facing the feed dogs. With a short stitch length (15–20 per inch) and one continuous stitching line, sew along the three printed seam lines, as shown. At the end of each seam line, with the needle in the up position, raise the presser foot and

move over the dashed and dotted lines to the next seam line. Short stitches perforate the paper so that it is easily removed. If stitches are too small it is difficult to remove the paper. Practice with the stitch length to find the best setting for your machine. Cut the connecting threads on both the front and backside.

4. Fold the fabric shapes A and D/DR over the seam lines and press. Use a pressing cloth to protect the iron and fabric in the event the photocopier toner melts.

5. Using the same technique, position glue, and stitch the next three shapes (A & D/DR). Several blocks can be sewn at one time, chain stitching and then pressing to save time and accelerate construction of the blocks. Fold the fabric shapes over the stitching line and press.

6. Add the final two background A triangles in the same manner. Lightly add glue to secure any loose tips of fabric to the paper pattern.

7. With the fabric sides facing each other, fold the completed block in half, along either center crease line.

8. Begin stitching at the top of the block, at least $1/8$" before the dashed line. Continue stitching to the end of the seam line on the top section. Do not stitch through the center seam allowances (which are parallel to the fold), but skip over this section and stitch along the seam allowance line of the bottom section. It is not necessary to backstitch.

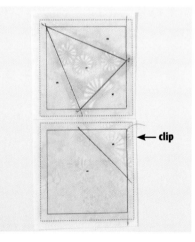

9. Use scissors to make a perpendicular clip into the foundation pattern at least $3/8$" from the folded edge, along the creased line.

10. Open the foundation paper and refold it in half along the other crease. This is possible because the intersection was clipped.

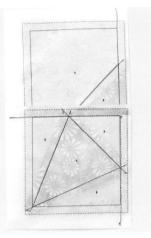

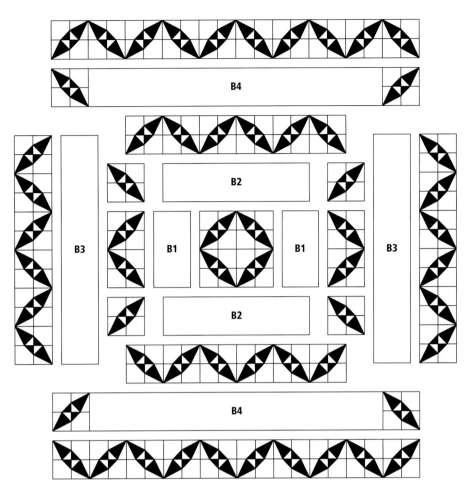

11. Repeat as in Step 2, stitching from top to bottom, but not through the upper and lower flaps in the center of the block. To make a smooth stitching line, raise the needle and move the flaps out of the way when skipping over them. Take a few backstitches before and after the skipped center intersection.

12. Using a pressing cloth, press the block on the paper side to set the seams within the folds.

13. Use a letter opener to make slits in the creased folds. Then remove the narrow strips of paper that enclose the seams.

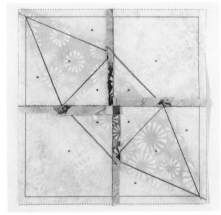

14. Press the seams again in whichever direction they want to go, pressing both on the wrong and right sides. Leave all of the remaining paper intact until the blocks have been joined together.

15. With the paper side facing up, place the block on the cutting board. Use the 6½" x 6½" ruler to trim the block, using the edge of the ruler as a guide. Do not rely on the printed edge of the pattern guide for this step as the paper can shrink during construction.

16. The completed block should measure 6½" x 6½". Do not remove the paper pattern.

ASSEMBLY

The blocks will be stabilized and less likely to stretch if the paper is placed next to the feed dogs during assembly. Refer to the diagram for exact position when joining the blocks together into the following sections:

Center: Four blocks

Inner sides: Two two-block strips

Inner top and bottom and outer sides: Four six-block strips

Outer top and bottom: Two 10-block strips

There will be eight remaining single blocks.

Refer to the assembly diagram (above) for help with joining the pieced strips and background strips.

1. To make the center section, sew the background B1 pieces to opposite sides of the center block. Then sew a two-block set to each side.

2. Sew a single block to opposite ends of each background B2 strips. Sew these strips to the top and bottom of the center section.

3. Sew a six-block strip to the top and bottom of the center section.

4. Sew a six-block strip to each background B3 strip. Then sew these to opposite sides of the center section.

5. Sew single blocks to opposite sides of the background B4 strips. Then sew these to the top and bottom edges.

6. Finally sew a 10-block strip to the top and bottom to complete the quilt top.

7. Remove all of the paper from the backside of all pieced blocks. No special tools are required. Since thin vellum and a No. 14 needle have been used, the paper will remove easily.

8. Attach the sides and then top and bottom border strips to complete the quilt top.

9. Layer and baste the quilt top with the batting and backing in preparation for quilting. The quilting design in the sample quilt is a diagonal grid stitched through only the background and not the red print fabric. Choose quilting thread in a color to match the background fabric.

10. Use the cutting tools to trim the excess batting and backing even with the edge of the quilt top.

147

11. Trim the corners to a gentle curve.

12. Attach the binding. Refer to page 68 for help. 🌀

Anita Grossman Solomon is known for her simpler approach to paper piecing and is the author of *Make It Simpler Paper Piecing* and *Perfect Blocks the Make It Simpler Way*. She likes to simplify quiltmaking as much as possible, from the piecing and assembly to the quilting, without compromising the quilt's design.

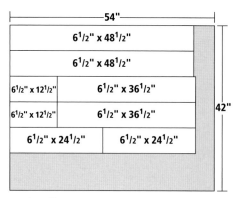

Cutting diagram

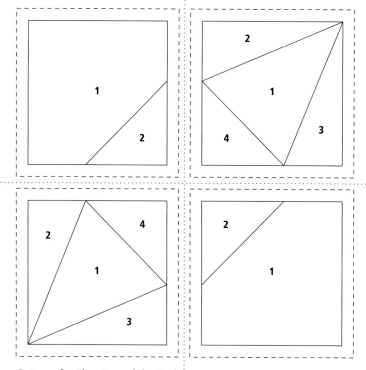

Patterns for Ring Around the Rosie. Enlarge pattern 200%.

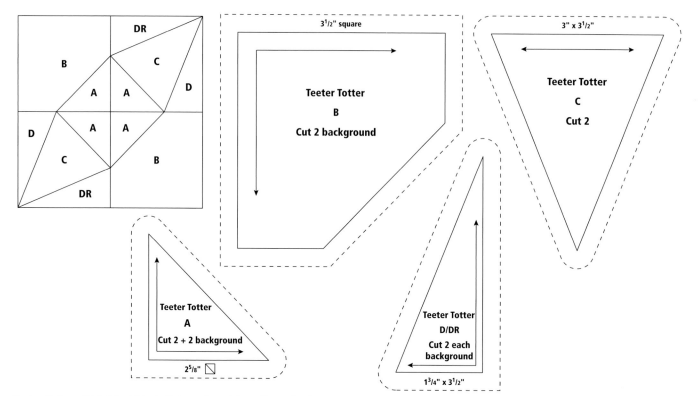

Teeter Totter—6" finished block. Enlarge template patterns 133%.

trapunto pillow

Trapunto, or stuffed quilting, is the technique of using extra batting to create dimension. On this pillow, hand embroidery beautifully outlines the raised design of a singing bird framed with leaves. The background is closely machine quilted to flatten it, lending even more distinction. Modern quilting supplies simplify this trapunto project.

DESIGNED AND MADE BY LINDA TIANO

Skill level: Intermediate
Finished pillow size: 16" x 16"
Techniques: Trapunto and hand embroidery

MATERIALS

Yardage: Based on 40" wide fabric (excluding selvages)

White fabric: 1/2 yard
Black fabric: 1/8 yard
Print fabric: 1/4 yard
Backing fabric: 3/8 yard
Extra-loft (1/2"-5/8" thick) polyester batting: 15" x 15"
Lightweight cotton batting: 15" x 15"
Water-soluble thread
Water-soluble fabric marker
Black embroidery floss
Black 1" wide fringe trim: 2 yards
Pillow form: 16" x 16"
Blunt-nose scissors
Safety-pins

CUTTING

Cut crosswise, from selvage to selvage. All measurements include seam allowances.

WHITE FABRIC:
2 squares 15" x 15"
BLACK FABRIC:
2 side inner borders 1 1/4" x 10 1/2"
2 top/bottom inner borders
   1 1/4" x 12"
PRINT FABRIC:
2 side outer borders 3" x 12"
2 top/bottom outer borders 3" x 17"
BACKING FABRIC:
2 pillow backs 10 1/2" x 17"

PREPARATION

1. Enlarge the entire bird and leaf border pattern, page 151, 125%.
2. Center 1 white fabric square over the full size pattern. Using the water-soluble fabric marker, trace the black lines of the design onto the fabric square.
3. With right side facing up, layer the traced fabric square over the polyester batting square. Avoiding the marked lines, secure layers with safety pins.
4. Using a darning foot and water-soluble thread, stitch just inside the traced lines where indicated in red on the pattern. **Note:** Do not stitch along the detail lines of the bird and leaves. Remove pins.
5. Using blunt-nose scissors, trim batting from all background areas, leaving batting behind the bird, branch, and leaves only.
6. With right side facing up, layer the basted square, cotton batting, and remaining white fabric square; secure the layers with safety pins.
7. Using 2 strands of floss and going through all the layers, Stem Stitch, page 111, over all traced lines.
8. Machine quilt all background areas with closely spaced meandering quilting, page 65.
9. Submerge the stitched piece in a sink of clear tepid water until basting thread is dissolved and fabric marker lines are no longer visible. Remove stitched piece from water, gently roll in a light-color towel, and squeeze to remove excess water. Dry flat, blocking as needed to square.

CONSTRUCTION

Match right sides and use 1/4" seam allowances unless otherwise noted.

1. Trim stitched piece to 10 1/2" x 10 1/2" to make the pillow top center.
2. Sew side then top/bottom inner borders to pillow top center.
3. Sew side then top/bottom outer borders to pillow top center.

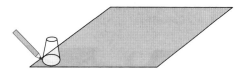

4. Place a small glass on one corner of the pillow top; draw around curve. Repeat for remaining corners. Trim each corner along drawn line.

1/2"

5. Beginning and ending at center bottom with a 1/2" overlap, match raw edges and pin fringe to the right side of the pillow top; baste in place.
6. Press 1 long edge of each pillow back 1/4" to the wrong side twice. Topstitch hem close to folded edges.

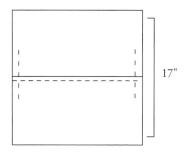

17"

7. With right sides facing up, overlap the 2 hemmed edges of the pillow backs until the overall measurement is 17" x 17". Baste the overlapped edges together. Trim corners as in Step 4.

8. Matching right sides and using a $1/2$" seam allowance, sew the pillow front and back together; clip curves.

9. Turn the pillow cover right side out and insert the pillow form.

Linda Tiano's years of sewing and designing for Leisure Arts have produced creations from the whimsical to the sublime. It's surprising to realize that Linda's creative skills were born of necessity. "I used to sew clothes for my three children, she says. "For me, the fun part of sewing began with the quilting boom about a decade later. I'm now a member of a guild and three quilt groups. I sew all kinds of projects, and I'm making sure my nine grandkids each have a quilt from me."

Enlarge pattern 125%.

jessi's holly basket

A tiskit a tasket, make a pretty basket. Lively colored fabrics make this charming wall hanging a perfect project for learning machine appliqué techniques. So gather up a bouquet of colorful fabrics and fill your home with flowers.

DESIGN BY SUE NICKELS
MADE BY SUE NICKELS AND ANNIE SMITH
Skill level: Intermediate
Finished quilt size: 28" x 28"
Techniques: Raw edge fusible machine appliqué and machine quilting

MATERIALS

Yardage: Based on 42" fabric, from selvage to selvage

Use prewashed 100% cotton fabric

Background: $3/4$ yard

Border: 1 yard

Appliqué shapes (flowers and leaves): 8–10 small pieces and fat quarters

Green for stems and leaves: $1/2$ yard

Backing: 1 yard

Batting, cotton or cotton blend: 30" x 30" piece

Binding, $1/4$" finished: $3/8$ yard

Lightweight paper-backed fusible web: 2 yards

Thread: 50 weight, in colors to match and contrast with appliqué shapes

Spray starch, regular weight

Scissors: fabric, paper, and small embroidery

Sewing machine with open toe embroidery foot

Teflon pressing sheet

PREPARATION

1. Trace a full-size pattern of the entire design onto a large piece of plain paper. If necessary, tape several sheets together.

2. Position the fusible web over the design pattern with the paper side facing up.

3. Use a sharp pencil to trace the individual shapes onto the fusible web. For asymmetrical shapes, the tracing must be done from the reverse side of the pattern. Be sure to mark the double hash marks on any shapes having them. These marks indicate that another shape will be positioned over it. **Note:** It is necessary to trace only the bottom curvy stems onto the fusible web as the other five stems are made using bias strips as instructed below.

CUTTING

Cut crosswise, from selvage to selvage

Background fabric: One 24" square

STEMS:

Center stem: One $1^1/_8$" x $7^1/_2$" strip, cut on the bias

Side tulip stems: Two 1" x 7" strips, cut on the bias

Side flower stems: Two 1" x 6" strips, cut on the bias

Bottom curvy stems: Use master pattern.

Appliqué shapes: Use paper scissors to cut the individual shapes from fusible web, cutting just outside the marked pencil lines. Then carefully cut all of the shapes (except the very small ones) $1/4$" inside the marked pencil line to remove the majority of the fusible web. There will remain a narrow paper outline of each shape.

Border fabric: 29" square

Binding: Four $1^7/_8$" strips

CONSTRUCTION
PREPARATION OF APPLIQUÉD FLOWERS AND STEMS

1. Apply spray starch to the backside of the background fabric. A few applications may be necessary to give the stiffness of paper. This will stabilize the fabric for appliqué.

2. Use one row of hand basting stitches to trifold the five bias stem pieces. Then press each stem very flat.

3. Press the backside (bumpy side) of the paper-backed fusible shapes to the wrong side of the corresponding appliqué fabrics.

4. Follow the manufacturer's instructions that accompany the fusible web for the recommended heat settings and length of pressing time.

5. Use the small embroidery scissors to cut all of the appliqué shapes, cutting exactly on the marked pencil lines. For those shapes with double hash marks, leave a $1/4$" extension beyond the pencil lines to allow for overlying shapes.

6. Remove the paper layer of the fusible web from the backside of all of the fabric shapes.

7. Working on a flat surface, center the background fabric over the master pattern. The marked lines on the pattern should be visible through the fabric and are used as a guide for placing all of the shapes. If they are not clear you may need to use a light box for this step.

8. Position and then hand baste the five bias stems in place.

9. Position all of the other shapes, using a straight pin as necessary to move shapes into their perfect placement. Refer to the master pattern for help with placing those shapes that overlap others.

10. Use an iron to carefully and firmly press all of the shapes onto the background fabric.

11. Follow the manufacturer's instructions that accompany the fusible web you are using for the correct setting on your iron.

STITCHING

1. For multiple layer units such as the flowers, stitch the small circles to the center before fusing the whole unit to the background fabric.

2. Use a machine blanket stitch to sew around the raw edges of all of the shapes (except the bias stems which will be stitched in step 3 below). Adjust the stitch just small enough to nicely cover the raw edge of the shapes, but not so short that it appears as a satin stitch. There should be approximately $1/16$" between bites as well as a $1/16$" bite onto the fabric shape. First, stitch all shapes with like colors, using the same color thread to avoid constantly changing color. For example, stitch all of the green leaves before changing to red thread for the flowers and pot. If you prefer, the thread color can contrast with the fabric to highlight the shape. Be sure to use the same color thread in both the top and bobbin. Refer to the diagrams on page 155 for correct placement of the stitches for inside and outside points and curves. For a smoother finish around the curves of the shapes, shorten the stitch length to 14–16 stitches per inch. Stitch close to the edge of the shape (about $1/16$" from the edge). Bring all of the thread ends to the backside and tie off. Bury the thread ends on the backside into the appliqué, if necessary.

3. After all raw edge blanket stitching is done, use a straight stitch along the folded edges of the bias strip stems.

REVERSE MACHINE APPLIQUÉ
TO BUILD A BASKET

When working with a complex unit such as the basket, which has multiple shapes and layers, it is helpful to join small pieces together before fusing the larger unit to the background fabric.

1. Place a Teflon pressing sheet over the basket pattern. The pattern will be visible through the sheet for use as a placement guide for the individual shapes.

2. Prepare the individual shapes with fusible web as described above, leaving just a thin outline of web around the edges of the shapes on the backside.

3. Accurately position the shapes onto the pressing sheet, using the full-size pattern as a guide. Press the shapes lightly onto the pressing sheet. Allow the shapes to cool completely before peeling the prepared basket away from the pressing sheet. The basket is now ready to be fused and stitched in place onto the background fabric.

FINISHING TOUCHES

THREAD STAMENS AND MACHINE EMBELLISHMENTS

The stamens of the tulips are made with a small zigzag stitch; use 50 weight cotton thread and the open toe embroidery foot. Set the machine to a narrow zigzag stitch and short length. The stitches should be close but not as close as a satin stitch. The stitches should still lie flat. Pull about one yard of thread off the spool and set aside. (Just pull to the side. Do not cut off.) Starting at the top of the stem, take one stitch and bring the bobbin thread to the top of the block. Bring the top and bobbin thread in front of the needle and toward you. Put the needle down into the block and raise the presser foot. Take the one yard of thread and fold it in half, then place it behind the needle and bring the thread in front and toward you with the other two threads. There will now be six threads in front of you. Drop the presser foot and begin zigzag stitching, couching the threads onto the background fabric. At the end of the stitching line, leave the threads long, thread them all to the backside of the block, and tie them off. This makes a nice dimensional thread stem.

The spiral at the top of the middle circle on the tulip is done with free motion stitching, using a darning foot with the feed dogs lowered. It is stitched to the background fabric before layering and basting.

Additional embellishing stitches can be added in other spaces, if desired.

SCALLOPED EDGE

The scalloped edge is prepared and stitched in place exactly as done for the other appliqué shapes. It is attached after all of the other stitching is complete.

1. Make a full size pattern of the scalloped edge. Use this pattern for all four sides. Prepare the fusible web in the same way as described in the general preparation section above.

2. Mark lines on the backside of the background fabric block for placement of the fusible web edgings. These lines should be centered and measure 19" x 19".

Thread stamens and machine embellishment on the tulip

machine needle

close-up of stamens (6 strands of thread with zigzag stitching on top)

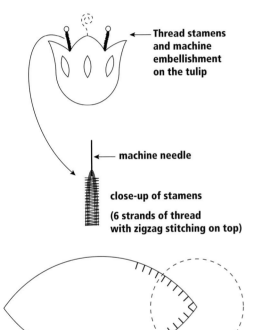

Outside Point

Inside Point

Outside curve, pivot with needle down in background

3. Carefully position the scalloped edging on the backside of the block, placing the guidelines along the marked lines on the backside of the fabric. Then press in place.

4. Use fabric scissors to accurately cut on the pencil lines to create the raw scalloped edge. Remove the paper pattern.

5. Apply spray starch to a 29" x 29" square of border fabric. Center and press the flower basket block onto the border fabric.

155

6. Blanket stitch around the scalloped edges.

7. Top stitch two parallel lines with a contrasting color thread, stitching close to the scalloped edge.

8. Press and stitch fabric circles in the corners using the circle pattern and a blanket stitch.

9. If desired, turn over to the backside and remove the border layer of fabric behind the center appliqué design up to the parallel stitching lines. This is only necessary if the underneath border fabric shows or shadows through to the front of the flower basket block. Otherwise it can be left in place.

FINISHING

1. Trim the excess border fabric to measure $4^{1}/_{2}$" from the topstitching lines to the outer edge. The quilt top should measure 28" x 28".

2. Layer and baste the quilt top in preparation for quilting.

3. Quilt as desired. Attach binding to complete the quilt.

Sue Nickels has been quilting for over 25 years, starting out by hand and gradually focusing on machine work. She is an internationally known instructor and has co-written books with her sister, Pat Holly. Their collaboration has won them many prestigious awards at several large quilt shows. Sue has written *Machine Appliqué: A Sampler of Techniques* and *Machine Appliqué: A Primer of Techniques.* She also designs machine quilting stencils.

Patterns for Jessi's Holly Basket. Enlarge patterns 200%.

Join here

• center

Scalloped Edge

pattern circle (for corners)

ulu pillow

*The Ulu or breadfruit is a food staple found throughout Hawaii and
the Pacific Islands. Many quilters believe that if your first quilt is an
Ulu design you will not want for anything in life. A favorite among the
island quilters, this design differs from other Hawaiian quilt patterns
in that it is formed from the border to its center.*

DESIGN BY JOHN SERRAO MADE BY CISSY SERRAO

Skill level: Intermediate
Finished size: 22" pillow
Techniques: Needle turn appliqué and hand quilting

MATERIALS

Yardage: Based on 42" fabric, selvage to selvage

Use prewashed 100% cotton fabric or a cotton-polyester blend.

Background: 22" x 22" square

Appliqué design: 22" x 22" square

Lining: 24" x 24" square

Backing: 22" x 22" square

Batting (5 oz.): 23" x 23" square

Pillow form: 22" x 22"

Covered cording: 2⅝ yards

Elastic (1" wide): 1 yard

Threads: One to match appliqué design, one for basting and quilting threads in colors to match background and design fabrics.

Additional supplies: Plain piece of paper, fabric scissors, safety pins (three medium size), straight pins, appliqué needles, quilting needle (Betweens), quilting hoop, and thimble.

PREPARATION
PREPARATION OF DESIGN FABRIC

1. Place the design fabric on a flat surface with the right side facing up.

2. Fold the fabric in half, having the raw edges even with each other and the fold at the bottom. Press the folded edge.

3. Fold the fabric again. There are now four thicknesses. Press the folded edge.

4. Fold the fabric to form a right angle triangle, aligning the edges. Each section of the folded fabric forms an eighth of the overall design.

PREPARATION OF DESIGN PATTERN

1. Use a pencil to trace all of lines of the design pattern (both dashed and solid) onto the plain piece of paper (see page 160).

2. Use paper scissors to cut the pattern, accurately cutting on the outer dashed lines on both sides. This pattern is one-eighth of the entire design.

3. Position the paper pattern onto the folded design fabric, carefully aligning the edges. The long angle of the paper pattern should be placed along the bias fold of the fabric, and the short angle of the paper pattern should be placed on the straight grain of the fabric. Check to see that the backside of the folded fabric lies flat without puckers. Pin to secure.

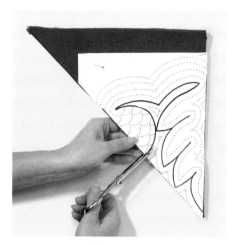

4. Use fabric scissors to carefully and accurately cut along all of the solid lines.

5. Remove the pins and pattern. Carefully remove the cutout section but do not unfold the fabric.

LAYING OUT THE DESIGN

1. Fold and press the background fabric piece into eighths, as was done above with the design fabric. Unfold and lay on a flat surface.

2. Position the folded design fabric over the background fabric, aligning the center points and creases of each.

3. Carefully unfold the design fabric to one-fourth of the entire design and then again to one-half of the entire design.

4. Finally unfold to expose the full design. Make sure that the design is centered on the background fabric as perfectly as possible.

CONSTRUCTION
PINNING AND BASTING THE DESIGN TO THE BACKGROUND

1. To secure the design to the background fabric, first pin the center, and then carefully pin out to the edges, gently smoothing the design as you pin. There should be no overlap; design edges may lay next to each other but never on top of each other.

2. When pinning is complete, use a long basting stitch and single strand of basting thread to stitch around the entire design. Be careful not to baste too closely to the outer edges of the design, as these will be turned under and appliquéd to the background fabric. Remove pins.

APPLIQUÉING THE DESIGN TO THE BACKGROUND FABRIC

1. Thread the appliqué needle. Don't make the thread too long; arms length from fingers to shoulder is perfect. Knot the end of the thread and cut off the excess after the knot. Use the needle to turn the edge of the design fabric under approximately 1/8". Use your thumb to hold approximately 1/2" to 1" under. The basting stitches should also help keep the turned edge under.

2. Make the first stitch by bringing the needle and thread between the design and background fabric. Bring the needle up into the folded edge of the design fabric. The knot will hide in the fold.

3. Position the needle under the previous stitch, pick up the bottom fabric with the needle; bringing it through the top fabric close to the folded edge. Refer to the photos at right for stitching points and inner corners.

4. When the thread becomes too short, pull it to the backside and knot off.

5. When the entire design has been appliquéd to the background fabric, remove all basting stitches. See photo of back at right.

STITCHING POINTS AND INNER CORNERS

POINTS: Stitch to the second to the last stitch from the point (about 1/8" from the point).

Use the needle to turn the whole point under the last stitch. Tuck under the opposite edge. Tug gently on the thread and the point will reappear. Then stitch the point.

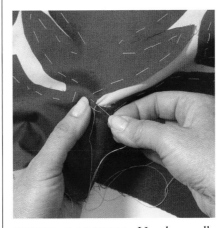

INNER CORNERS: Use the needle to tuck the fabric under and into the inner corner as far as possible only on one side.

Next tuck under from the opposite edge into the corner. The fabric should automatically fold under, so you can continue with the appliqué stitch.

PREPARATION FOR QUILTING

1. Place the lining fabric onto a flat surface. Use tape around the edges to secure.

2. Position first the batting and then the finished appliqué design on top.

3. Use basting stitches to hold the layers together.

4. Place the prepared pillow top into the quilting hoop.

159

QUILTING

Refer to the general instructions for hand quilting on pages 63-64 for help if needed. Refer to the design pattern for placement of the quilting stitches.

Add quilting stitches in the following order:

1. Stitch the leaves first. Make a quilting line down the center of each leaf, then branch out from the center to show veins of the leaf.

2. Quilt in the ditch, stitching around the leaves on the background fabric close to the edge of the design. Try to make the stitches invisible.

3. Next outline the leaf with echo quilting lines on the background fabric.

4. Quilt the breadfruit portion of the design. The breadfruit looks like a green pineapple without the crown, so you can easily crisscross the quilting stitches. Also quilt in the ditch and echo quilt around the breadfruit.

5. Finally quilt the outside portion of the design with echo quilting. When you have reached the outside edge of the quilt, fasten the edges with elastic and safety pins. Wrap the elastic around the hoop to the back of the quilt top. Secure with a safety pin on the top section of the quilt top. This will hold the fabric tight and help with quilting the corners and edges of the design.

6. When all of the quilting is complete, trim the excess lining and batting even with the edge of the background fabric.

PILLOW CONSTRUCTION

1. Use a zipper foot to sew purchased covered cording around the edge of the pillow top.

2. With right sides facing, use a $1/4"$ seam allowance to sew the quilted pillow top to the backing, leaving a large enough opening for turning and inserting the pillow form. Carefully turn the pillow right side out.

3. Insert the pillow form, working it around and into the corners for a full, smooth finished look. Hand stitch the opening closed to complete the pillow.

John Serrao and his wife Poakalani have been teaching Hawaiian quilting since 1972. They are descendants of Hawaiian quilters and quilt designers, who handed down to them their own spiritual culture and knowledge of quilting. Today they continue the art of quilting and design and have also passed on their knowledge to their daughter W. Cissy Serrao. Cissy teaches with them in their many classes.

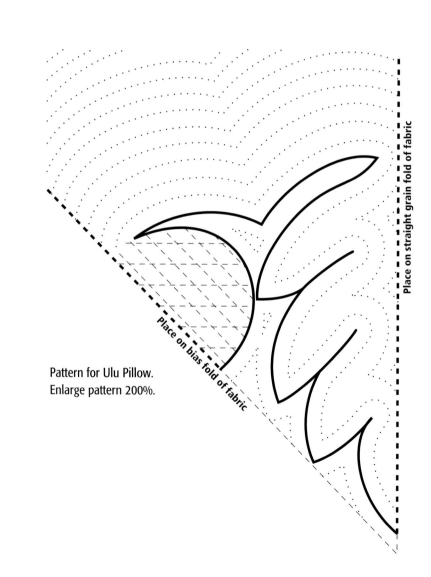

Pattern for Ulu Pillow.
Enlarge pattern 200%.

Place on bias fold of fabric

Place on straight grain fold of fabric

old tulips

Beauty and warmth combine in this lovely quilt made with a repeated tulip design. The invisible machine appliqué technique provides the precision required when working with flannel. Enjoy creating the traditional pattern, which may bring back memories of bygone days.

MADE BY NANCY BUSBY

Skill level: Intermediate
Finished size: 53" x 53"
Technique: Invisible machine appliqué

The pattern named Rare Old Tulip is a design taken from an old quilt pattern book from the 1930s. The book indicated that the quilt was copied from one that was over 100 years old at that time. The colors were "red, yellow, and orange with green" as quoted from *A Quilter's Companion* by Dolores A. Hinson. To successfully make this project using invisible machine appliqué techniques, you will need a machine with a setting for hem stitching that will allow you to override any programmed settings.

MATERIALS

Yardage: Based on 42" fabric, without selvages

This quilt is made from 100% cotton flannel. Since flannel stretches more easily than other cotton fabrics, the fabric was not washed until after the project was finished.

Background: $2^3/_4$ yards
Green print for stems: $^1/_2$ yard
Green prints for leaves, two each: $^1/_2$ yard
Red prints for tulips, eight each: $^1/_4$ yard
Red print for center circle: $^3/_8$ yard
Gold print for tulip centers: $^1/_8$ yard
Red print for inner frame: $^3/_8$ yard
Backing: $3^1/_4$ yards
Batting: 60" x 60"
Binding, $^1/_2$" finished: $^1/_2$ yard
Nonwoven, lightweight, iron-on interfacing: 2 yards
#8 gauge translucent upholstery vinyl: $^5/_8$ yard
17" x 17" piece of plain paper
Invisible, monofilament thread
50 weight machine embroidery thread or bobbin fill thread for bobbin (color to match background fabric)
Water soluble fabric glue stick
Sheet of fine-grit sandpaper
$^1/_2$" bias bar
Open toe embroidery presser foot
#10 universal sewing machine needle
Sharpie permanent pen

CUTTING

Cut crosswise from selvage to selvage. Cut through only two thicknesses of flannel at a time for a more accurate cut.

BACKGROUND: For center blocks: Four $18^1/_2$" x $18^1/_2$" squares For corner triangles: Two $27^1/_2$" x $27^1/_2$" squares.

RED INNER FRAME: Two $1^1/_2$" x $36^1/_2$" strips; two $1^1/_2$" x $38^1/_2$" strips

BINDING: Six $2^1/_2$" strips

Vinyl for overlay, $18^1/_2$" x $18^1/_2$" square

PREPARATION

1. Enlarge the design pattern 300%. Center the full-size pattern on the 17" x 17" paper by matching the center of the paper with the center mark on the pattern.

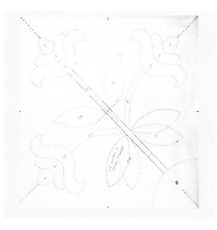

2. Place the piece of vinyl over the master pattern and use the Sharpie pen to carefully trace around the shapes. This will be an overlay used for the placement of the shapes onto the background fabric. Be sure to trace both the solid and dashed lines for the leaves. The solid lines indicate the placement for the center blocks and the dashed lines are used for placement in the corner blocks.

3. The fusible interfacing is used to make templates for the appliqué shapes. Place the interfacing over the master design pattern and use the Sharpie pen to trace all of the individual shapes, leaving at least $^3/_4$" between each one. Mark onto the wrong (rough) side of the interfacing for all shapes except those marked with an "R". These should be marked on the right (smooth) side. To prevent the permanent pen from bleeding through the interfacing onto the master pattern, place a scrap piece of vinyl between the layers.

MARKING GUIDE:
C: 8 and 8R*
D: 8 and 8R*
E: 24—mark the bottom curve with a dashed line to indicate that it will be overlapped by piece F
F: 24—mark the bottom curve with a dashed line to indicate that it will be overlapped by piece G
G: 24
*R = Reverse
Center circle: Make a circle pattern with a 9" diameter then cut one from fabric.

Note: Stems A, AR, and B are not required as they are made using bias strips—see Step 8 below.

4. Use fabric scissors to cut each fusible interfacing shape, cutting just outside the marked lines. Stack similar pieces together with rough side facing down.

5. Press the rough side of the fusible template shapes onto the wrong side of the corresponding fabrics.

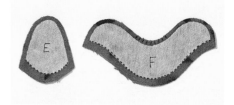

6. Use fabric scissors to cut each shape, cutting $^3/_{16}$" beyond all solid lines and $^1/_4$" beyond the bottom sides of shapes E and F).

7. Use the fabric glue stick to turn the seam allowances to the wrong side of the shape and secure them to the interfacing. Do not turn back the seam allowances on the bottom sides of shapes E and F. It is helpful to place the shape onto the sandpaper during this step. The sandpaper will grip the small shape

allowing you to neatly turn back the seam allowances. To prepare shapes with points, turn and glue the point first. Then use a long quilter's pin to turn and glue one side of the point and then the other, holding the edge in place until set.

Check to be certain that the fabric glue stick will wash out before preparing the shapes.

8. To make stems, cut enough 1½" wide bias strips to make the following:

(a) Sixteen 9" pieces for side stems

(b) Four 12" pieces for center stems on corner triangles

(c) Four 14" pieces for center stems on center blocks

For help with cutting bias strips, refer to pages 44-45.

Fold strips in half lengthwise with the right side facing out; stitch along the length of each strip ¼" from the cut edges.

Insert the bias bar into the tube, rotating the seam allowance so it is centered onto the flat side of the bar. Press to set the creases. Be careful if you are using a metal bar as it gets hot. Remove the bias bar and the strip is ready for appliqué.

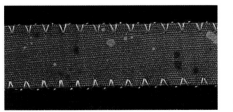

9. Set your machine for blind hem stitching and then make a practice piece before stitching on your project.

(a) Insert the No. 10 Universal needle

(b) Thread the top with monofilament thread and the bobbin with either bobbin fill thread or machine embroidery thread. If your bobbin case has an eye at the end of the curved "finger," thread the bobbin thread through it to prevent the upper thread from pulling the bobbin thread to the surface. If not, you may need to lower the upper tension.

(c) Set the machine for the blind hem stitch. Adjust the stitch width to halfway between zero and the next higher setting. Adjust the stitch length to halfway between zero and the next higher setting. If your machine will not adjust down to the needed length and width, you will have to use a narrow zigzag stitch, using the same settings.

(d) Attach the open toe embroidery foot.

10. Lay one of the center background blocks onto a flat surface. Place the vinyl overlay on top of the fabric, aligning center points. Don't worry that the

overlay is smaller than the background fabric. Just be certain that it is centered.

11. Position 14" stems by applying glue to the wrong side of two side stem pieces. Firmly hold the background and vinyl overlay together with one hand while sliding the stems into position on the background fabric. Press firmly so that the glue will hold them in place.

12. Use the same technique to position the center stem.

APPLIQUÉING SHAPES TO THE BACKGROUND

1. Position the stems under the presser foot so that the straight line of the stitch runs along the edge of the stems and the stitch catches the edge of the stem fabric. Stitch the side stems first, then the center stem. Leave at least 3" of thread tails which will be pulled to the backside and tied off with a square knot.

163

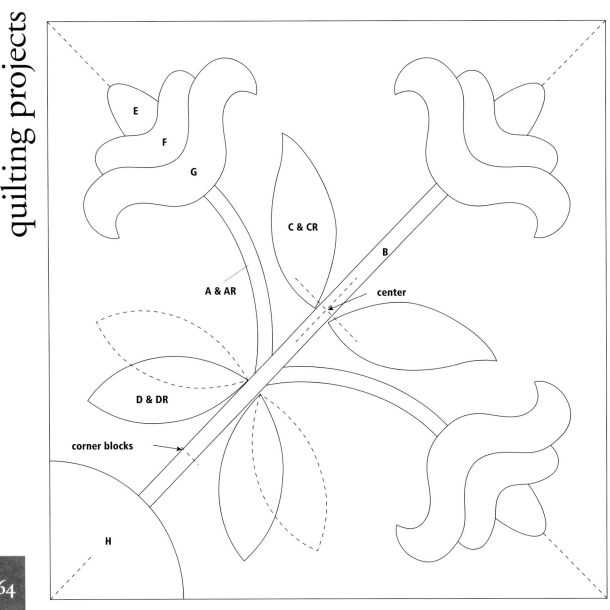

E

F

G

C & CR

B

A & AR

center

D & DR

corner blocks

H

**Pattern for Old Tulips.
Enlarge pattern 300%.**

2. Use the overlay and glue to position and secure the leaves to the background fabric. Then stitch around the edges, starting on one side, stitching up to the point, raising the presser foot to pivot, and continuing around the shape.

3. Use the overlay and glue to position and secure the flowers to the background fabric; overlapping F onto E and G onto F. Stitch the upper curve of E, then upper curve of F and finally all the way around G.

4. To make the corner triangles: appliqué the shapes onto the squares first before cutting the background fabric in half diagonally to make triangles. This will prevent stretching. First determine the diagonal center of the background fabric by folding in half and pressing a crease. Run a machine basting stitch along the crease. You will later cut along this stitching line to make two corner triangles.

5. Use the vinyl overlay to position the shapes (flowers, stems, and leaves) onto the background fabric. The only differences are that the finished length of the center stem is 11 1/2" for corner triangles and also the position of the lower leaves changes (indicated by the dashed lines on the master pattern).

6. After all of the shapes are appliquéd to the background fabric, carefully cut along the center diagonal basting line. Repeat for the other large background square to make the four corner triangles.

ASSEMBLY

1. Sew the four center blocks together.

2. Appliqué the large red circle in the center of the blocks.

3. Sew the two shorter red frame strips to opposite sides of the center blocks, trimming the center to fit, if necessary.

4. Sew the two remaining longer frame strips to complete the center section.

5. Sew the four corner blocks onto the center section, matching center points and easing in any fullness. Stitch with the center section on top to prevent stretching along the bias edge of the corner blocks. Straighten the edges if necessary.

6. Layer and baste the quilt in preparation for quilting. This quilt was machine quilted using an all over meandering design and outline stitching around the appliquéd shapes. Attach the binding to complete the quilt. Refer to page 68 for help. ✿

Nancy Busby began making quilt tops in 1979. Appliqué captured her interest about 10 years later and both hand and machine appliqué became her passion. She enjoys teaching and sharing her love for appliqué with her appreciative students.

kaleidoscope sampler

When it comes to samplers, this is the icing on the cake! Use a variety of fabrics and different techniques to construct the colorful blocks; assemble them, and you're ready to have fun quilting. The quilting patterns (kites, balloons, butterflies, hearts, and more) add a whimsical touch to this delightful quilt and all are included in the pattern gallery.

DESIGNED AND MADE BY APRIL OLIVEIRA-WARD

Skill level: Intermediate
Finished size: 51" x 51"
Techniques: Piecing and appliqué

MATERIALS

Yardage for blocks: Variety of ¹/₈–¹/₄ yard pieces
Sashings: Inner (black with white dots) ¹/₄ yard
Sashings: Sawtooth Star blocks (white with black dots): ¹/₈ yard each of four fabrics
Corner triangles: ¹/₈ yard
Borders: Inner–¹/₄ yard each of two fabrics; Middle–¹/₄ yard; Outer–³/₄ yard
Pom-pom trim: 6 yards
Backing: 3 yards
Batting: 54" x 54"
Binding: (¹/₄" finished) ³/₈ yard (matches backing fabric)

CUTTING AND CONSTRUCTION

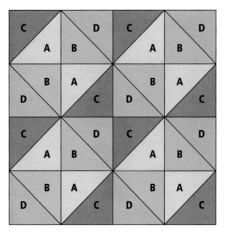

BROKEN DISHES
10" finished block

CUTTING
A, B, C, and D: Four 3³/₈" squares each of four fabrics.

CONSTRUCTION

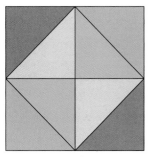

Make four

1. Use one of the methods on pages 49-50 for making half-square triangles.

2. Join four half-square triangles together to make four units.

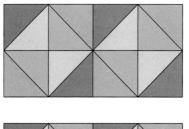

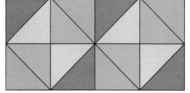

3. Sew the four units together in rows.

4. Sew the rows together, alternating the pressing direction of the seams.

5. Give the finished block a final press. It should accurately measure 10¹/₂" square.

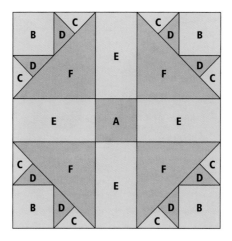

CROSS AND CROWN
10" finished block

CUTTING
A: One 2¹/₂" square
B: Four 2¹/₂" squares
C: Two 3¹/₄" squares, cut into quarters diagonally to make eight triangles
D: Two 3¹/₄" squares, cut into quarters diagonally to make eight triangles
E: Four 2¹/₂" x 4¹/₂" rectangles
F: Two 4⁷/₈" squares, each cut in half diagonally to make four triangles

CONSTRUCTION

Make four each

1. Join the C and D triangles together in pairs.

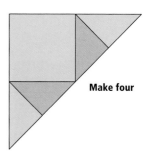

Make four

2. Join two pairs with a B square.

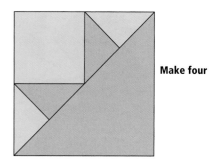

Make four

3. Sew the F triangles to the units made in Step 2.

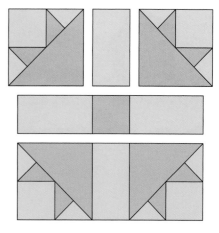

4. Sew all of the pieces together in rows. Press the seams in the direction of the E pieces.

5. Sew the rows together to complete the block.

6. Give the finished block a final press. It should accurately measure 10¹/₂" square.

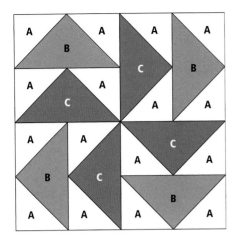

DUTCHMAN'S PUZZLE
10" finished block

CUTTING
Measurements are given for making the flying geese units using either method one or method two on pages 53–54.

A: Sixteen 3" squares (method one) or eight 3" squares (method two)

B: Four 3" x 5½" rectangles (method one) or one 6¼" square (method two)

C: Four 3" x 5½" rectangles (method one or one 6¼" square (method two)

CONSTRUCTION
1. Make the flying geese units using one of the methods on pages 53–54.

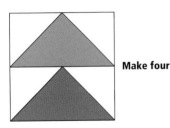

Make four

2. Join the flying geese units together in pairs.

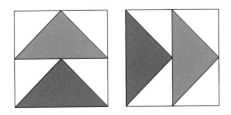

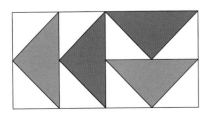

3. Sew the pairs together in rows.

4. Sew the rows together, pressing the seams in alternate directions.

5. Give the block a final press. It should accurately measure 10½" square.

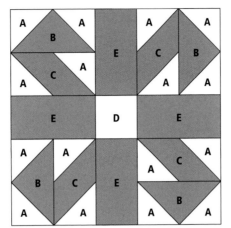

JACK IN THE BOX
10" finished block

CUTTING
Measurements are given for making the flying geese units using method one on pages 53-54.

A: Sixteen 2½" squares

B and C: Eight 2½" x 4½" rectangles

D: One 2½" square

E: Four 2½" x 4½" rectangles

CONSTRUCTION

Make four

Make four

Make four

1. Make the A/B/A units exactly as described on page 53. Make the A/C/A units, using a variation of this technique.

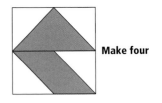

Make four

2. Join the two combinations of flying geese units together in pairs.

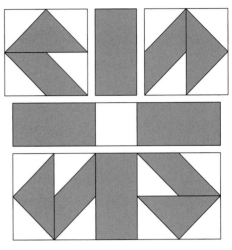

3. Sew all of the pieces together in rows, pressing the seams in the direction of the E pieces.

4. Sew the rows together to complete the block.

5. Give the block a final press. It should accurately measure 10½" square.

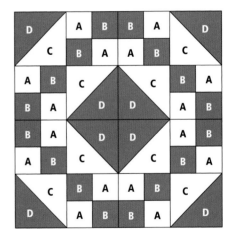

JEWEL BOX
10" finished block

CUTTING
A and B: One 1¾" strip, from each of two fabrics.

C: Four 3⅜" squares. Cut the squares in half to make triangles.

D: Two 3⅜" squares, from each of two fabrics. Cut the squares in half to make triangles.

CONSTRUCTION

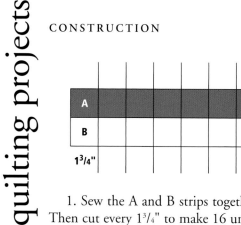

1. Sew the A and B strips together. Then cut every 1³/₄" to make 16 units.

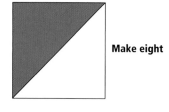

Make eight

2. Sew the units together to make eight four-patches.

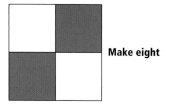

Make eight

3. Sew the C & D triangles together in pairs to make eight half-square triangles.

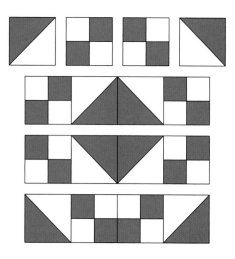

4. Sew all of the units together in rows, alternating the pressing direction of the seams in each row.

5. Sew the rows together to complete the block.

6. Give the block a final press. It should accurately measure 10¹/₂" square.

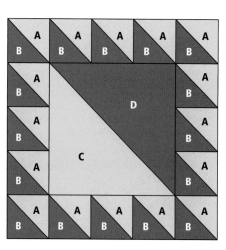

LADY OF THE LAKE
10" finished block

CUTTING

A: Eight 2⁷/₈" squares. Cut the squares in half to make triangles.

B: Eight 2⁷/₈" squares. Cut the squares in half to make triangles.

C: One 6⁷/₈" square. Cut the square in half to make triangles. Need only one.

D: One 6⁷/₈" square. Cut the square in half to make triangles. Need only one.

CONSTRUCTION

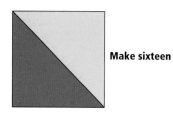

Make sixteen

1. Join the A and B triangles together in pairs to make half-square triangle units. They should each measure 2¹/₂" square.

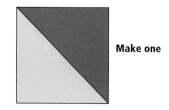

Make one

2. Join the C and D triangles together. The unit should measure 6¹/₂" square.

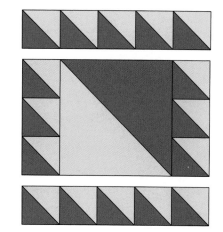

3. Sew the units together in rows.

4. Sew the rows together to complete the block.

5. Give the block a final press. It should accurately measure 10¹/₂" square.

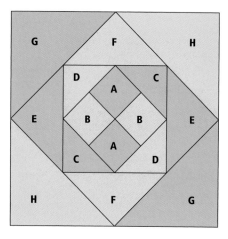

MONKEY WRENCH
10" finished block

CUTTING

A: Two 2¹/₄" squares

B: Two 2¹/₄" squares

C: One 3¹/₂" square, cut in half diagonally.

D: One 3¹/₂" square, cut in half diagonally.

E: One 4¹/₂" square, cut in half diagonally.

F: One 4¹/₂" square, cut in half diagonally.

G: One 6" square, cut in half diagonally.

H: One 6" square, cut in half diagonally.

CONSTRUCTION

1. Join the A and B squares together to make the center unit.

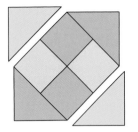

2. Sew the C and then D triangles to the center unit.

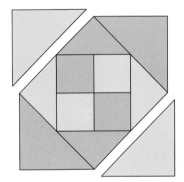

3. Sew the E and then F triangles.

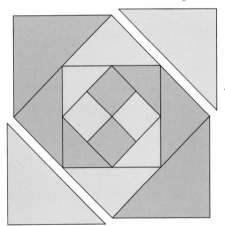

4. Sew the G and then H triangles to complete the block.

5. Give the block a final press. It should accurately measure 10½" square.

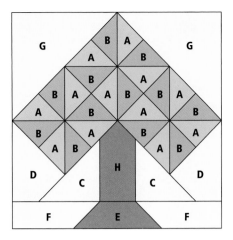

PINWHEEL PINE
10" finished block

CUTTING

A: Six 2¾" squares, cut in half diagonally.

B: Six 2¾" squares, cut in half diagonally.

C: One 3¼" square, cut in half diagonally.

D: One 6¼" square, cut in half diagonally. Use the template pattern to cut one and one reversed (see page 171).

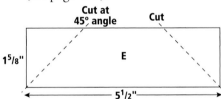

E: One 1⅝" x 5½" piece. Cut the ends at 45-degree angles.

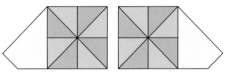

F: One 1⅝" x 9¾" piece. Cut in half and then cut the ends at 45-degree angles.

G: One 6" square, cut in half diagonally.

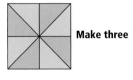

H: One 2½" x 4½" piece. Cut one end at 45-degree angles.

CONSTRUCTION

1. Join the A and B triangles together to make 12 half-square triangle units.

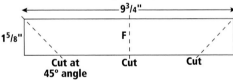

Make three

2. Sew four half-square triangles together to make three pinwheel units.

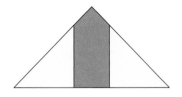

3. Sew a D piece to two of the pinwheel units.

4. Sew the C triangles to the H trunk piece.

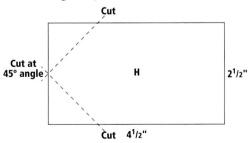

5. Sew the E and F pieces together.

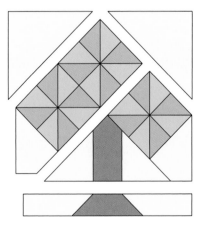

6. Sew the units together in the order shown to complete the block.

7. Give the block a final press. It should accurately measure 10½" square.

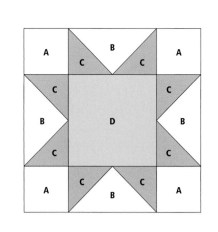

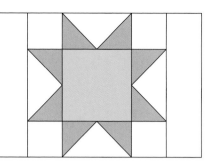

3. Sew the rows together to complete the star. Give it a final press. It should accurately measure 6$\frac{1}{2}$" square.

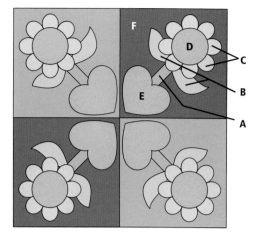

SAWTOOTH STAR

6" finished block. 10" finished block with sashing

CUTTING

Cutting is given for making the flying geese units using either method one or method two on pages 53–54.

To make four blocks:

D: Four 3$\frac{1}{2}$" squares

C: Thirty two 2" squares (method one) or sixteen 2$\frac{3}{8}$" squares (method two)

B: Sixteen 2" x 3$\frac{1}{2}$" pieces (method one) or four 4$\frac{1}{4}$" squares (method two)

A: Sixteen 2" squares

Sashing strips: Four 2$\frac{1}{2}$" x 6$\frac{1}{2}$" pieces
Four 2$\frac{1}{2}$" x 10$\frac{1}{2}$" pieces

Corners: Eight 2$\frac{1}{2}$" squares. Use method one on page 53 for making flying geese units to attach corner triangles to sashing strips.

CONSTRUCTION

1. Make 16 flying geese units using one of the methods described on pages 53-54.

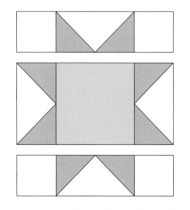

2. Arrange all of the units and sew the pieces together in rows, pressing all seams away from the star points.

4. Sew sashing strips to two sides of each star block.

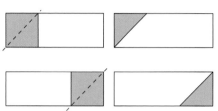

5. Add corner triangles to one end of each remaining sashing strip.

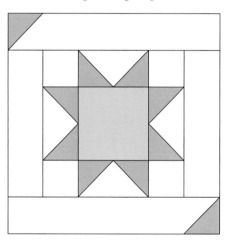

6. Sew the sashing strips to top and bottom of each star with triangles at opposite sides to complete the blocks.

7. Give the blocks a final press. They should each accurately measure 10$\frac{1}{2}$"square.

HEARTS AND SUNFLOWERS

16" finished block

CUTTING

Use template patterns on page 222 to cut:

A: Four

B: Four and four reversed

C: 32

D: Four

E: Four

F: Four 8$\frac{1}{2}$" squares (two fabrics used).

Refer to pages 55–56 for help with appliqué.

Inner sashing strips (around Hearts and Sunflowers block):

Cut two 2$\frac{1}{2}$" x 16$\frac{1}{2}$" pieces (sides)

Cut two 2$\frac{1}{2}$" x 20$\frac{1}{2}$" pieces (top and bottom)

Corner triangles: 12 2$\frac{1}{2}$" squares

CONSTRUCTION

1. Sew the four F squares together to make a 16$\frac{1}{2}$" square background.

2. Prepare the shapes for raw edge machine appliqué using fusible web. Refer to pages 55-56 for help.

3. Position the shapes on the background fabric and then stitch around the edges with a machine blanket stitch.

INNER PIECED BORDER: Cut three 1$\frac{1}{2}$" strips from each fabric. Sew the strips together in pairs. Cut apart every 1$\frac{1}{2}$". Then sew the units together to measure the length of each side.

MIDDLE BORDER: Cut five 1$\frac{1}{2}$" strips. Cut one strip into four equal pieces and use these to add the needed length to the other four strips.

FINISHING

1. Refer to page 61 for help with layering and basting the quilt in preparation for machine quilting.

2. Machine quilt. Designs for these blocks are shown on pages 227-231.

3. Attach the pom-pom trim around the edges of the quilt top.

4. Attach the binding strip. Turn the entire strip to the back and hand stitch to the backing.

April Oliveira-Ward started sewing in a 4-H clothing project in the sixth grade. After much success making outfits for 4-H contests, April knew she wanted to pursue fashion design. After studying design at UC Davis and The Fashion Institute of Technology in NYC she worked for several years in the fashion industry. Then she and her husband started their own children's clothing company, "Chicken Noodle," which is now celebrating its 15th year in business. April first fell in love with quilting about six years ago and always finds creating sampler quilts the most fun and challenging. Quilting combines the things April likes to do best—precision sewing and using her trained eye to mix unique fabric color and print combinations.

OUTER BORDER: Cut five 3³/₄" strips crosswise. Cut one strip into four equal pieces and use these to add the needed length to the other four strips.

ASSEMBLY

1. Sew the side inner sashing strips to the Hearts and Sunflowers block.

2. Use method one of flying geese units on pages 53-54 to attach the corner triangles to the top and bottom sashing strips. Then sew them to the Hearts and Sunflowers block.

3. Sew the side blocks together in pairs (Jewel Box to Dutchman's Puzzle and Pinwheel Pine to Broken Dishes) and then sew them to the center block.

4. Join the top and bottom rows of blocks together. Then sew them to the top and bottom of the center section.

5. Sew two pieced inner border strips to the top and bottom. Then sew the two remaining inner border strips to the sides.

6. Sew two middle border strips to the top and bottom edges. Then sew the two remaining strips to the sides.

7. Sew two outer border strips to the top and bottom edges. Then sew the two remaining strips to the sides to complete the quilt top.

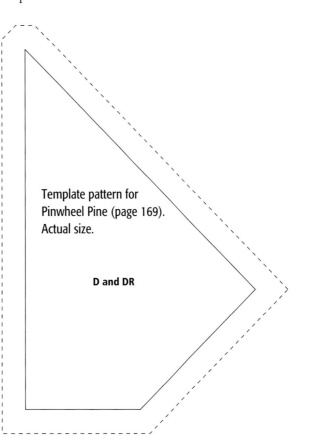

Template pattern for Pinwheel Pine (page 169). Actual size.

D and DR

quilt pattern gallery

ULTIMATELY, QUILTING IS SIMPLE GEOMETRY plus pattern repetition. Break a square into components and recombine the shapes. Slice the squares and create triangles. Add, subtract, multiply, and divide and then add color. It is that simple—really it is.

A trip through the *quilt pattern gallery* finds block, appliqué, and quilting patterns. Since many blocks have one name in Kansas and another in California, the gallery identifies each block with the most common name, known variations, and any know origin.

For instance, a Four-Patch and Nine-Patch are both quite straightforward, but if you add triangles for wings or claws it might become Flying Geese or Bear's Paw. This is what makes quilting so interesting. When you add blocks or patterns together, they become small parts of a larger design. Creative repetition, scale, and color are the components that add imagination and make your quilt distinctly your own.

QUILT PATTERN GALLERY

The gallery is a sampling of the many thousands of pieced, appliquéd, and quilting patterns available to quilters. Most are traditional patterns that have been enjoyed by quilters for many years. The pieced patterns are presented in alphabetical order according to a given category. Some of the categories are referred to as grid categories. The grid provides a framework of the pattern; defining the individual shapes within the quilt block. Quilt historians have been defining and categorizing patterns for years and there is often some discrepancy as to the exact naming and placement of some of the blocks within grid categories.

The blocks in this gallery have been organized into categories that provide the easiest reference to assist you with drafting the pattern. Recognizing the grid category of a quilt block makes drafting the pattern easier. An accurately drafted pattern is helpful for block construction.

EACH OF THE PIECED QUILT PATTERNS INCLUDES:

1. The name(s) given to the pattern.
2. The oldest published source of the pattern name(s), when available.
3. A color line diagram of the block or pattern.
4. A color line diagram of the quilt block or pattern with letters that refer to cutting instructions.
5. A construction diagram indicating a suggested order for sewing the individual fabric shapes together.
6. A color diagram showing four blocks joined together. This is helpful in planning a quilt. Most quilts consist of more than one block or pattern, and it is important to preview an expanded version of the design. There is often a surprise secondary design that is created where the blocks join together.
7. The number of fabric pieces to cut from each fabric for one block.
8. Helpful suggestions for block construction. References are given for specific techniques that can be used to make construction easier.

EACH OF THE APPLIQUÉ DESIGNS INCLUDE:

1. The name(s) given to the pattern or design.
2. The oldest published source of the pattern or design, when available.
3. A color line diagram of the pattern.
4. A color diagram with letters that refer to the cutting instructions.
5. The number of fabric pieces to cut from each fabric for one pattern or design.
6. Helpful suggestions for appliqué.

EACH OF THE QUILTING DESIGNS INCLUDE:

1. The name(s) given to the designer on which project the design was used.
2. A line diagram of the outline of the design.
3. Any helpful tips for stitching, if necessary.

HOW TO USE THE PATTERN GALLERY

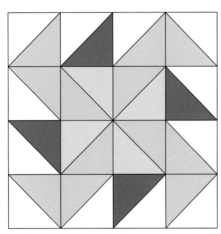

Yankee Puzzle Quilt Block

TO MAKE PIECED QUILT BLOCKS FROM THE PATTERNS

MAKE A DRAFT OF THE PATTERN

It is suggested that the pattern you wish to make first be drafted onto graph paper in the desired finished size. Use the grid category of the pattern you desire to make to assist with this process. Then refer to the instructions for Drafting Patterns in the general instructions on page 42.

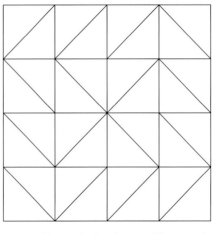

For example, to make a 12" Yankee Puzzle quilt block, begin by marking a 12" square on a piece of graph paper.

Next subdivide the square into 16 equal squares (4 x 4). Each square measures 3" x 3".

Finally mark the diagonal lines within the grid, as shown.

For further help with drafting, refer to the General Instructions on page 175.

GRID CATEGORIES FOR PIECED BLOCKS
(included in this gallery)

4-PATCH

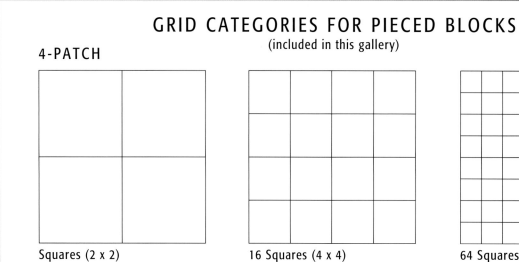

Squares (2 x 2)

16 Squares (4 x 4)

64 Squares (8 x 8)

5-PATCH

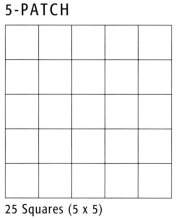

25 Squares (5 x 5)

7-PATCH

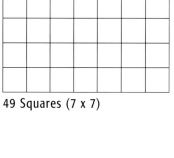

49 Squares (7 x 7)

8-POINTED STAR DESIGNS

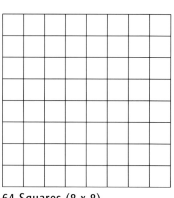

9-PATCH

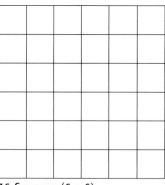

9 Squares (3 x 3)

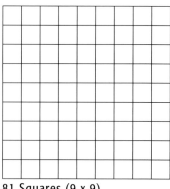

36 Squares (6 x 6)

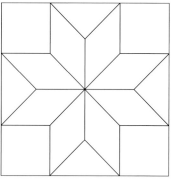

81 Squares (9 x 9)

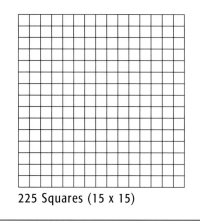

225 Squares (15 x 15)

DRAFTING A QUILT BLOCK IN ANY SIZE

It is easy to draft a quilt block when the finished block size is evenly divisible by the grid size. For example, a Five-Patch Cross and Crown can be drafted as a 10" block because the grid is 5 x 5 and each square measures 2". There may be instances when the grid size of a block does not fit evenly (stay on the lines of the graph paper) into the finished block size. Drafting a Cross and Crown as a 12" block is a little more difficult as 12 is not evenly divisible by 5. Here's an exercise to help you. Use a ruler that is at least 18" long. Draft a 12" Cross and Crown block.

1. Mark a 12" square on a piece of graph paper.

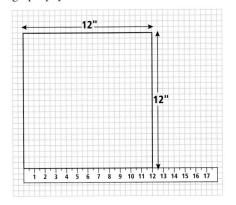

2. Position the ruler with the left edge in line with the bottom left corner of the square.

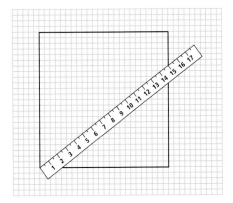

3. Next determine the next whole number greater than 12 that is evenly divisible by 5. The answer is 15. Keeping the left edge of the ruler in place, rotate the ruler to position the 15" marking along the right edge of the marked square.

If the next whole number extends beyond the right edge of the square, it will be necessary to extend the line on that side.

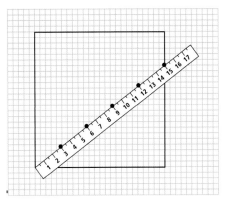

4. When you divide 15 by 5, the answer is 3. Next, mark points along the ruler every 3".

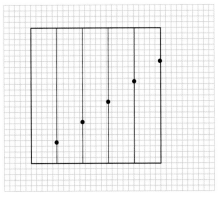

5. With the ruler perpendicular to the edges of the square, mark vertical lines through the four points.

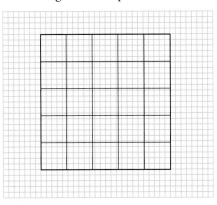

6. To complete the grid, turn the graph paper a quarter turn and repeat steps 2–5.

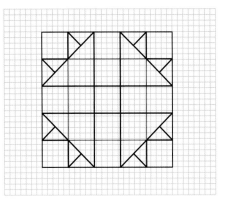

7. The grid is now ready to fill in with the Cross and Crown block.

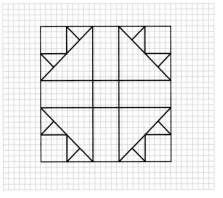

8. Erase any unnecessary grid lines.

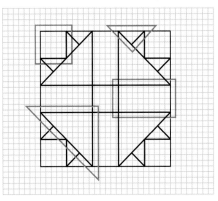

9. Mark a $1/4$" seam allowance around the four different shapes to determine their cut sizes. See page 42 for help.

175

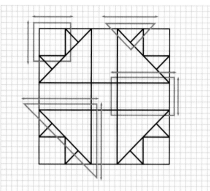

10. Measure the red marked lines to determine the cut sizes for each fabric shape. The cutting instructions with each block pattern will indicate the number of pieces to cut from each fabric. It will be helpful to make a cutting chart on the piece of graph paper to use as an easy reference when it is time to begin cutting.

CUT FABRIC SHAPES FOR DRAFTED CROSS AND CROWN BLOCK

SQUARE: Length of a side. Cut a strip this measurement then cut the strip into squares. Need five per block.

SMALL TRIANGLE: Length of longest side. (This measurement keeps the straight grain of fabric around the outer edge of the block.) Cut a strip this measurement. Cut the strip into squares and then cut the squares into quarters diagonally. For Cross and Crown, two squares each of two fabrics will make the needed triangles. These are quarter-square triangles.

LARGE TRIANGLE: Length of one of the legs (shorter sides). Cut a strip this measurement, cut the strip into squares, then cut the squares in half to make triangles. For Cross and Crown, two squares will make the four triangles needed for one block.

RECTANGLE: Length of short side, cut a strip this measurement then cut into rectangles using the length of the longer sides. For Cross and Crown, need four for one block.

Antique hand pieced quilt blocks with original cardboard templates.

It is a good idea to make a practice block before cutting fabric for an entire quilt. The practice block gives you the opportunity to check your cutting measurements, preview color and fabric choices, and fine-tune your sewing skills before starting on a large project.

Many of the fabric shapes can be cut using quick-cutting techniques with the cutting tools, while others will require the use of templates. The number of fabric shapes required is listed with each pattern. Suggested techniques for cutting accompany each pattern however many of them can be made using a variety of techniques. Many quilters use only quick-cutting methods, while others prefer to make and use templates. The choice is yours. Refer to page 45 for help with quick cutting or page 43 for making templates and making fabric shapes using templates.

CONSTRUCT THE QUILT BLOCK

Refer to the construction diagrams that accompany each pattern to determine the order in which all of the shapes are sewn together to make a completed block.

TO MAKE APPLIQUÉ DESIGNS

1. Use a photocopy machine to enlarge the pattern to the size you want for your quilt.

2. Prepare the fabric for either hand or machine appliqué referring to pages 54–56 for help, if needed.

FOR QUILTING DESIGNS

1. Use a photocopy machine to enlarge the pattern to the size you want for your quilt.

2. Use one of the methods on page 61 to transfer the design to your fabric for either hand or machine quilting.

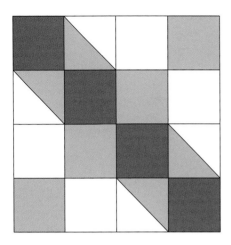

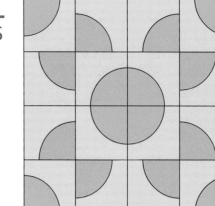

← – – – – – – – – – –

ARKANSAS CROSSROADS

Arkansas Crossroads, *Kansas City Star, 1941*

Category: 16-square Four-Patch

CUTTING
A – Cut 4
B – Cut 4
C – Cut 4
D – Cut 4
E – Cut 4

SUGGESTED TECHNIQUES
Quick cutting, strip piecing, and half-square triangles

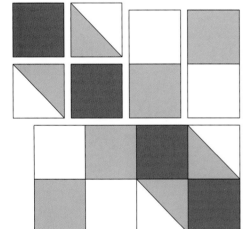

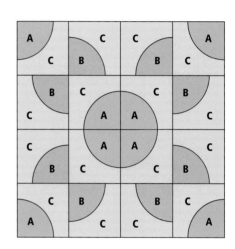

– – – – – – – – – – – →

AROUND THE WORLD

Around the World, *Hall*
'Round the World, *Capper's*

Category: 16-square Four-Patch

CUTTING
A – Cut 8
B – Cut 8
C – Cut 16

SUGGESTED TECHNIQUES
Quick cutting; templates for A, B, and C; and curved piecing

NOTE
Use same pattern for A and B.

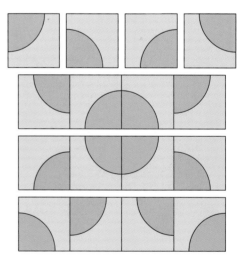

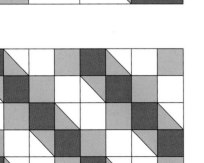

quilt pattern gallery

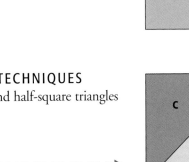

BARRISTER'S BLOCK

Barrister's Block, *Ladies' Art Company, 1898*

Category: 64-square Four-Patch

CUTTING
    A – Cut 4
    B – Cut 24
    C – Cut 24
    D – Cut 4
    E – Cut 4

SUGGESTED TECHNIQUES
Quick cutting and half-square triangles

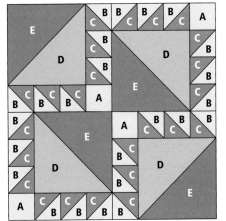

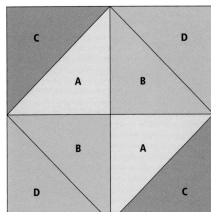

BROKEN DISHES

Broken Dishes, *McKim*
A Simple Quilt Block
The Double Square, *Kansas City Star*

Category: Four-Patch

CUTTING
    A – Cut 2
    B – Cut 2
    C – Cut 2
    D – Cut 2

SUGGESTED TECHNIQUES
Quick cutting and half-square triangles

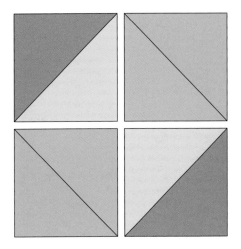

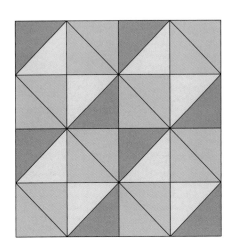

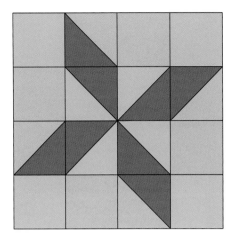

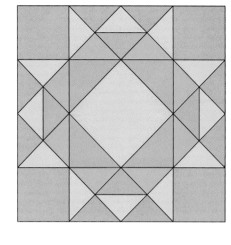

← – – – – – – – –

CLAY'S CHOICE

Clay's Choice, *Finley*
Beauty Patch, *OCS Bk. 116*
Clay's Favorite, *Nancy Cabot, 1937*
Clay's Star, *McKim 101*
Harry's Star, *Finley*
Henry of the West, *Finley*
Star of the West, *Finley*

Category: 16-square Four-Patch

CUTTING

      A – Cut 4
      B – Cut 4
      C – Cut 4
      D – Cut 4
      E – Cut 8

SUGGESTED TECHNIQUES

Quick cutting, strip piecing, and half-square triangles

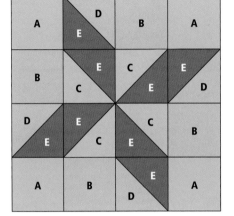

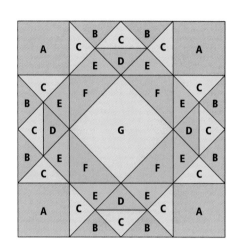

– – – – – – – – →

CROWN OF THORNS

Crown of Thorns, *Finley*
Georgetown Circle, *Finley*
Georgetown Puzzle, *Nancy Cabot*
Memory Fruit, *attributed to Nancy Cabot*
Memory Wreath, *Hall*

Category: Unequal Nine-Patch with large center square (use 16-square Four-Patch grid for drafting)

CUTTING

      A – Cut 4
      B – Cut 8
      C – Cut 12
      D – Cut 4
      E – Cut 8
      F – Cut 4
      G – Cut 1

SUGGESTED TECHNIQUES

Quick cutting and half-square triangles

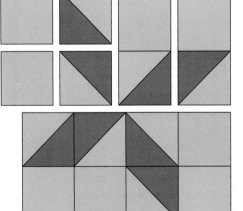

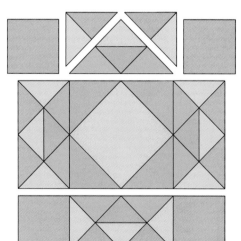

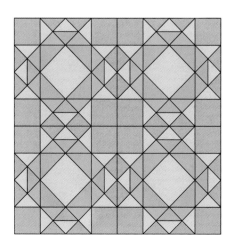

quilt pattern gallery

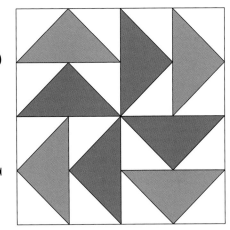

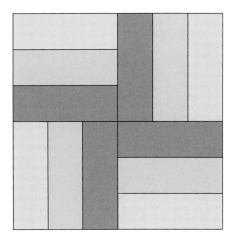

← – – – – – – – – – – – –

DUTCHMAN'S PUZZLE

Dutchman's Puzzle, *Ladies' Art Company, 1898*
Dutchman's Wheel, *Ohio Farmer, 1898 Mosaic*
Wheel, *Ohio Farmer, 1894*
Wild Goose Chase, *Gutcheon*

Category: Four-Patch (use 16-square Four-Patch grid for drafting)

CUTTING
   A – Cut 16
   B – Cut 4
   C – Cut 4

SUGGESTED TECHNIQUES
Quick cutting

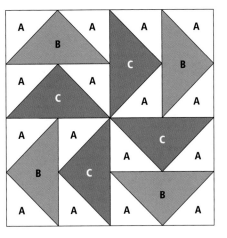

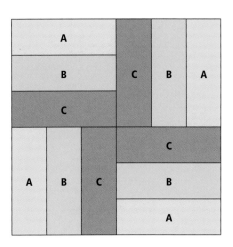

– – – – – – – – – – – – →

INTERLOCKED SQUARES

Interlocked Squares, *Kansas City Star*
Four Part Strip Block, *Kansas City Star*

Category: Four-Patch

CUTTING
   A – Cut 4
   B – Cut 4
   C – Cut 4

SUGGESTED TECHNIQUES
Quick cutting and strip piecing

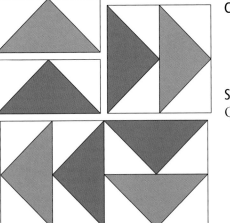

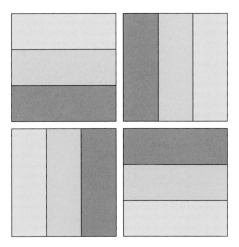

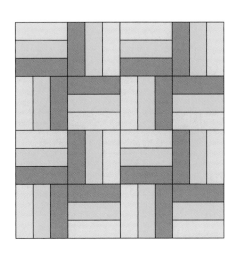

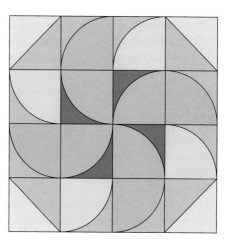

←----------------------------------

JEWEL BOX

Category: 16-square Four-Patch

CUTTING
A – Cut 16
B – Cut 16
C – Cut 8
D – Cut 8

SUGGESTED TECHNIQUES
Quick cutting, strip piecing, and half-square triangles

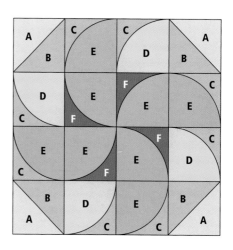

----------------------------------→

JUNGLE FLOWER

Jungle Flower, *Electric Quilt 5 Block Book*

Category: 16-square Four-Patch

CUTTING
A- Cut 4
B- Cut 4
C- Cut 8
D- Cut 4
E- Cut 8
F- Cut 4

SUGGESTED TECHNIQUES
Quick cutting, half-square triangles, templates for C and D, and curved piecing

NOTE
C and F are the same and D and E are the same.

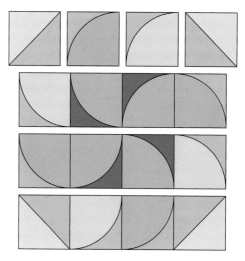

quilt pattern gallery

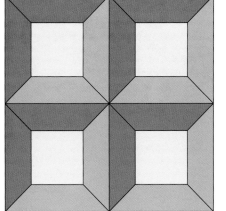

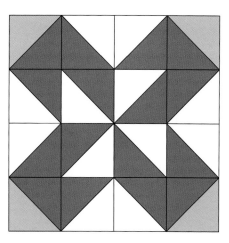

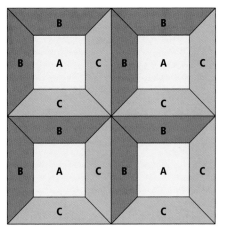

← ─ ─ ─ ─ ─ ─ ─ ─ ─ ─ ─ ─ ─

LATTICE SQUARE

Lattice Square, *Nancy Cabot*

Category: 16-square Four-Patch

CUTTING

A – Cut 4
B – Cut 8
C – Cut 8

SUGGESTED TECHNIQUES

Quick cutting, templates for B and C, and Y-seam construction

─ ─ ─ ─ ─ ─ ─ ─ ─ ─ ─ →

LUCKY PIECES

Lucky Pieces, *Nancy Page*

Category: 16-square Four-Patch

CUTTING

A – Cut 12
B – Cut 4
C – Cut 16

SUGGESTED TECHNIQUES

Quick cutting and half-square triangles

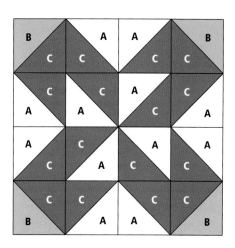

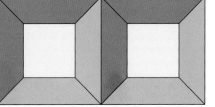

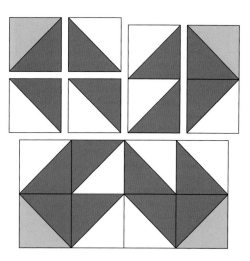

182

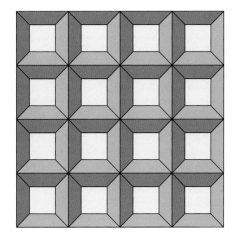

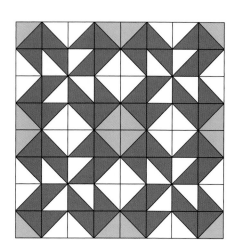

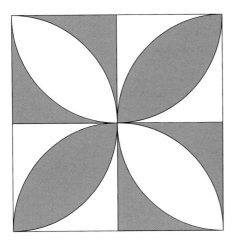

← - - - - - - - - - - - - - - - - - - →

MELON PATCH

Melon Patch, *Finley*
Flower Petals, *Woman's World*

Category: Four-Patch with Curves

CUTTING
A – Cut 2
B – Cut 2
C – Cut 4
D – Cut 4

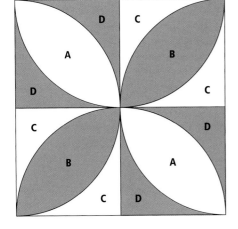

SUGGESTED TECHNIQUES
Templates for A and D and curved piecing

NOTE
A and B are the same and C and D are the same.

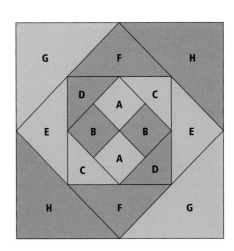

- - - - - - - - - - - - - - - - - - - →

MONKEY WRENCH

Monkey Wrench, *McKim 101*
Snail's Trail, *McKim 101*
Indiana Puzzle, *Quilter's Newsletter Magazine, 1976*

Category: Square in a Square (use 16-square Four-Patch grid for drafting)

CUTTING
A through H – Cut 2 each

SUGGESTED TECHNIQUES
Quick cutting and strip piecing

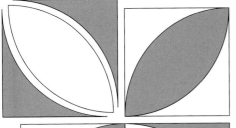

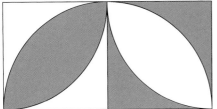

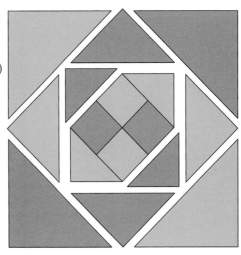

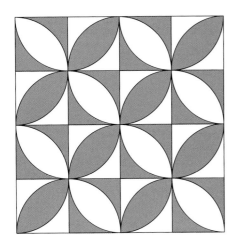

quilt pattern gallery

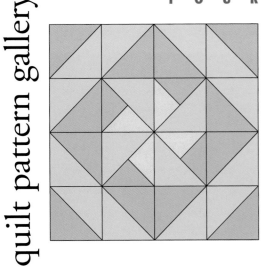

MOSAIC NO.2

Mosaic, No. 2, *Ladies' Art Company #330, 1898*

Category: Square in a Square (use 16-square Four-Patch grid for drafting)

CUTTING
A – Cut 4
B – Cut 16
C – Cut 4
D – Cut 12

SUGGESTED TECHNIQUES
Quick cutting and half-square triangles

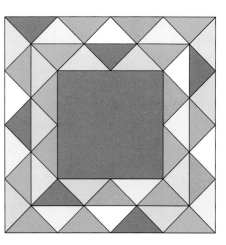

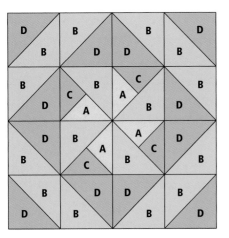

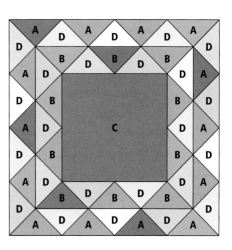

OCEAN WAVES

Ocean Waves, *The Romance of the Patchwork Quilt in America, 1935*
Our Village Green, *Progressive Farmer 33/35*

Category: Square in a Square (use 16-square Four-Patch grid for drafting)

CUTTING
A – Cut 14
B – Cut 10
C – Cut 1
D – Cut 24

SUGGESTED TECHNIQUES
Quick cutting and half-square triangles

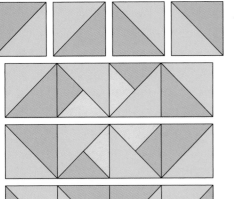

184

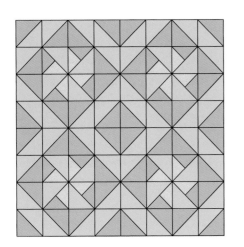

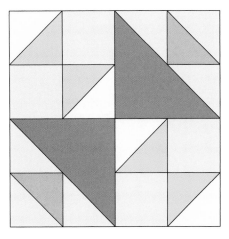

OLD MAID'S PUZZLE

Old Maid's Puzzle, *Ladies' Art Company*

Hour Glass, *Grandma Dexter*

School Girl's Puzzle, *Needlecraft Supply, 1936*

Category: 16-square Four-Patch

CUTTING

A – Cut 4
B – Cut 2
C – Cut 4
D – Cut 4
E – Cut 6
F – Cut 2

SUGGESTED TECHNIQUES

Quick cutting and half-square triangles

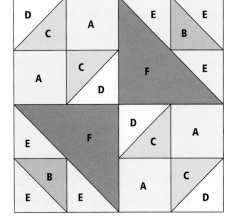

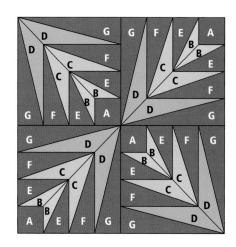

PALM LEAF

Palm Leaf, *McKim and Grandmother Clark*

Palm, *Ladies' Art Company*

Hosannah, *McKim*

Category: 64-square Four-Patch

CUTTING

A – Cut 4
B – Cut 4 & 4R*
C – Cut 4 & 4R*
D – Cut 4 & 4R*
E – Cut 4 & 4R*
F – Cut 4 & 4R*
G – Cut 4 & 4R*
*R= reverse template on fabric for marking

SUGGESTED TECHNIQUES

Quick cutting and templates for B through G, and Y-seam construction

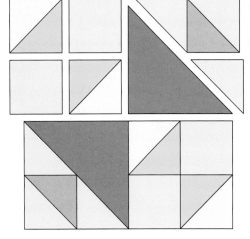

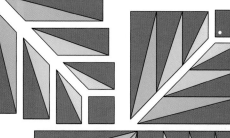

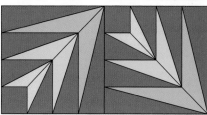

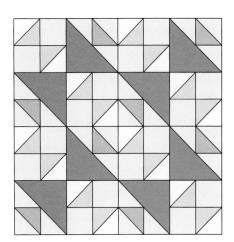

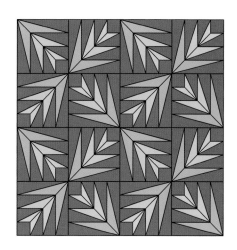

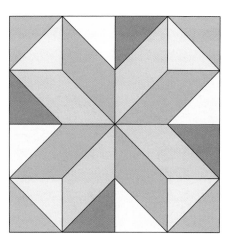

← - - - - - - - - - - - - - - - - -

PINWHEEL PINE
Pinwheel Pine, *Electric Quilt Block Book*

Category: 16-square Four-Patch

CUTTING
    A – Cut 12
    B – Cut 12
    C – Cut 2
    D – Cut 1 and 1R*
    E – Cut 1
    F – Cut 1 and 1R*
    G – Cut 2
    H – Cut 1
    *R= reverse template on fabric for marking

SUGGESTED TECHNIQUES
Quick cutting, half-square triangles, and templates for D, E, and F

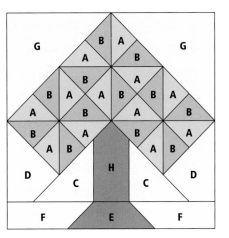

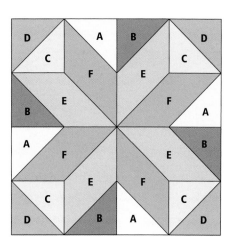

- - - - - - - - - - - - - - - - - →

RED AND WHITE CROSS
Red and White Cross, *Nancy Cabot*

Category: 16-square Four-Patch

CUTTING
    A – Cut 4
    B – Cut 4
    C – Cut 4
    D – Cut 4
    E – Cut 4
    F – Cut 4

SUGGESTED TECHNIQUES
Quick cutting, half-square triangles, templates for E and F, and Y-seam construction

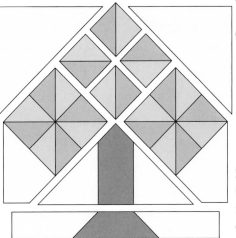

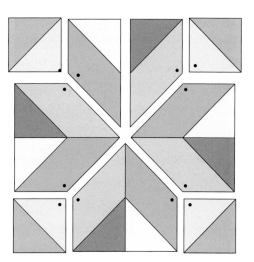

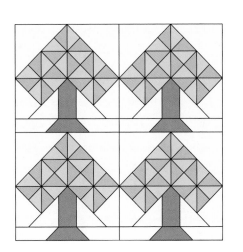

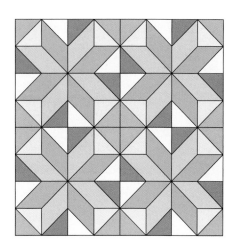

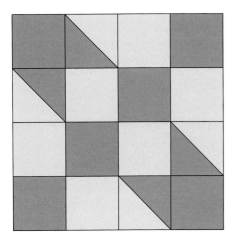

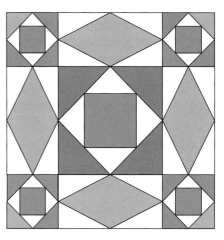

ROAD TO OKLAHOMA
Road to Oklahoma, *Hall*

Category: 16-square Four-Patch

CUTTING
A – Cut 6
B – Cut 6
C – Cut 4
D – Cut 4

SUGGESTED TECHNIQUES
Quick cutting and half-square triangles

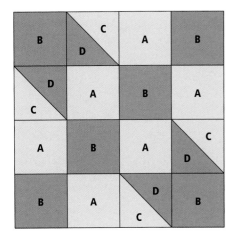

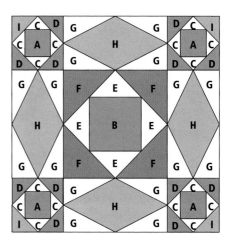

ROLLING STONE
Storm at Sea, *Ladies' Art Company, 1898*

Category: 16-square Four-Patch

CUTTING
A – Cut 4
B – Cut 1
C – Cut 16
D – Cut 12
E – Cut 4
F – Cut 4
G – Cut 16
H – Cut 4
I – Cut 4

SUGGESTED TECHNIQUES
Quick-cutting and templates for G and H

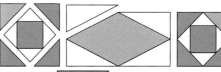

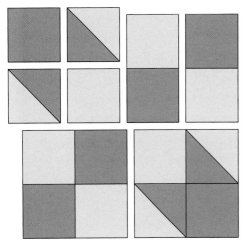

187

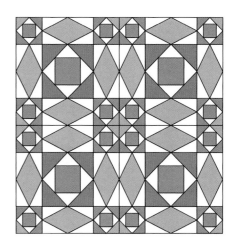

quilt pattern gallery

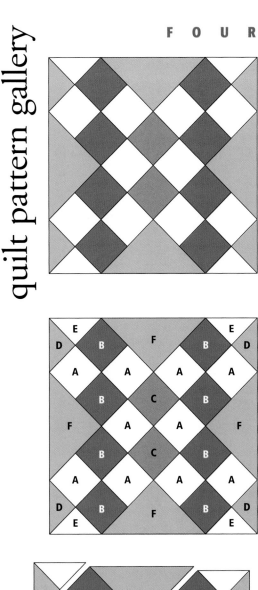

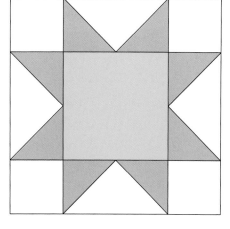

SARAH'S FAVORITE

Sarah's Favorite, *Ladies' Art Company, 1898*
Sally's Favorite, *Nancy Page*

Category: Four X (use 16-square Four-Patch grid for drafting)

CUTTING
A – Cut 10
B – Cut 8
C – Cut 2
D – Cut 4
E – Cut 4
F – Cut 4

SUGGESTED TECHNIQUES
Quick cutting and strip piecing

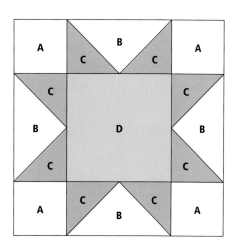

SAWTOOTH

Sawtooth, *The Farm and Fireside, 1884*
A Smaller Star
Cluster of Stars
Evening Star
Nameless Star, *Nancy Cabot*
Sawtooth Star, *Dubois*

Category: 16-square Four-Patch

CUTTING
A – Cut 4
B – Cut 4
C – Cut 8
D – Cut 1

SUGGESTED TECHNIQUE
Quick cutting and flying geese units

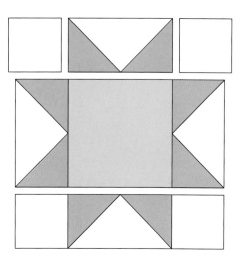

188

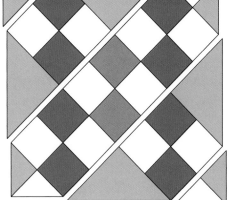

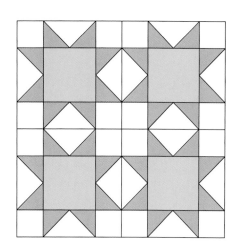

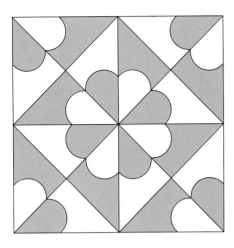

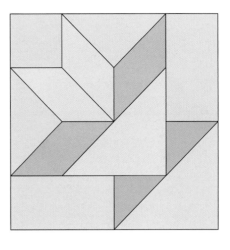

SPRINGTIME BLOSSOMS

Springtime Blossoms, *Hinson, Quilter's Magazine*

Category: 16-square Four-Patch with Curves

CUTTING
- A – Cut 8
- B – Cut 8
- C – Cut 8
- D – Cut 8

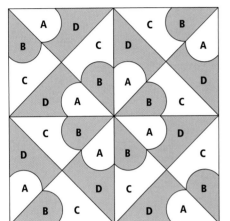

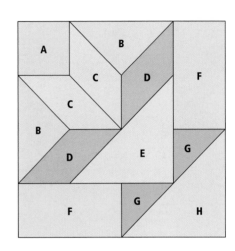

SUGGESTED TECHNIQUES
Templates for A and D and curved piecing

NOTE
A and B are the same and C is the reverse of D.

THE DISK

The Disk, *Ladies' Art Company, 1898*
Basket of Diamonds, *Kansas City Star, 1936*
Flower Basket, Kansas City Star, *1935*
Flower Pot, *Hearth and Home and Rural New Yorker*
Jersey Tulip, *Mary McElwain*
Rainbow Cactus, *Mary McElwain*

Category: 16-square Four-Patch

CUTTING
- A – Cut 1
- B – Cut 2
- C – Cut 1 and 1R*
- D – Cut 1 and 1R*
- E – Cut 1
- F – Cut 2
- G – Cut 2
- H – Cut 1
- *R= reverse template on fabric for marking

SUGGESTED TECHNIQUES
Quick cutting and templates for C and D

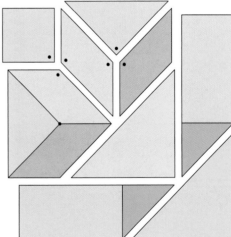

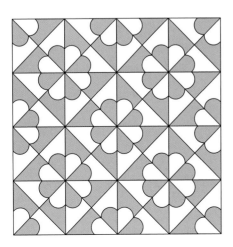

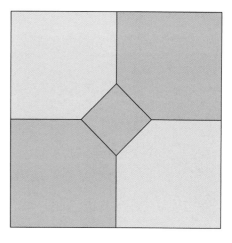

← – – – – – – – – – – – – – –

TRIANGLE SQUARES

Triangle Squares, *Grandma Dexter*

Category: 16-square Four-Patch

CUTTING
- A – Cut 4
- B – Cut 1
- C – Cut 12
- D – Cut 4
- E – Cut 4

SUGGESTED TECHNIQUES
Quick cutting and half-square triangles

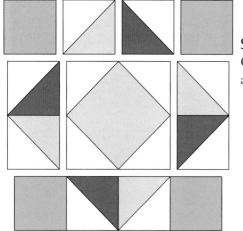

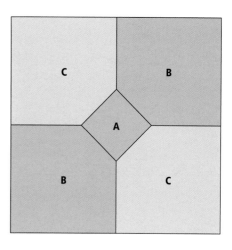

– – – – – – – – – – – – – – →

TRUE LOVER'S KNOT

True Lover's Knot, *Ladies' Art Company #262*
Bowtie

Category: Four-Patch

CUTTING
- A – Cut 1
- B – Cut 2
- C – Cut 2

SUGGESTED TECHNIQUES
Quick cutting, templates for B and C, and Y-seam construction

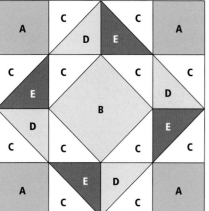

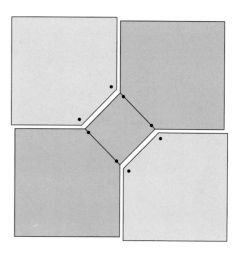

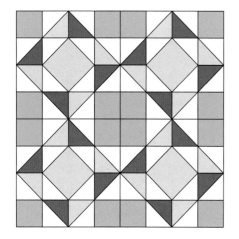

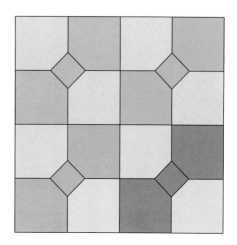

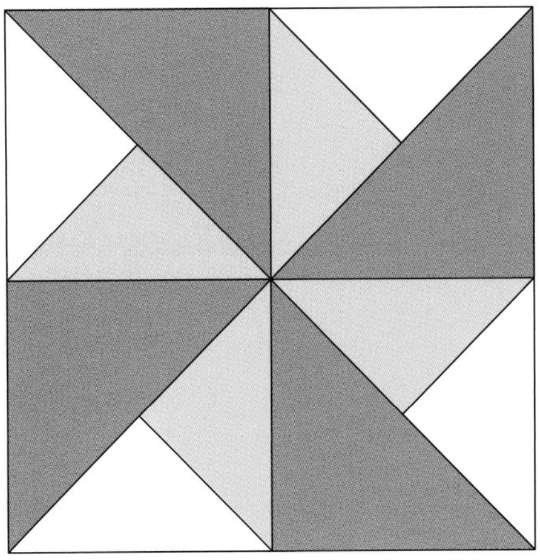

WINDMILL

Turnstile, *Ladies' Art Company, 1928*
Churn Dash
Old Windmill
Whirligig

Category: Four-Patch

CUTTING

A – Cut 4
B – Cut 4
C – Cut 4

SUGGESTED TECHNIQUE

Quick cutting

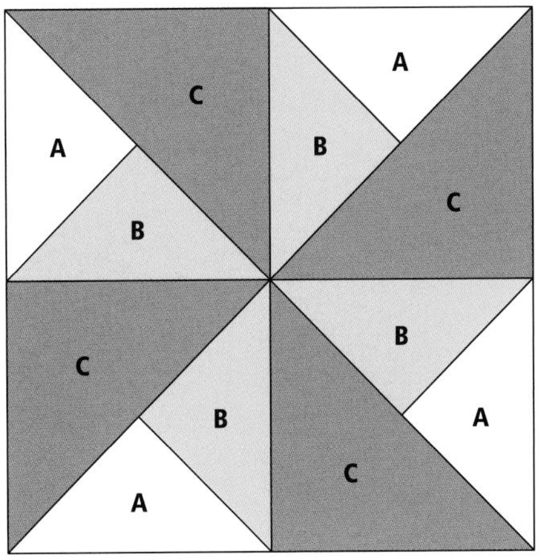

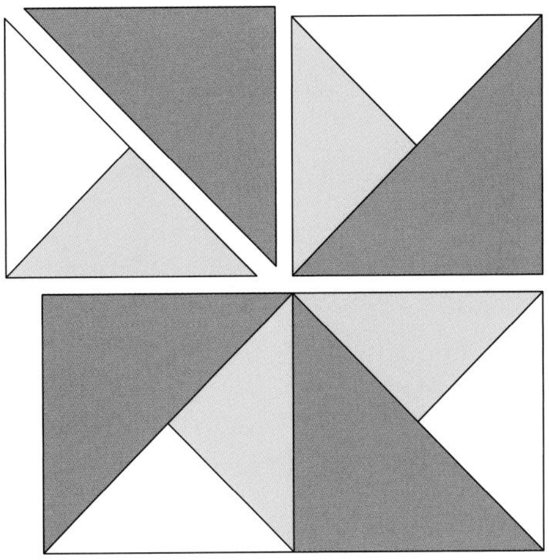

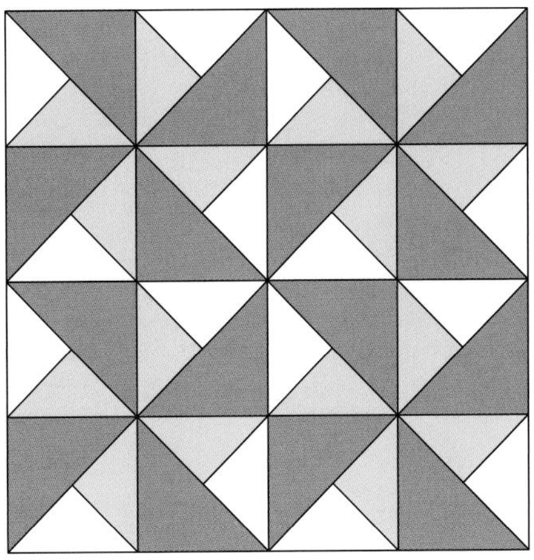

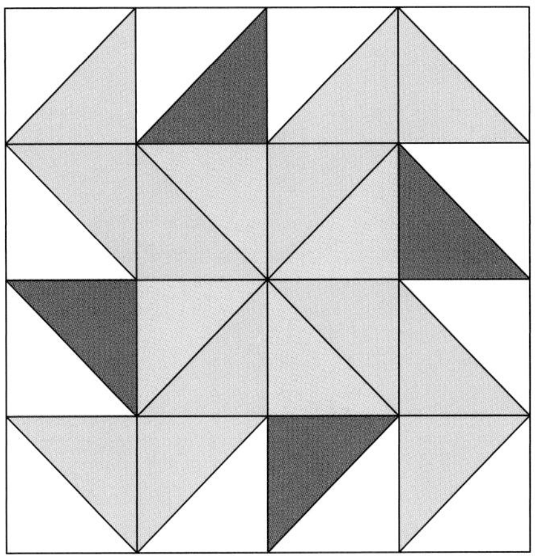

YANKEE PUZZLE

Yankee Puzzle, *Ladies' Art Company, 1898*

Category: 16-square Four-Patch

CUTTING

A – Cut 4
B – Cut 4
C – Cut 12
D – Cut 12

SUGGESTED TECHNIQUES

Quick cutting and half-square triangles

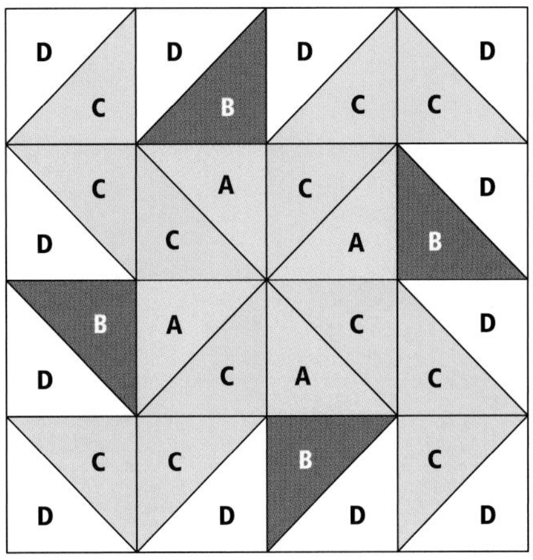

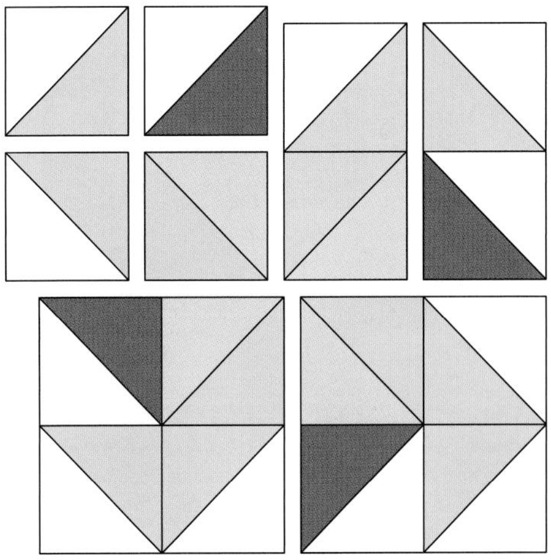

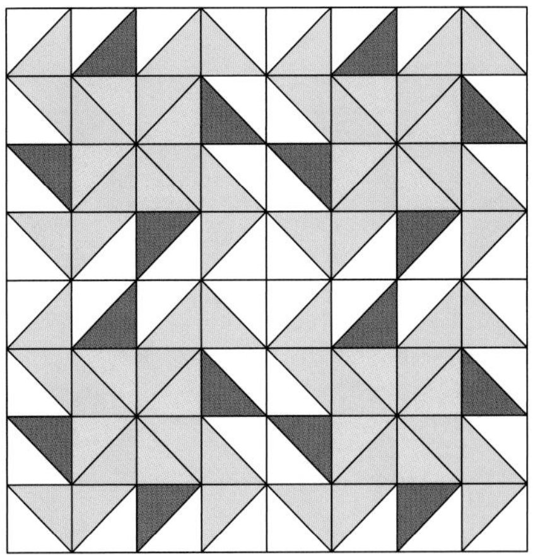

quilt pattern gallery

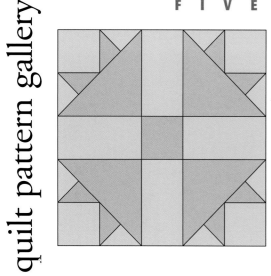

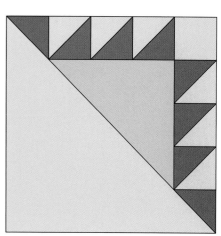

CROSS AND CROWN

Cross and Crown, *Ladies' Art Company*
Bouquet's Quilt, *Nancy Page*
Goose Tracks
Tulip Wreath, *Pennsylvania Farmer*

Category: Five-Patch

CUTTING
A – Cut 1
B – Cut 4
C – Cut 8
D – Cut 8
E – Cut 4
F – Cut 4

SUGGESTED TECHNIQUE
Quick cutting

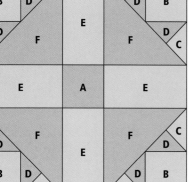

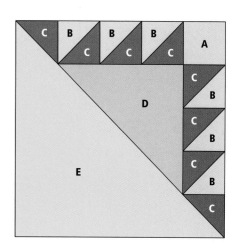

DELECTABLE MOUNTAINS

Category: Five-Patch

CUTTING
A – Cut 1
B – Cut 6
C – Cut 8
D – Cut 1
E – Cut 1

SUGGESTED TECHNIQUES
Quick cutting and half-square triangles

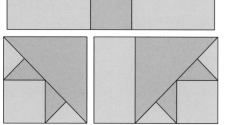

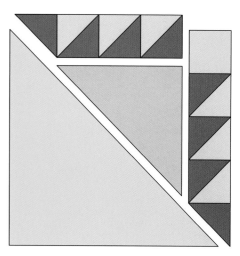

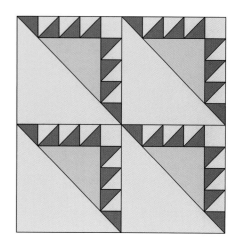

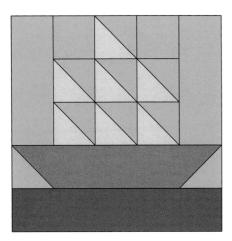

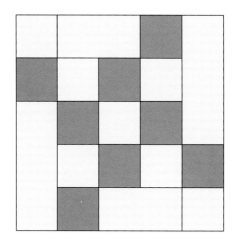

DREAM SHIP

Dream Ship, *Nancy McElwain*
Ships in the Night

Category: Five-Patch

CUTTING

A – Cut 2
B – Cut 1
C – Cut 2
D – Cut 9
E – Cut 7
F – Cut 1

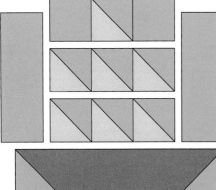

SUGGESTED TECHNIQUES

Quick cutting and half-square triangles

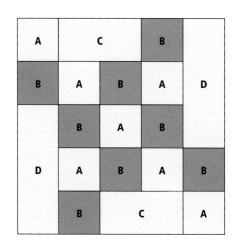

FLYING SQUARES

Flying Squares, *Ladies' Art Company*

Category: Five-Patch

CUTTING

A – Cut 7
B – Cut 8
C – Cut 2
D – Cut 2

SUGGESTED TECHNIQUES

Quick cutting and strip piecing

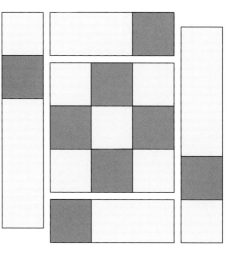

193

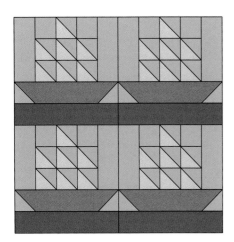

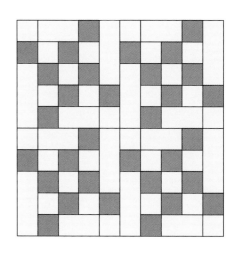

quilt pattern gallery

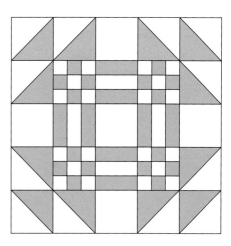

FOUR X STAR

Four X Star, *Ladies' Art Company, 1898*

Category: Five-Patch

CUTTING
A – Cut 1
B – Cut 4
C – Cut 4
D – Cut 4
E – Cut 4
F – Cut 8
G – Cut 8

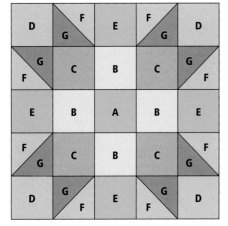

SUGGESTED TECHNIQUES
Quick cutting, strip piecing, and half-square triangles

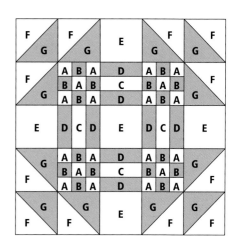

GOOSE IN THE POND

Goose in the Pond, *Ladies' Art
  Company #202*
Gentleman's Fancy, *Household
  Magazine, 1929*
Geometric Garden, *Grandma Dexter*
Mrs. Wolf's Red Beauty, *Mrs. Danner,
  1970*
Patchwork Fantasy, *Household
  Magazine*
Scrap Bag, *Kansas City Star, 1935*
Unique Nine-Patch, *Wallace's Farmer,
  1928*
Unnamed, *Comfort, 1923*
Young Man's Fancy, *Finley*

Category: Five-Patch

CUTTING
A – Cut 20
B – Cut 16
C – Cut 4
D – Cut 8
E – Cut 5
F – Cut 12
G – Cut 12

SUGGESTED TECHNIQUES
Quick cutting, strip piecing, and half-square triangles

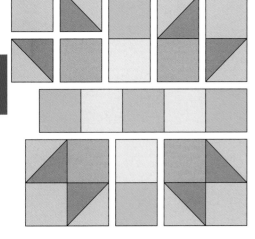

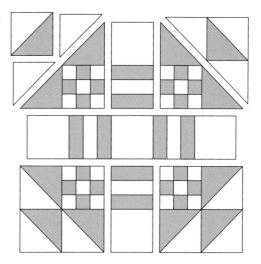

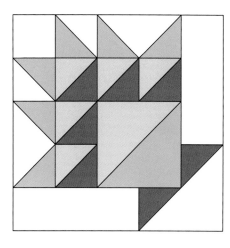

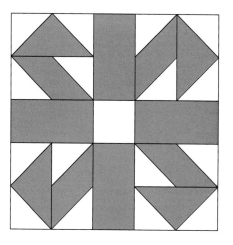

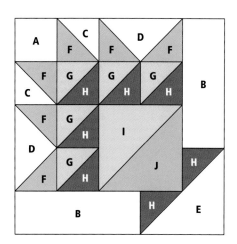

← - - - - - - - - - - - - - -

GRAPE BASKET

Grape Basket, *Ladies' Art Company*

Category: Five-Patch

CUTTING
- A – Cut 1
- B – Cut 2
- C – Cut 2
- D – Cut 2
- E – Cut 1
- F – Cut 6
- G – Cut 5
- H – Cut 7
- I – Cut 1
- J – Cut 1

SUGGESTED TECHNIQUES
Quick cutting and half-square triangles

- - - - - - - - - - - - - - →

JACK IN THE BOX

Jack in the Box, *101 Patchwork Patterns, 1931*
Wheel of Fortune

Category: Five-Patch

CUTTING
- A – Cut 16
- B – Cut 4
- C – Cut 4
- D – Cut 1
- E – Cut 4

SUGGESTED TECHNIQUE
Quick cutting and flying geese units

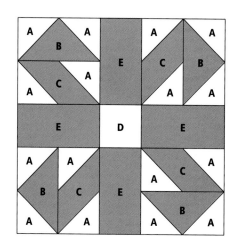

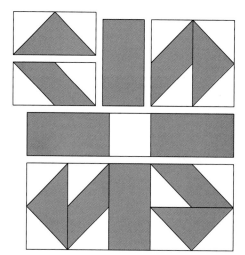

195

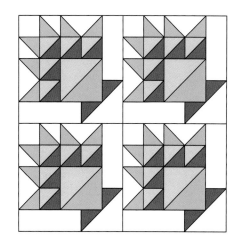

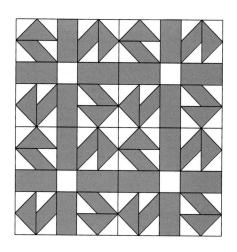

quilt pattern gallery

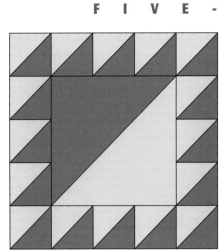

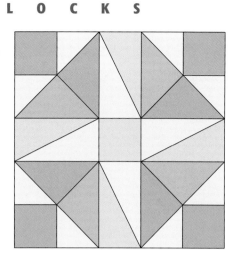

LADY OF THE LAKE

Lady of the Lake, *Ladies' Art Company, 1898*

Category: Five-Patch

CUTTING
A – Cut 16
B – Cut 16
C – Cut 1
D – Cut 1

SUGGESTED TECHNIQUES
Quick cutting and half-square triangles

NOTE
Rotate the block when constructing the sampler quilt.

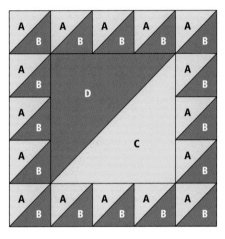

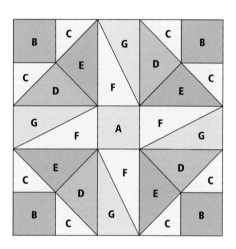

PINWHEEL SQUARE

Pinwheel Square, *Ladies' Art Company*

Category: Five-Patch

CUTTING
A – Cut 1
B – Cut 4
C – Cut 8
D – Cut 4
E – Cut 4
F – Cut 4
G – Cut 4

SUGGESTED TECHNIQUES
Quick cutting and template for F and G

NOTE
G is the reverse of F.

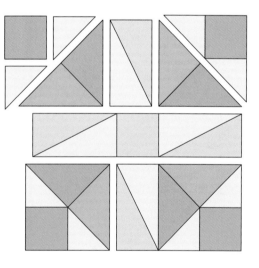

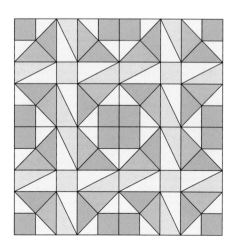

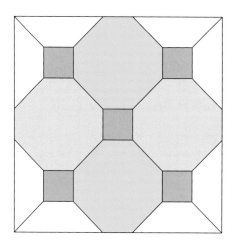

← - - - - - - - - - - - - - - - -

BEAR'S PAW
Bear's Paw, *Finley*
Bear's Foot, *Ladies' Art Company*
Batsche, *Graeff*
Cat's Paw, *Nancy Page*
Duck's Foot in the Mud, *Finley*
Hand of Friendship, *Finley*
Illinois Turkey Track, *Mrs. Danner, 1958*
Small Hand, *Graeff*
Tea Leaf Design, *The Farmer's Wife*
The Best Friend, *Finley*

Category: Seven-Patch

CUTTING
A – Cut 1
B – Cut 4
C – Cut 16
D – Cut 16
E – Cut 4
F – Cut 4

SUGGESTED TECHNIQUES
Quick cutting, strip piecing, and half-square triangles

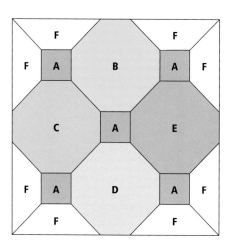

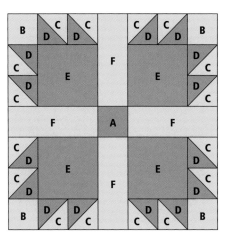

- - - - - - - - - - - - - - - - →

MEADOW FLOWER
Meadow Flower, *Old Chelsea Station Needlecraft Service/Wheeler*

Category: Seven-Patch

CUTTING
A – Cut 5
B – Cut 1
C – Cut 1
D – Cut 1
E – Cut 1
F – Cut 8

SUGGESTED TECHNIQUES
Quick cutting and templates for B, C, D, E, and F.

NOTE
B, C, D, and E are the same.

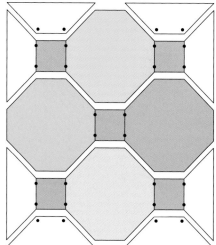

197

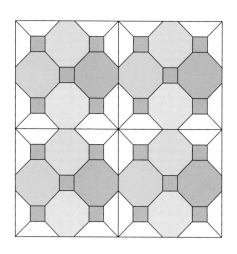

quilt pattern gallery

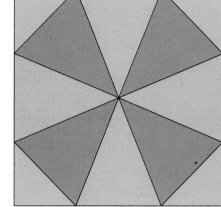

KALEIDOSCOPE

Kaleidoscope, *Holstein*
Octagons, *Nancy Page*
Semi-Octagon, *Household Journal*
The Windmill, *Kansas City Star*
Will of the Wisp, *Farm Journal*

Category: Eight-Pointed Star Design

CUTTING

    A – Cut 4
    B – Cut 4
    C – Cut 4

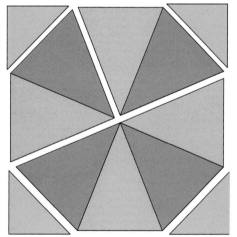

SUGGESTED TECHNIQUES

Quick cutting and template for A and B

NOTE

A and B are the same.

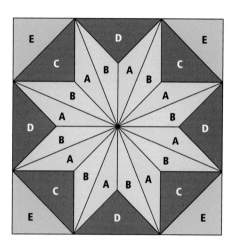

SILVER AND GOLD

Silver and Gold, *Kansas City Star, Hearth and Home*
Gold and Silver, *Nancy Cabot*
Winter Stars, *Nancy Cabot*

Category: Eight-Pointed Star Design

CUTTING

    A – Cut 8
    B – Cut 8
    C – Cut 4
    D – Cut 4
    E – Cut 4

SUGGESTED TECHNIQUES

Quick cutting, strip piecing, template for A and B, and Y-seam construction

NOTE

Shapes A and B can be combined to make one pattern.

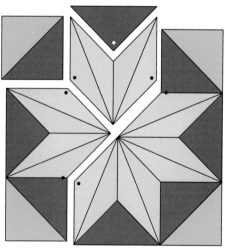

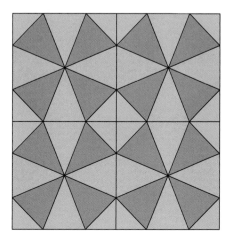

198

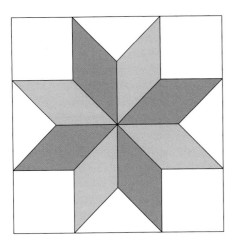

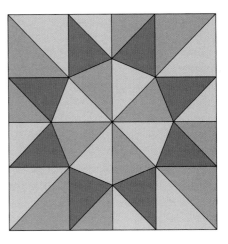

LE MOYNE STAR

Star of LeMoyne, *Finley*
Puritan Star Quilt, *Joseph Doyle*
Lemon Star, *Finley*
Diamond Design, *Woman's World, ca. 1930*
The Star, *Kansas City Star, 1936*
Eastern Star, *McCall's, ca. 1930*
Idaho Star, *Nancy Cabot*
Hanging Diamonds, *Denver Art Museum*
Diamond, *Vote*

Category: Eight-Pointed Star Design

CUTTING
A – Cut 4
B – Cut 4
C – Cut 4
D – Cut 4

SUGGESTED TECHNIQUES
Quick cutting and Y-seam construction

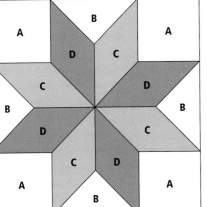

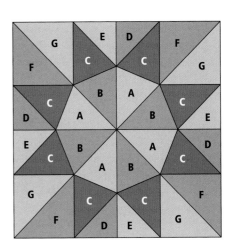

STAR VARIATION

Star Variation, *Electric Quilt 5 Block Book*

Category: Eight-Pointed Star Design

CUTTING
A – Cut 4
B – Cut 4
C – Cut 8
D – Cut 4
E – Cut 4
F – Cut 4
G – Cut 4

SUGGESTED TECHNIQUES
Quick cutting, half-square triangles, and template for A, B, and C

NOTE
One template can be used for all three shapes.

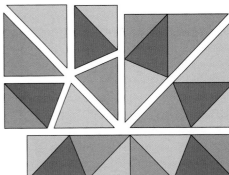

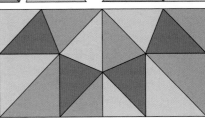

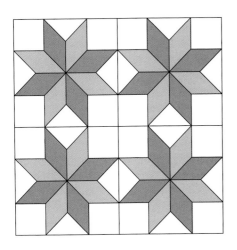

quilt pattern gallery

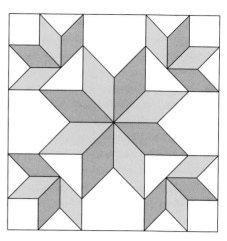

WHIRLING STAR

Whirling Star, *Old Chelsea Station Needlecraft*

Category: Eight-Pointed Star Design

CUTTING
- A – Cut 4
- B – Cut 4
- C – Cut 4
- D – Cut 4
- E – Cut 4
- F – Cut 4

SUGGESTED TECHNIQUES
Quick cutting; template for B, D, E, and F; and Y-seam construction.

NOTE
One template can be used for all four shapes.

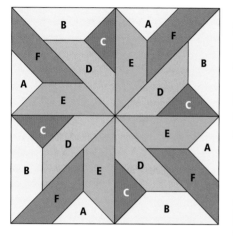

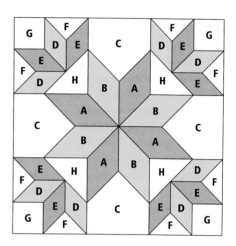

BLAZING STAR

Blazing Star, *Kansas City Star, 1930*

Category: Eight-Pointed Star Design

CUTTING
- A – 4
- B – 4
- C – 4
- D – 8
- E – 8
- F – 8
- G – 4
- H – 4

SUGGESTED TECHNIQUES
Quick cutting, template for C, and Y-seam construction

200

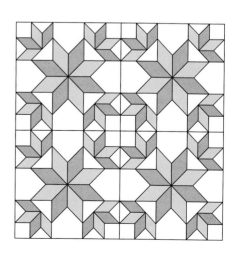

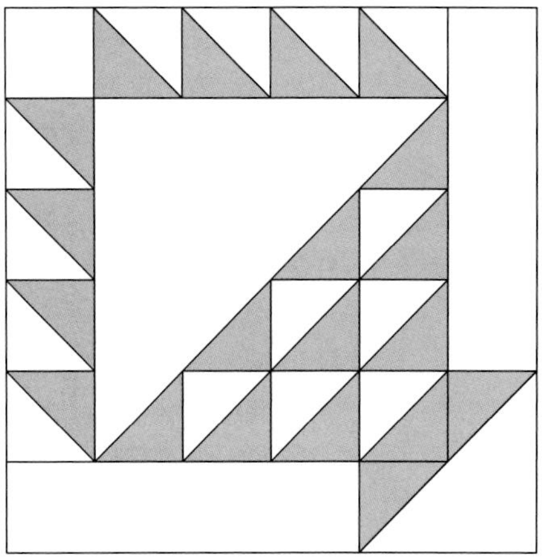

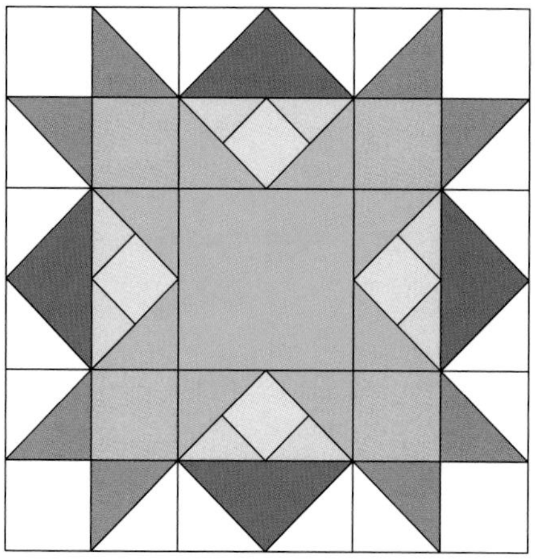

BASKET QUILT

A Basket Quilt in Triangles, *Kansas City Star, 1942*

Category: 36-square Nine-Patch

CUTTING

- A – Cut 1
- B – Cut 14
- C – Cut 1
- D – Cut 2
- E – Cut 20
- F – Cut 1

SUGGESTED TECHNIQUES

Quick cutting and half-square triangles

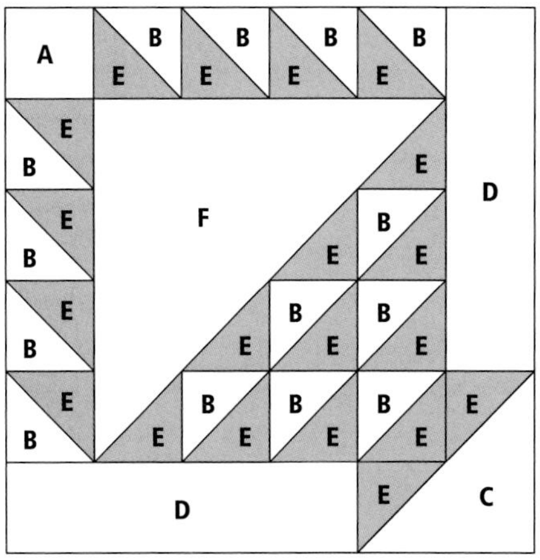

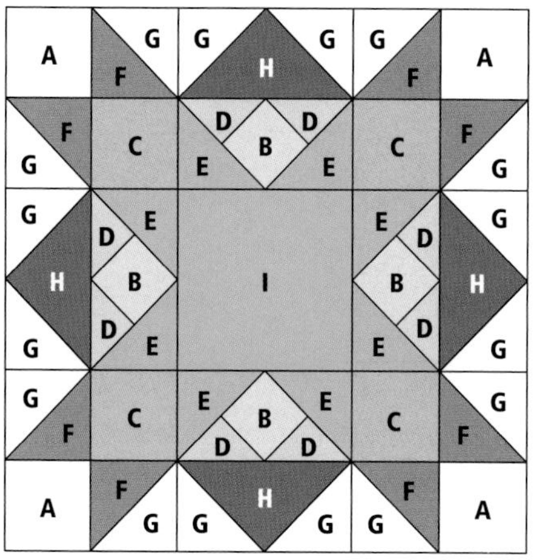

BEST OF ALL

Best of All, *Clara Stone*

Christmas Star, *Workbasket, 1950*

Category: 36-square Nine-Patch

CUTTING

- A – Cut 4
- B – Cut 4
- C – Cut 4
- D – Cut 8
- E – Cut 8
- F – Cut 8
- G – Cut 16
- H – Cut 4
- I – Cut 1

SUGGESTED TECHNIQUES

Quick cutting

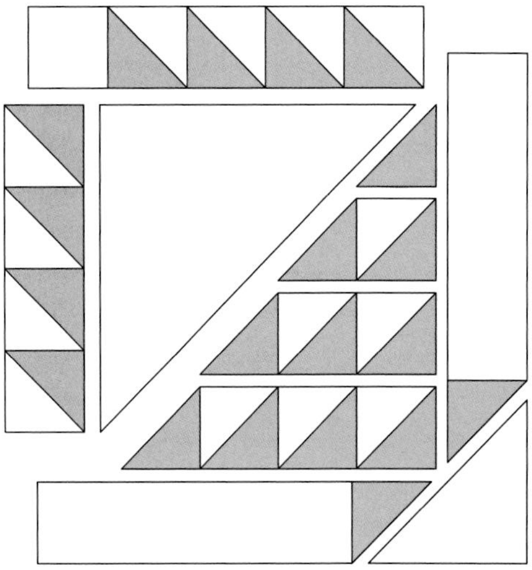

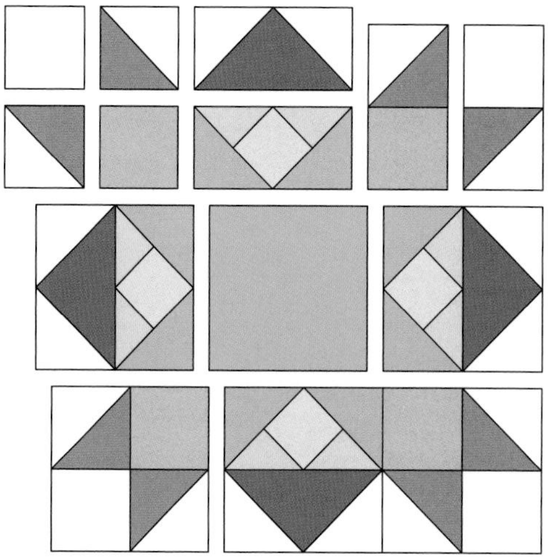

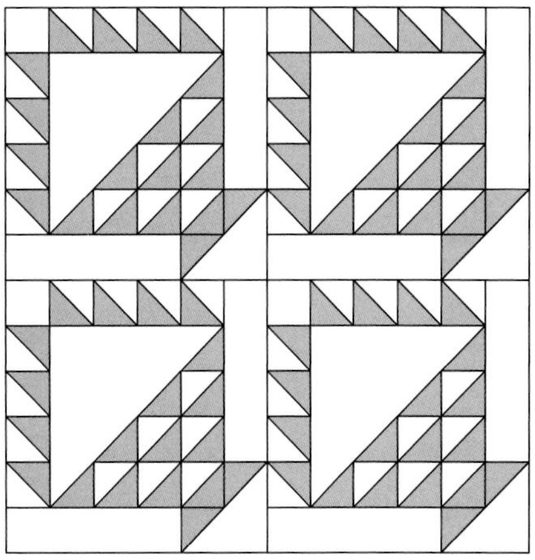

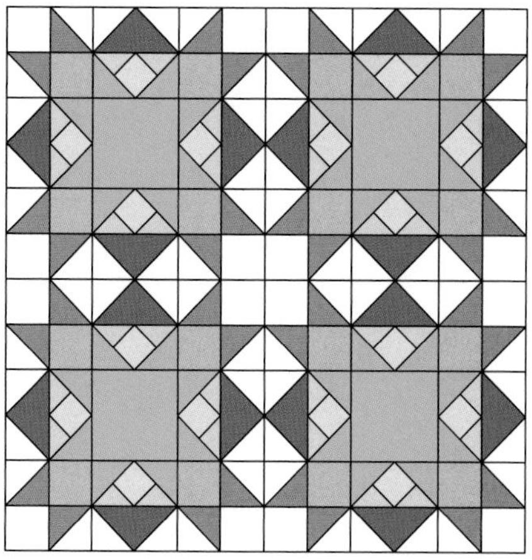

quilt pattern gallery

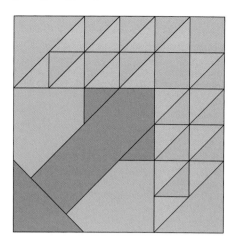

BURGOYNE SURROUNDED

Burgoyne Surrounded, *Household Magazine, ca. 1930*
An Odd Patchwork, *Ladies' Art Company #285*
Beauregard's Surroundings, *Ohio Farmer, ca. 1890*
Burgoyne's Puzzle, *Home Art*
Burgoyne's Quilt, *101 Patchwork Patterns, 1931*
Coverlet Quilt, *Capper's*

Category: Nine-Patch

CUTTING
A – Cut 28
B – Cut 33
C – Cut 12
D – Cut 8
E – Cut 4
F – Cut 8
G – Cut 4

SUGGESTED TECHNIQUE
Quick cutting and strip piecing

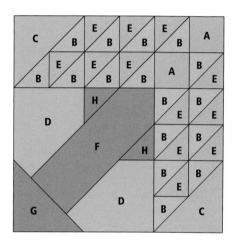

202

CENTENNIAL TREE

Centennial Tree, *Clara Stone and Hearth and Home*

Category: 36-square Nine-Patch

CUTTING
A – Cut 2
B – Cut 16
C – Cut 2
D – Cut 1 and 1R*
E – Cut 12
F – Cut 1
G – Cut 1
H – Cut 2
*R= reverse template on fabric for marking

SUGGESTED TECHNIQUES
Quick cutting, half-square triangles, and template for F

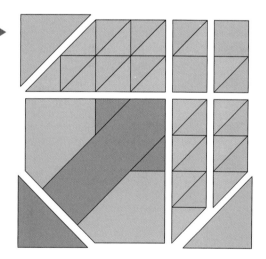

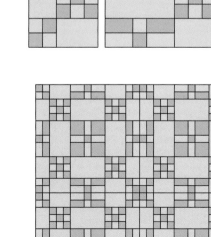

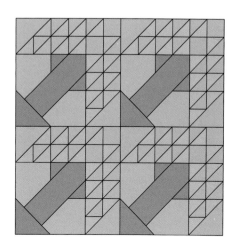

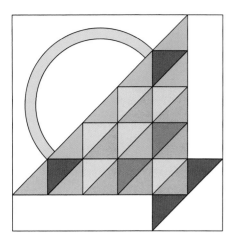

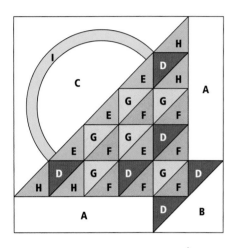

CHERRY BASKET

Cherry Basket, *Ladies' Art Company, 1898*
Berry Basket, *Coats and Clark*
Fruit Basket, *Comfort*
Pieced Basket

Category: 36-square Nine-Patch

CUTTING

A – Cut 2
B – Cut 1
C – Cut 1
D – Cut 6
E – Cut 4
F – Cut 7
G – Cut 6
H – Cut 4
I – Cut 1

SUGGESTED TECHNIQUES

Quick cutting, half-square triangles, appliqué, and template for I

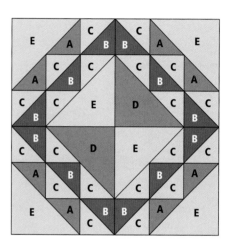

CORN AND BEANS

Corn and Beans, *Ladies' Art Company*
Ducks and Ducklings, *Hall*
Handy Andy, *Hall*
Hen and Chickens, *Hall*
Hen and Chicks, *Grandmother Clark, 1931*
Shoo Fly, *Hall*

Category: 36-square Nine-Patch

CUTTING

A – Cut 8
B – Cut 12
C – Cut 20
D – Cut 2
E – Cut 6

SUGGESTED TECHNIQUE

Quick cutting and half-square triangles

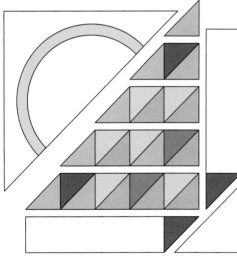

203

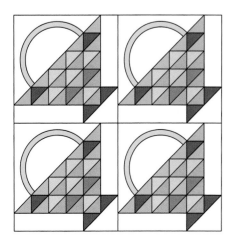

quilt pattern gallery

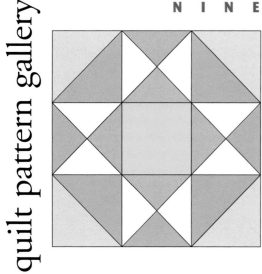

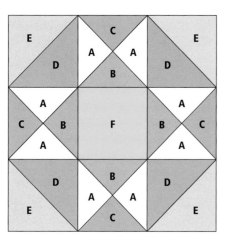

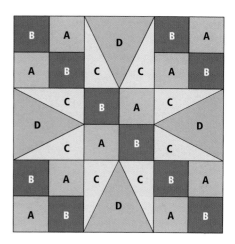

GODEY DESIGN

Godey Design, *Godey's Lady's Book, 1858*
Swamp Patch
The Four-X Quilt, *Mrs. Danner*

Category: Nine-Patch

CUTTING
A – Cut 8
B – Cut 4
C – Cut 4
D – Cut 4
E – Cut 4
F – Cut 1

SUGGESTED TECHNIQUES
Quick cutting and half-square triangles

GRANDMA'S STARS

Grandma's Star, *Practical Needlework ca. 1910*
Blue Meteors
54-40 or Fight
The Railroad Quilt

Category: 36-square Nine-Patch

CUTTING
A – Cut 10
B – Cut 10
C – Cut 4 and 4R*
D – Cut 4
*R– reverse template on fabric for marking

SUGGESTED TECHNIQUES
Quick cutting, strip piecing, and templates for C and D

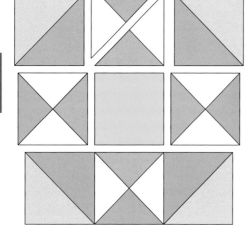

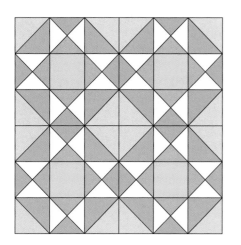

204

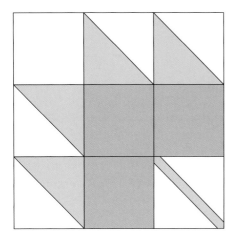

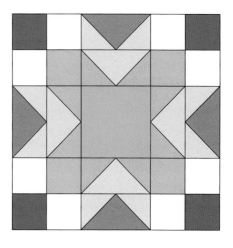

← - - - - - - - - - - - -

MAPLE LEAF

Maple Leaf, *Clara Stone*
Album, *Comfort*
Apple Leaf
Magnolia Leaf, *Practical Needlework,*
 ca. 1910
Tea Leaves

Category: Nine-Patch

CUTTING
A – Cut 1
B – Cut 2
C – Cut 4
D – Cut 3
E – Cut 4
F – Cut 1

SUGGESTED TECHNIQUES
Quick cutting and half-square triangles

- - - - - - - - - - - - - - →

MERRY KITE

Merry Kite, *Ladies' Art Company, 1928*
Friendship Block, *Hearth and Home*
Mrs. Fay's Favorite

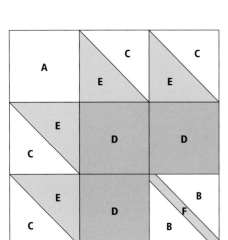

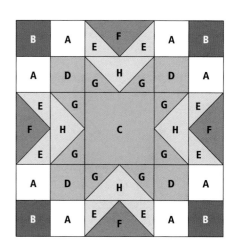

Category: 36-square Nine-Patch

CUTTING
A – Cut 8
B – Cut 4
C – Cut 1
D – Cut 4
E – Cut 8
F – Cut 4
G – Cut 8
H – Cut 4

SUGGESTED TECHNIQUES
Quick cutting, strip piecing, and half-square triangles

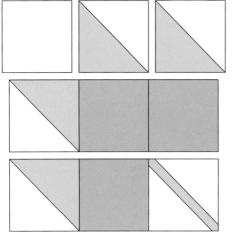

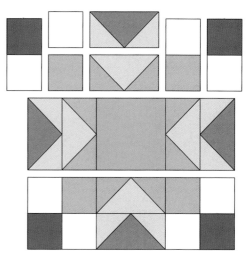

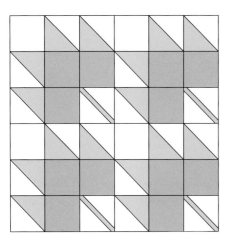

quilt pattern gallery

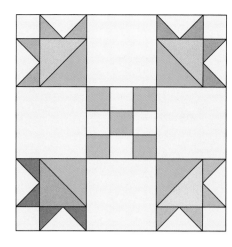

NINE-PATCH

Nine Patch, *Ohio Farmer, 1896*
Checkerboard Design, *Woman's World, 1931*

Category: Nine-Patch

CUTTING
A – Cut 5
B – Cut 4

SUGGESTED TECHNIQUES
Quick cutting and strip piecing

NOTE
Half of blocks have light corners and half have dark.

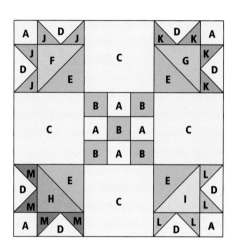

PICNIC BOUQUET

Picnic Bouquet, *Electric Quilt Block Book*

Category: 81-square Nine-Patch

CUTTING
A – Cut 8
B – Cut 5
C – Cut 4
D – Cut 8
E – Cut 4
F – Cut 1
G – Cut 1
H – Cut 1
I – Cut 1
J – Cut 4
K – Cut 4
L – Cut 4
M – Cut 4

SUGGESTED TECHNIQUES
Quick cutting, strip piecing, and half-square triangles

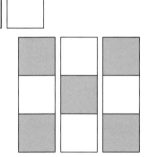

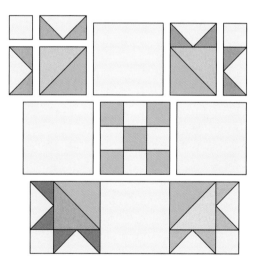

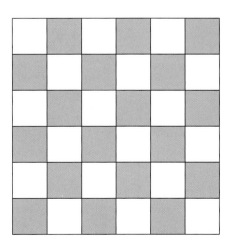

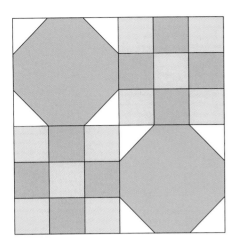

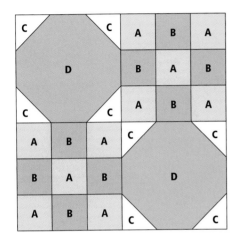

SNOWBALL

Snowball, *Doyle*
Flagstones, *Ladies' Art Company*
Four and Nine-Patch, *Nancy Cabot*
Tile Puzzle
Improved Nine-Patch, *Aunt Martha, 1932*
New Snowball, *Hearth and Home*
Delaware's Flagstones, *Workbasket, 1935*
Federal Chain, *Nancy Cabot*
Aunt Patty's Favorite, *Farm Journal*
Aunt Patsy's Pet, *Nancy Cabot*
Nine and Four-Patch, *Progressive Farmer*
The Snowball and Nine-Patch, *Evelyn Brown, 1978*
Grandmother Short's Quilt, *Goodspeed*
Dutch Mill, *Lady's Circle Patchwork Quilts*
Pullman Puzzle, *Lady's Circle Patchwork Quilts*

Category: 36-square Nine-Patch

CUTTING

    A – Cut 10
    B – Cut 8
    C – Cut 8
    D – Cut 2

SUGGESTED TECHNIQUES

Quick cutting, strip piecing, and template for D

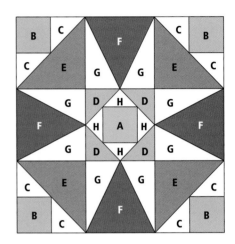

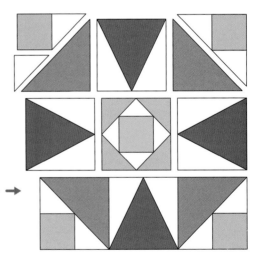

STORM AT SEA

Category: 36-square Nine-Patch

CUTTING

    A – Cut 1
    B – Cut 4
    C – Cut 8
    D – Cut 4
    E – Cut 4
    F – Cut 4
    G – Cut 4 and 4R*
    H – Cut 4
    *R = reverse template on fabric for marking

SUGGESTED TECHNIQUES

Quick cutting and templates for F and G

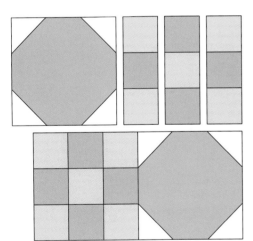

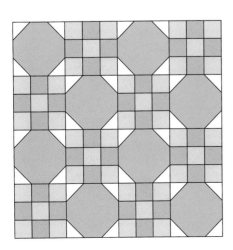

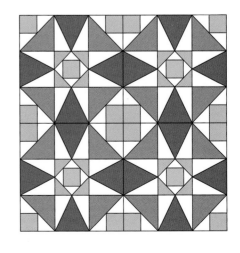

207

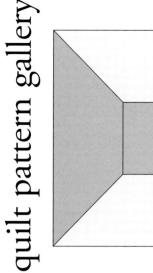

quilt pattern gallery

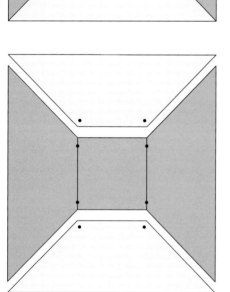

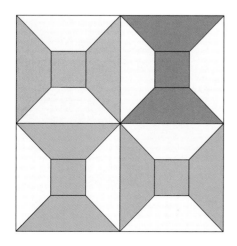

THE SPOOL

The Spool, *McKim 101*
Fred's Spool, *Clara Stone*

Category: Nine-Patch

CUTTING
A – Cut 1
B – Cut 2
C – Cut 2

SUGGESTED TECHNIQUE
Quick cutting and template for B and C

NOTE
One template can be used for both B and C.

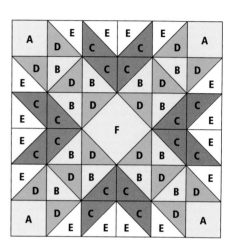

WYOMING VALLEY

Wyoming Valley, *Nancy Cabot*

Category: 36-square Nine-Patch

CUTTING
A – Cut 4
B – Cut 12
C – Cut 16
D – Cut 16
E – Cut 16
F – Cut 1

SUGGESTED TECHNIQUES
Quick cutting and half-square triangles

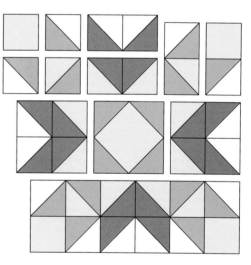

CIRCLE STAR

Circle Star, *Khin*

Category: Wheels

CUTTING
A – Cut 1
B – Cut 4
C – Cut 4
D – Cut 8
E – Cut 16
F – Cut 4

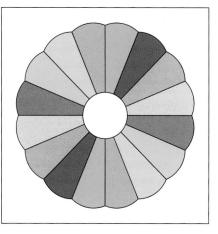

SUGGESTED TECHNIQUES
Templates and curved piecing

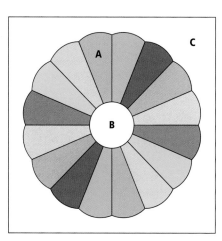

DRESDEN PLATE

Dresden Plate, *McKim, Home Art*
Friendship Ring, *Coats and Clark*
Aster, *McKim*
Chrysanthemum, *Ladies' Art Company,
1898*

Category: Wheels

CUTTING
A – Cut 16 (variety)
B – Cut 1
C – Cut 1

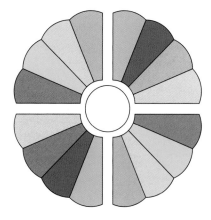

SUGGESTED TECHNIQUES
Templates and appliqué

NOTES
Sew plates together in sets of four. Join sets together to complete the circle. Turn curved edges under and appliqué to the background fabric. Appliqué circle to the center.

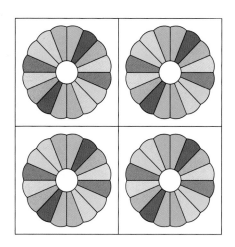

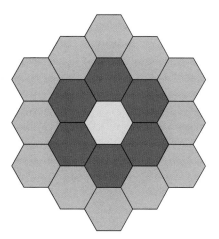

DOUBLE WEDDING RING

Double Wedding Ring, *Ladies' Art Company, 1928*

Category: Curved Designs

CUTTING (FOR ONE RING)

A – 8
B – 8
C – 4
D – 4
E – 4
F – 1

SUGGESTED TECHNIQUES

Templates and curved piecing

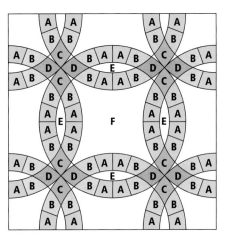

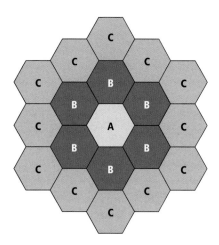

GRANDMOTHER'S FLOWER GARDEN

Grandmother's Flower Garden, *Aunt Martha*

Category: Hexagon

CUTTING

A – Cut 1
B – Cut 6
C – Cut 12

SUGGESTED TECHNIQUE

English paper piecing

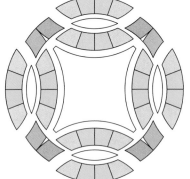

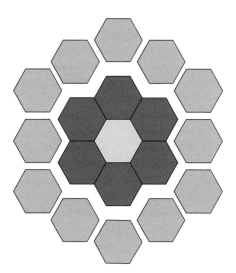

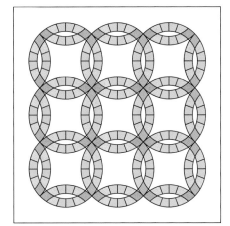

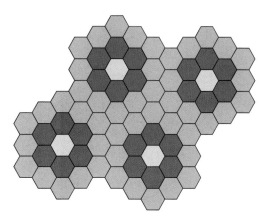

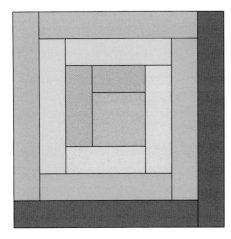

- - - - - - - - - - - - - - - - ←

LOG CABIN

Log Cabin, *Square in a Square*
The Log Patch, *Ladies' Art Company*
American Log Patchwork, *Ladies' Art Company*

Category: Square in a Square

CUTTING
A through M – Cut 1 each

SUGGESTED TECHNIQUE
Quick cutting

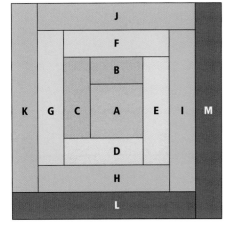

- - - - - - - - - - - - - - - - →

MEXICAN STAR

Mexican Star, *101 Patchwork Patterns*
Dallas Star
Mexican Rose, *Ickis*
Panama Block, *Nancy Cabot*

Category: Nine X or Isolated Square Design

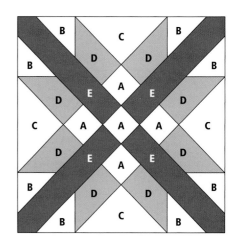

CUTTING
A – Cut 5
B – Cut 8
C – Cut 4
D – Cut 4 and 4R*
E – Cut 4
*R= reverse template on fabric for marking

SUGGESTED TECHNIQUES
Quick cutting and templates for D and E

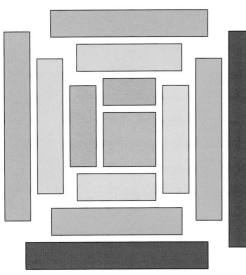

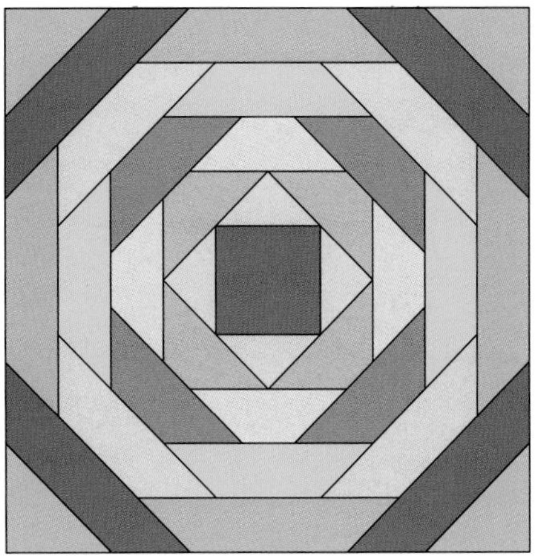

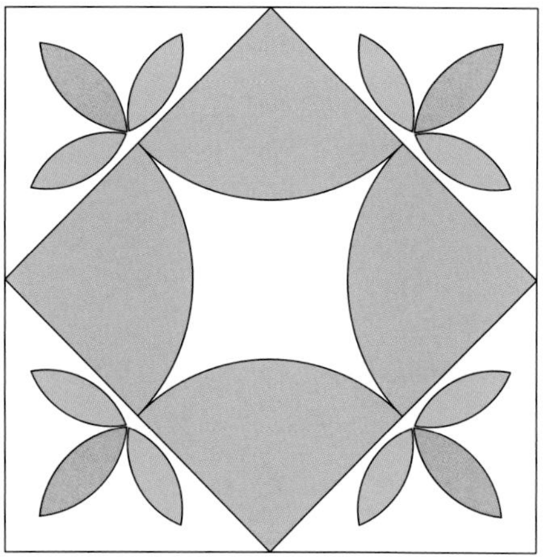

PINEAPPLE

Pineapple, *Ladies' Art Company 1898*

Category: Square in a Square (use 100-Patch grid for drafting)

CUTTING

A – Cut 1
B through J – Cut 4 each

SUGGESTED TECHNIQUES

Foundation method or paper piecing with quick cutting

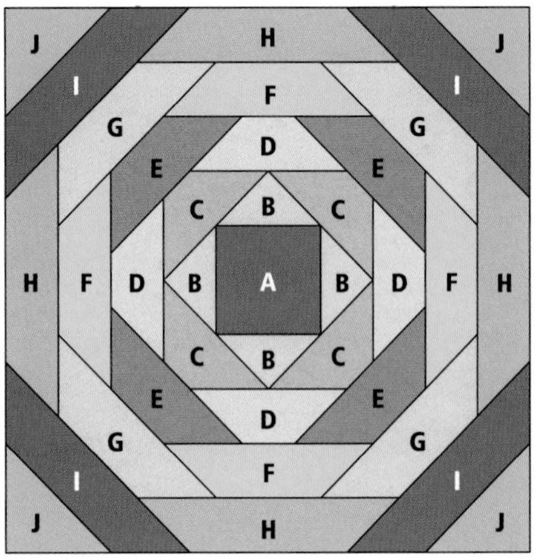

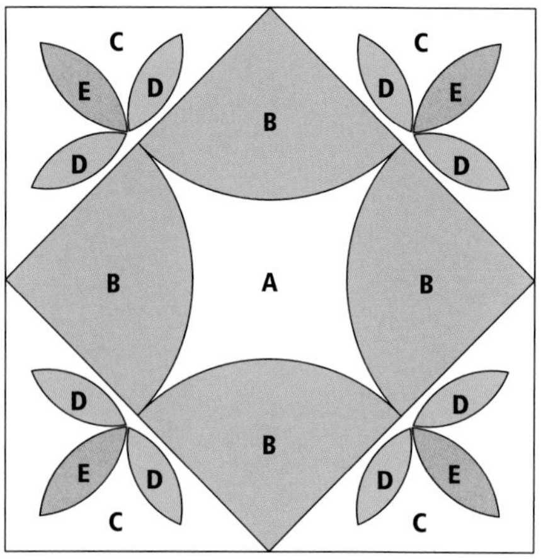

SWEETHEART GARDEN

Sweetheart Garden, *Nancy Cabot*

Category: Blocks with Curves

CUTTING

A – Cut 1
B – Cut 4
C – Cut 4
D – Cut 8
E – Cut 4

SUGGESTED TECHNIQUES

Quick cutting; templates for A, B, D, and E; curved piecing; and appliqué

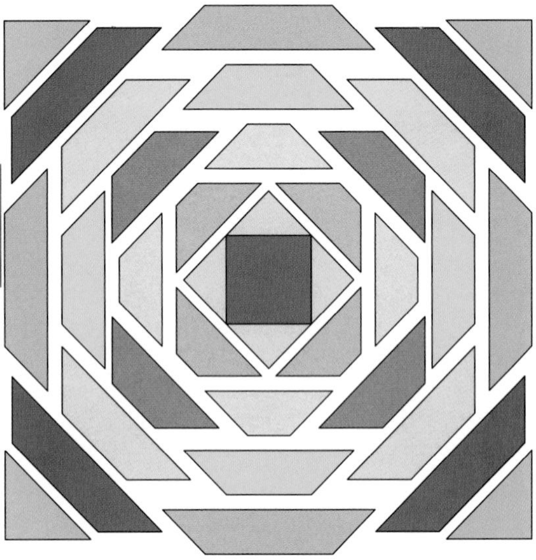

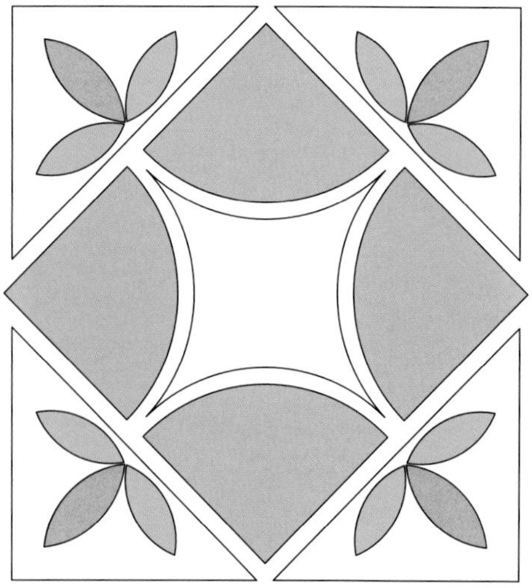

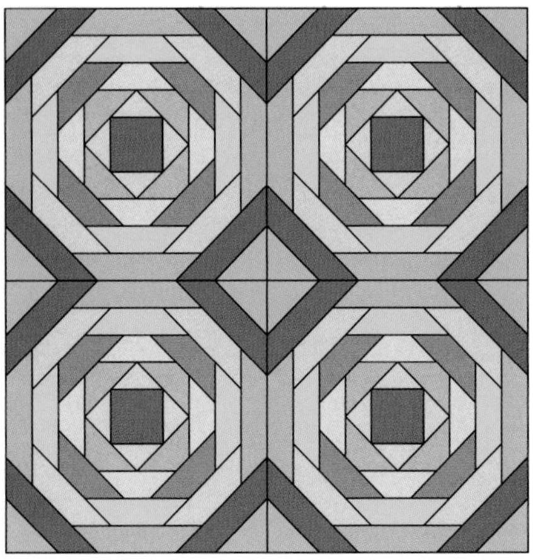

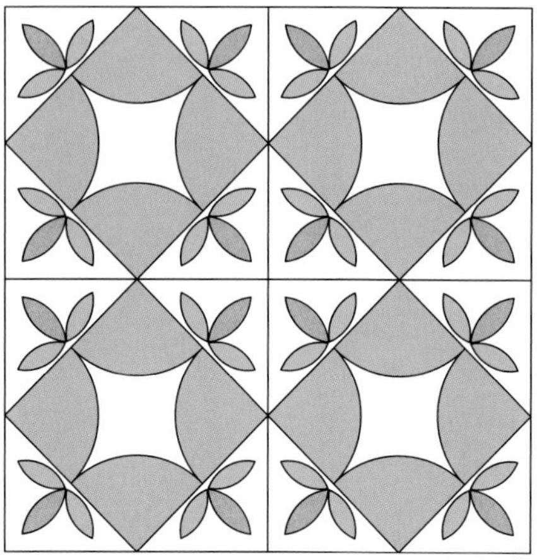

← - - - - - - - - - - - - - -

TUMBLING BLOCKS

Baby Blocks
Building Blocks
Cubes and Stars
Cube Work
Diamond Cube
Godey Design, *Godey's Lady's Book,*
1851
Variegated Diamonds

Category: Hexagon

CUTTING
    A – Variety of lights
    B – Variety of mediums
    C – Variety of darks

SUGGESTED TECHNIQUES
Quick cutting, Y-seam construction, or
English paper piecing

- - - - - - - - - - - - - - →

WINDING WAYS

Winding Ways, *Ladies' Art Company,*
1922
Four Leaf Clover, *Nancy Cabot*
Nashville, *Hearth and Home*
Wheel of Mystery, *Kansas City Star,*
1931, Grandmother Clark, 1932

Category: Curved Designs

CUTTING
    A – Cut 4
    B – Cut 4
    C – Cut 4

SUGGESTED TECHNIQUES
Templates for A, B, and C and curved
piecing

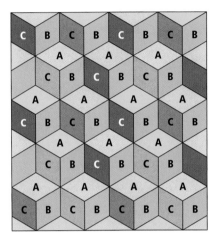

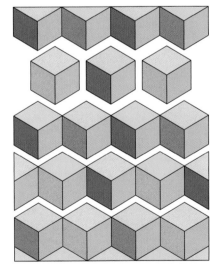

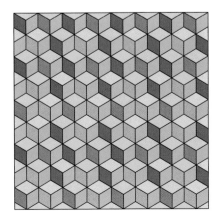

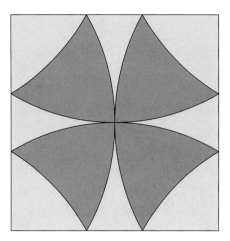

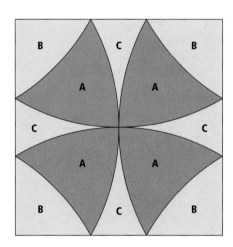

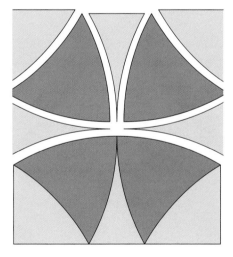

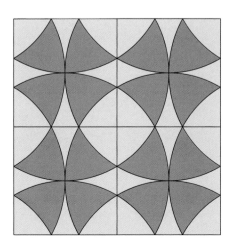

213

quilt pattern gallery

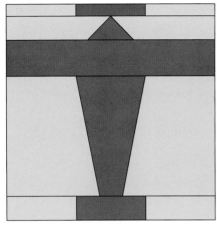

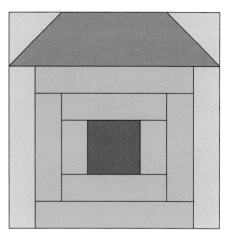

AIRPLANE

Category: Realistic

CUTTING

A – Cut 2
B – Cut 1 and 1R*
C – Cut 1 and 1R*
D – Cut 2
E – Cut 1
F – Cut 1
G – Cut 1
H – Cut 1
I – Cut 1
*R= reverse template on fabric for marking

SUGGESTED TECHNIQUES

Quick cutting and templates for B, C, and H

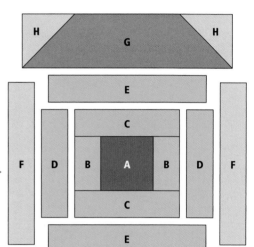

BIG BIRD HOUSE

Category: Realistic

CUTTING

A – Cut 1
B – Cut 2
C – Cut 2
D – Cut 2
E – Cut 2
F – Cut 2
G – Cut 1
H – Cut 2
I – Cut 1
J – Cut 2

SUGGESTED TECHNIQUES

Quick cutting

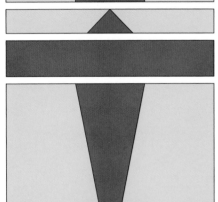

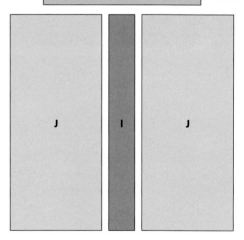

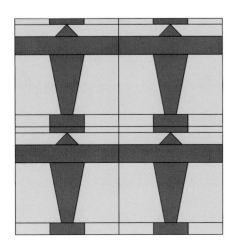

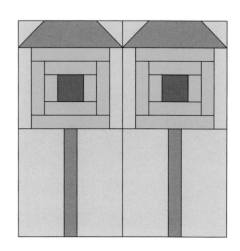

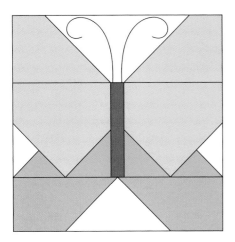

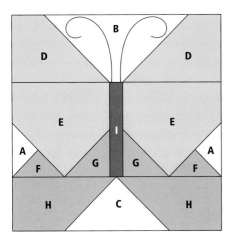

BUTTERFLY

Butterfly Quilt, *McKim*

Category: Realistic

CUTTING

    A – Cut 2
    B – Cut 1
    C – Cut 1
    D – Cut 1 and 1R*
    E – Cut 2
    F – Cut 2
    G – Cut 2
    H – Cut 1 and 1R*
    I – Cut 1
    *R= reverse template on fabric for marking

SUGGESTED TECHNIQUES

Quick cutting; templates for D, E, and H; appliqué or embroidery for antennae

CHARM BASKET

Charm Basket, *Electric Quilt 5 Block Book*

Category: Realistic (use 16-square Four-Patch grid for drafting)

CUTTING

    A – Cut 4
    B – Cut 6
    C – Cut 2
    D – Cut 1 and 1R*
    E – Cut 1 and 1R*
    F – Cut 2
    G – Cut 2
    H – Cut 1 and 1R*
    I – Cut 1
    J – Cut 2
    *R= reverse template on fabric for marking

SUGGESTED TECHNIQUES

Quick cutting, strip piecing, and templates for D, E, and H

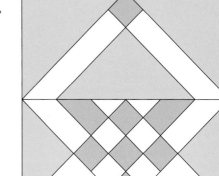

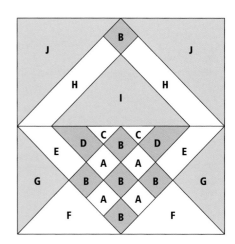

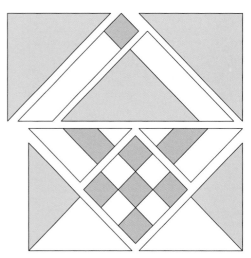

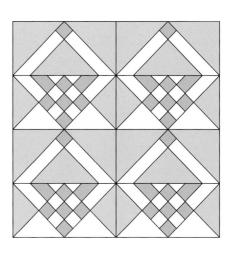

quilt pattern gallery

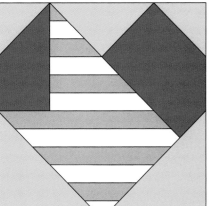

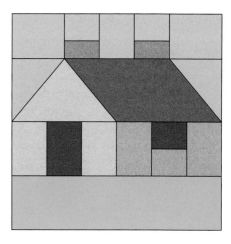

HEART FLAG

Heart Flag, *Electric Quilt 5 Block Book*

Category: Realistic

CUTTING
A – Cut 2
B – Cut 2
C – Cut 1
D – Cut 1
E through Q – Cut 1 each

SUGGESTED TECHNIQUES
Quick cutting and strip piecing

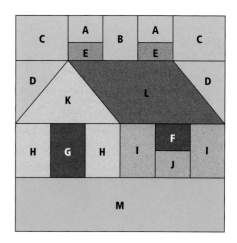

HOUSE ON THE HILL

House on the Hill, *McKim*
The Star's Exhibition House Quilt
    Block Pattern, *McKim Kansas City
    Star, 1929*
Little White House on a Hill, *Nancy
    Cabot*

Category: Realistic

CUTTING
A – Cut 2
B – Cut 1
C – Cut 2
D – Cut 2
E – Cut 2
F – Cut 1
G – Cut 1
H – Cut 2
I – Cut 2
J – Cut 1
K – Cut 1
L – Cut 1
M – Cut 1

SUGGESTED TECHNIQUES
Quick cutting, strip piecing

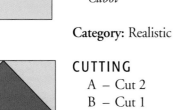

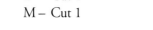

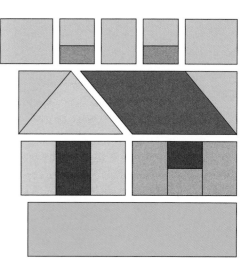

216

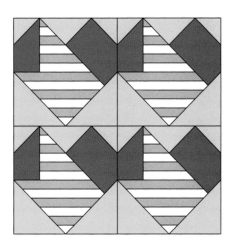

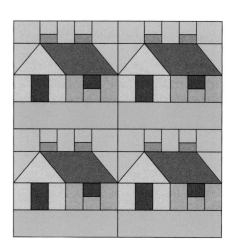

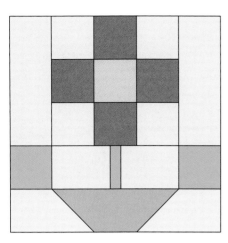

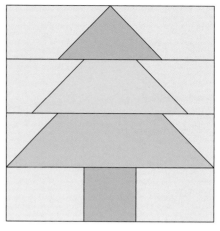

THE FLOWER POT QUILT
The Flower Pot, *Aunt Martha*

Category: Realistic

CUTTING
A – 4
B – 2
C – 2
D – 1 and 1R*
E – 1
F – 4
G – 2
H – 1
I – 1
*R= reverse template on fabric for marking and cutting

SUGGESTED TECHNIQUES
Quick cutting, strip piecing, and templates for D and H

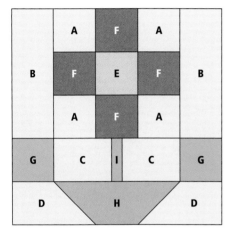

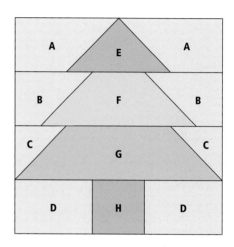

TREE
Tree, *Electric Quilt 5 Block Book*

Category: Realistic

CUTTING
A – Cut 1 & 1R*
B – Cut 1 & 1R*
C – Cut 2
D – Cut 2
E – Cut 1
F – Cut 1
G – Cut 1
H – Cut 1
*R= reverse template on fabric for marking

SUGGESTED TECHNIQUES
Quick cutting and templates for A, B, C, E, F, and G

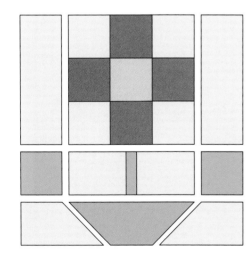

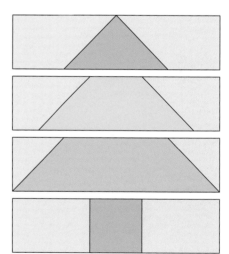

217

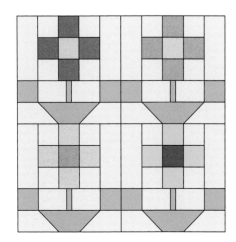

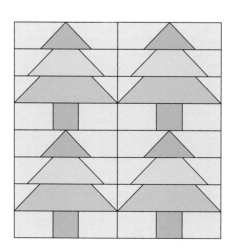

ANN'S ANGEL

Ann's Angel, *Electric Quilt 5 Block Book*

CUTTING

A – Cut 1
B – Cut 1
C – Cut 1
D – Cut 1
E – Cut 2
F – Cut 1

SUGGESTIONS

Allow an extension on the slashed sides of shape A for underlay.

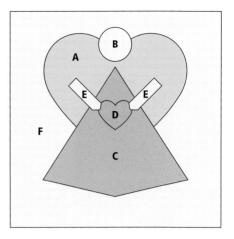

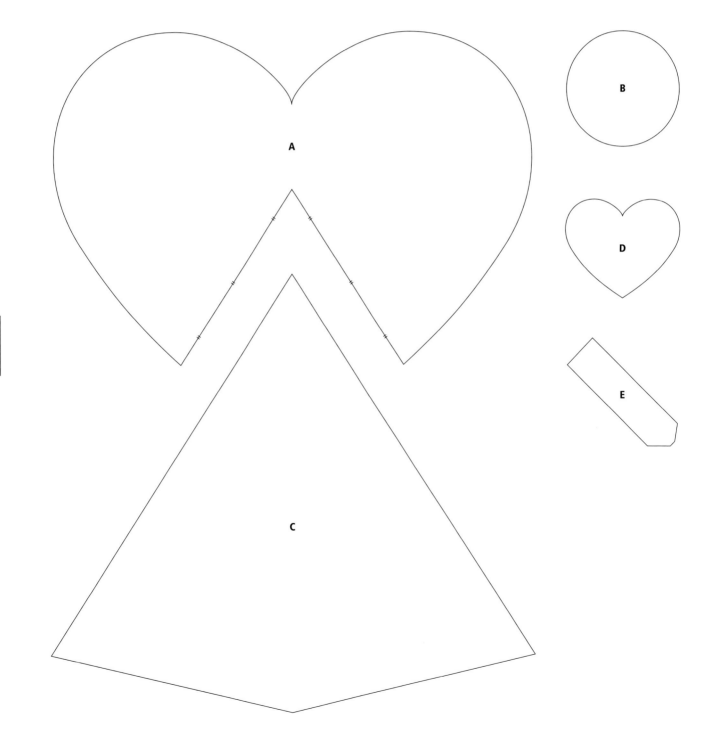

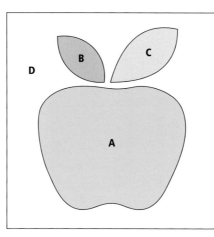

APPLE
Apple, *Electric Quilt 5 Block Book*

CUTTING
A – Cut 1
B – Cut 1
C – Cut 1
D – Cut 1

quilt pattern gallery

DOVE
Dove, *Electric Quilt 5 Block Book*

CUTTING
A – Cut 1
B – Cut 1
C – Cut 1
D – Cut 1
E – Cut 5
F – Cut 1

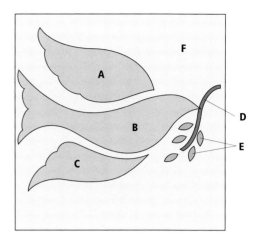

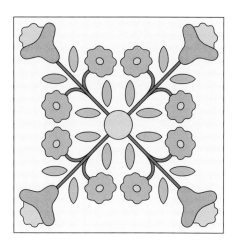

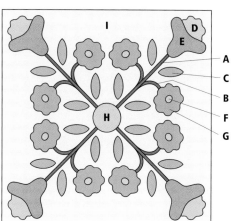

ENGLISH ROSE

English Rose II, *Electric Quilt 5 Block Book*

CUTTING

A and B – Cut long enough length of bias strips for all stems

C – Cut 16

D – Cut 4

E – Cut 4

F – Cut 8

G – Cut 8

H – Cut 1

I – Cut 1

SUGGESTIONS

Allow extension on slashed side of D for underlay. Cut I 1" larger to allow for any shrinkage during appliqué. Then trim to size.

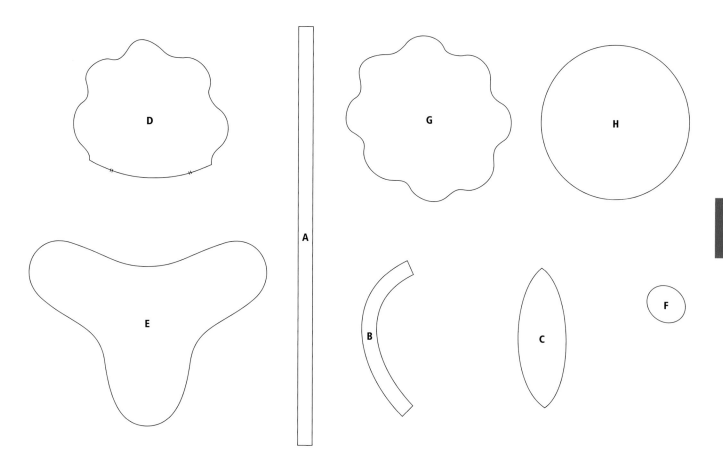

quilt pattern gallery

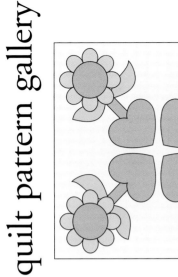

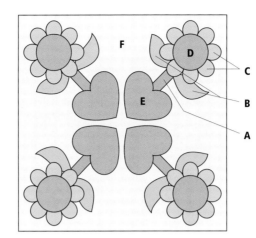

HEARTS & SUNFLOWERS

Hearts and Sunflowers, *Electric Quilt 5 Block Book*

CUTTING

A – Cut 4
B – Cut 4 and 4R*
C – Cut 32
D – Cut 4
E – Cut 4
F – Cut 1
*R= reverse template on fabric for marking

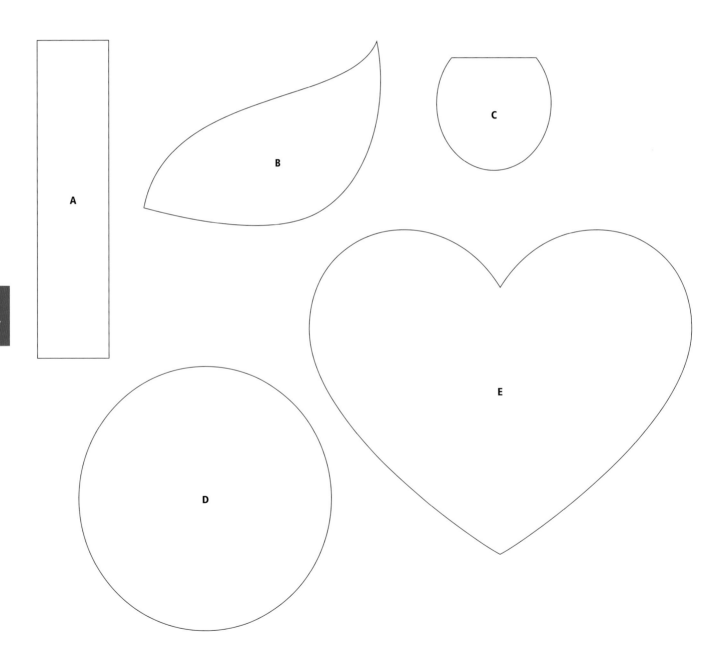

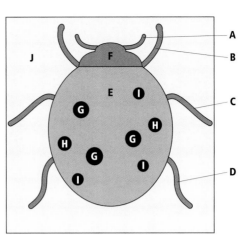

LADYBUG
Ladybug, *Electric Quilt 5 Block Book*

CUTTING
A – Cut 1 and 1R*
B – Cut 1 and 1R*
C – Cut 1 and 1R*
D – Cut 1 and 1R*
E – Cut 1
F – Cut 1
G – Cut 3
H – Cut 2
I – Cut 3
J – Cut 1
*R= reverse template on fabric for marking

SUGGESTIONS
Allow an extension on the slashed edges of shapes A, B, C, D, and E for under-lay.

223

quilt pattern gallery

ORANGE

Orange, *Electric Quilt 5 Block Book*

CUTTING

A – Cut 1 and 1R*
B – Cut 1
C – Cut 1

*R= reverse template on fabric for marking

GRAPES

Grapes, *Electric Quilt 5 Block Book*

CUTTING

A – Cut 1
B – Cut 1
C – Cut 1
D – Cut 4
E – Cut 5
F – Cut 1

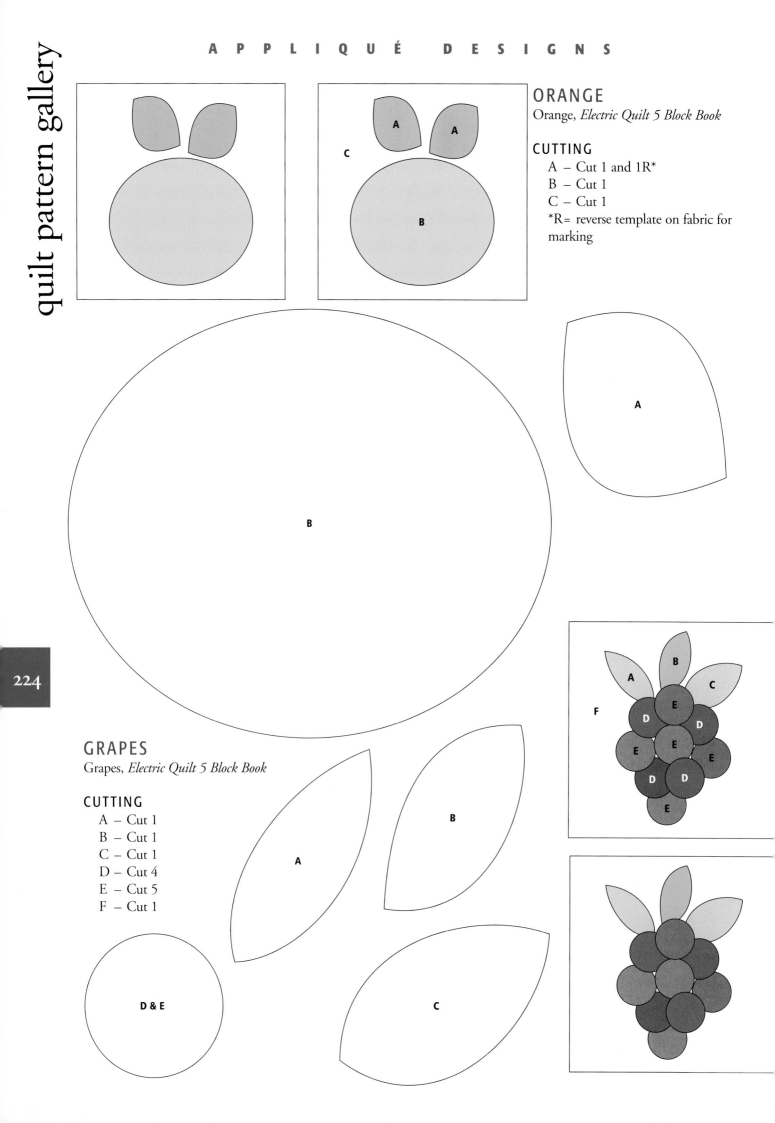

PEAR
Pear, *Electric Quilt 5 Block Book*

CUTTING
A – Cut 1
B – Cut 1
C – Cut 1
D – Cut 1

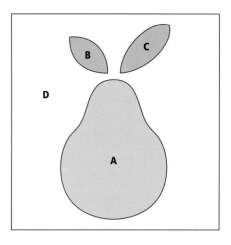

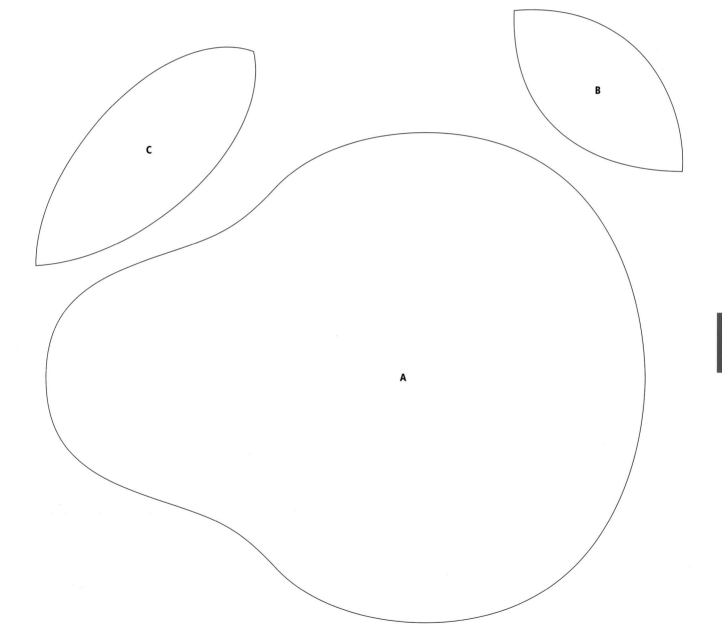

225

quilt pattern gallery

SUNBONNET SUE

Sunbonnet Sue, *Electric Quilt 5 Block Book*

A – Cut 1
B – Cut 1
C – Cut 1
D – Cut 1
E – Cut 1
F – Cut 1
G – Cut 1

SUGGESTIONS

Allow an extension on the slashed edges of shapes A and D for underlay.

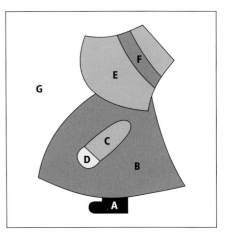

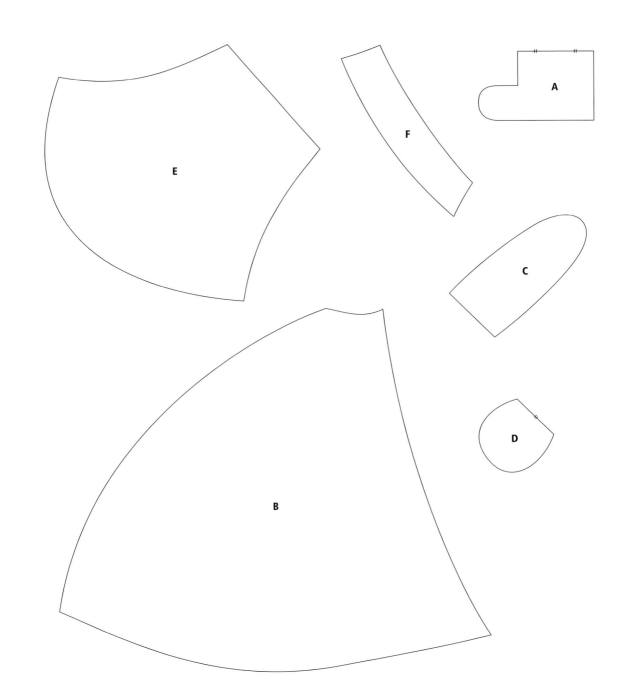

quilting designs

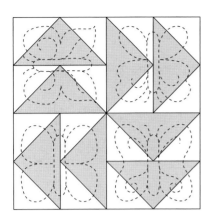

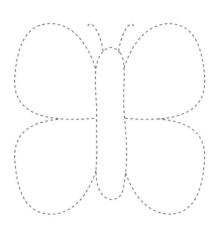

Quilting design used on Dutchman's Puzzle block in sampler quilt on page 167.
1. Quilt in the ditch first.
2. Use free-motion quilting for the butterflies.

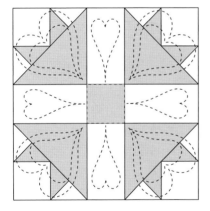

Enlarge all patterns 200%

Quilting design used on Cross and Crown block in sampler quilt on page 166.
1. Quilt in the ditch first.
2. Use free-motion quilting for the hearts.

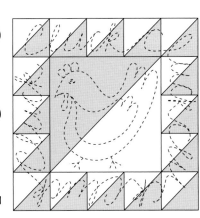

Quilting design used on Lady of the Lake block in sampler quilt on page 168.

1. Quilt in the ditch first.
2. Use free-motion quilting for the rooster and words.

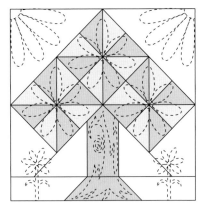

Quilting design used on Pinwheel Pine block in sampler quilt on page 169.

1. Quilt in the ditch first.
2. Use free-motion quilting for the flowers and trunk.

Enlarge all patterns 200%

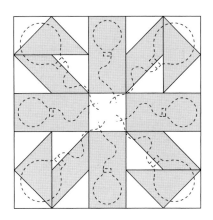

Quilting design used on Jack in the Box block in sampler quilt on page 167.
1. Quilt in the ditch first.
2. Use free-motion quilting for the balloons. Stitch lines as shown then stitch around them again.

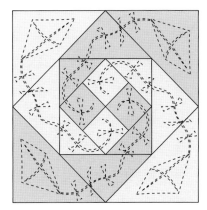

Quilting design used on Monkey Wrench block as well as in the outer border of the sampler quilt on page 168.
1. Quilt in the ditch first.
2. Use free-motion quilting for the kites.

Quilting design used on Hearts and Sunflowers block in sampler quilt on page 170.
1. Quilt in the ditch first.
2. Use free-motion quilting for the leaves and hearts.

Enlarge all patterns 200%

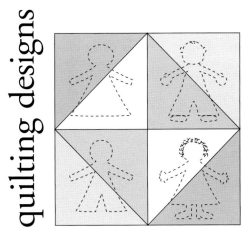

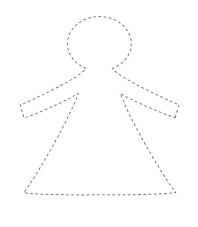

Quilting design used on Broken Dishes block in sampler quilt on page 166.
1. Quilt in the ditch first.
2. Use free-motion quilting to double-stitch the children as shown.

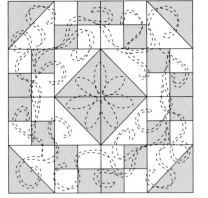

Quilting design used on Jewel Box block in sampler quilt on page 167.
1. Quilt in the ditch first.
2. Use free-motion quilting for the flowers and ribbon.

Enlarge all patterns 200%

Quilting design used on Sawtooth Star
block in sampler quilt on page 170.
1. Quilt in the ditch first.
2. Use free-motion quilting for the star,
cat and words.

Enlarge all patterns 200%

Quilting design used on Miniature Bear's Paw Quilt.
Photo on page 123. Actual size

Quilting designs used on Joseph's Coat string quilt.
Photo on page 115.
Enlarge both patterns 140%

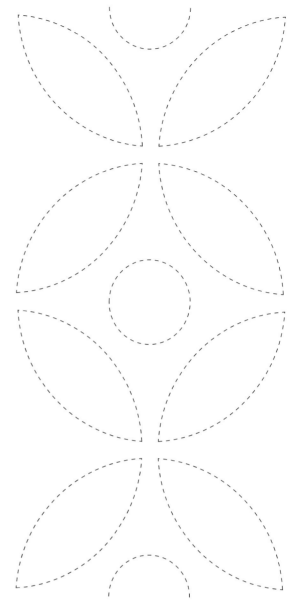

for your information

234

NOTES FOR THE HISTORY OF QUILTING

1. Webster, Marie D., *Quilts: their story and how to make them*; Santa Barbara, CA, 1990, Practical Patchwork, p. 22.
2. Orlofsky, Patsy and Myron, *Quilts in America*, NY, 1974, McGraw-Hill, p. 1.
3. Shown in a color plate between pp. 42-52; Chung Chien, "Perfect preservation after 2100 years", in *New Archaeological Finds in China*, Peking, 1974, Foreign Language Press.
4. Batterbury, Michael and Ariane; *Fashion: the Mirror of History*, NY, 1982, Greenwich House, p. 85.
5. Payne, Blanche; *History of Costume*, NY, 1965, Harper and Row, p. 268.
6. *ibid.*, p. 421; and Webster, *op.cit.*, pp. 67-69.
7. Orlofsky, *op.cit.*, p. 5.
8. Kiracofe, Roderick, The American Quilt: *A History of Cloth and Comfort 1750–1950*, NY, 2004, Clarkson Potter, p. 54.
9. Orlofsky, *op.cit.*, p. 8.
10. *ibid.*, p. 159.
11. Payne, *op.cit.*, p. 263.
12. Battenbury, *op.cit.*, p.160.
13. Kiracofe, *op.cit.*, p.53
14. Clarke, Duncan, *The Art of African Textiles*, London, 1997, Grange Books, p. 8.
15. Lane, Rose Wilder; *Woman's Day Book of American Needlework*, NY, 1963, Simon and Schuster, p. 52.
16. Orlofsky, *op.cit.*, p. 32–33
17. Kiracofe, *op.cit.*, p. 140, fig. 142.
18. Clarke, *op.cit.*, pp. 22, 48.
19. Clarke, *op.cit.*, p. 26.
20. Clarke, *op.cit.*, p. 12.
21. Clarke, *op.cit.*, p. 10.
22. Clarke, *op.cit.*, p. 13.
23. Spring, Christopher, *African Textiles*, NY, 1989, Crescent Books, p.8.
24. Sieber, Roy, *African Textiles and Decorative Arts*, NY, 1972, Museum of Modern Art, p. 11.
25. Taylor, Roderick, *Ottoman Embroidery*, NY, 1993, Interlink Books, pp. 133–139.
26. *Grandes Heures of Jean, Duke of Berry*; NY, 1971, George Braziller, plate 52.
27. Clarke, *op.cit.*, p. 8.
28. Sieber, *op.cit.*, p. 196.
29. Fry, Gladys-Marie, *Stitched from the Soul: slave quilts from the antebellum south*, 1990, Chapel Hill, University of North Carolina, pp. 32–34.
30. Orlofsky, *op.cit.*, p. 31.
31. Swan, Susan Burrows; *Plain and Fancy*, NY, 1977, Holt Rhinehart Winston, p. 54.
32. Swan, *op.cit.*, p.184.
33. Orlovsky, *op.cit.*, p. 226.
34. Orlofsky, *op.cit.*, pp. 226–7.
35. Tobin, Jacqueline L. and Raymond G. Dobard; *Hidden in Plain View*, NY, 1999, Anchor Books.
36. Orlofsky, op.cit., pp. 260–263.
37. Beardsley, John, et al.,*The Quilters of Gee's Bend*, Atlanta, 2002, Tinwood Books in association with The Museum of Fine Arts, Houston, pp. 9–11.
38. Webster, *op.cit.*, p. 35

GENERAL BIBLIOGRAPHY

Anderson, Alex. *Shadow Redwork with Alex Anderson*. C&T Publishing, Inc., Lafayette, CA, 2001.

___. *Start Quilting with Alex Anderson*. C&T Publishing, Inc., Lafayette, CA, 2001.

Armstrong, Carol. *Appliqué, Inside the Lines*. C&T Publishing, Inc., Lafayette, CA, 2003.

Batterbury, Michael and Ariane. *Fashion: the Mirror of History*. Greenwich House, NY, 1982.

Beardsley, John, et al. *The Quilters of Gee's Bend*. Tinwood Books in association with The Museum of Fine Arts Houston, Atlanta, 2002.

Becker, Joyce R. *Luscious Landscapes*. C&T Publishing, Inc., Lafayette, CA, 2003.

Beyer, Jinny. *Color Confidence for Quilters*. The Quilt Digest Press, Gualala, CA, 1992.

___. *Patchwork Patterns*. EPM Publications, Inc., McLean, VA, 1979.

___. *The Quilter's Album of Blocks & Borders*. EPM Publications, Inc., McLean, VA, 1980.

___. *Quiltmaking by Hand*. Breckling Press, Elmhurst, IL, 2004.

Boutté, Karen D. *Delightful Diva Designs*. Remembrance Design Publications, Lafayette, CA, 2004.

Bowser, Tammie. *More Amazing Quilted Photography*. Mosaic Quilt Studio, South Pasadena, CA, 2004.

___. *Simply Amazing Quilted Photography*. Bowser Publications, South Pasadena, CA, 2003.

Brackman, Barbara. *Encyclopedia of Appliqué*. EPM Publications, Inc., McLean, VA, 1993.

___. *Encyclopedia of Pieced Quilt Patterns*. EPM Publications, Inc., McLean, VA, 1993.

Bradkin, Cheryl Greider. *The Seminole Patchwork Book*. A Yours Truly Publication, Atlanta, GA, 1980.

C&T Publishing, Inc., Quilter's Newsletter Magazine, Quiltmaker Magazine. *All About Quilting from A to Z*. C&T Publishing, Inc., Lafayette, CA, 2002.

Causee, Linda. *101 Patchwork Potholders*, American School of Needlework, Inc., San Marcos, CA, 1997.

___. *400 Quilt Blocks*. American School of Needlework, Inc., San Marcos, CA, 2003.

___. *Teach Yourself Foundation Piecing*. Leisure Arts, Inc., Little Rock, AR, 2004.

Christopherson, Darlene C. *A Perfect Union of Patchwork & Appliqué*. C&T Publishing, Inc., Lafayette, CA, 2003.

Clarke, Duncan. *The Art of African Textiles*. Grange Books, London, 1997.

Collins, Sally. *The Art of Machine Piecing*. C&T Publishing, Inc., Lafayette, CA, 2001.

Cory, Pepper. *Mastering Quilt Marking*. C&T Publishing, Lafayette, CA, 1999.

Craig, Sharyn. *Great Sets*. C&T Publishing, Inc., Lafayette, CA, 2004.

___. *Setting Solutions*. C&T Publishing, Inc., Lafayette, CA, 2001.

Daniel, Nancy Brenan. *Learn To Do Hand Quilting In Just One Day*. American School of Needlework, San Marcos, CA, 1996.

___. *Stitch it, Snip it & Flip it*. American School of Needlework, San Marcos, CA, 1993.

Doak, Carol. *Your First Quilt Book (or it should be!)*. Martingale & Company, Woodinville, Washington, 1997.

Donna Kooler. *Donna Kooler's Quilting for the First Time*. Sterling Publishing Co., Inc., New York, NY, 2003.

Dunn, Sarah Sacks (editor). *Rodale's Successful Quilting Library, Innovative Piecing*. Rodale, Inc., Emmaus, PA, 2000.

___. *Rodale's Successful Quilting Library, Rotary Cutting & Speed Piecing*, Rodale, Inc., Emmaus, PA, 2000.

The Electric Quilt Company, *EQ5 Block Book*. The Electric Quilt Company, Bowling Green, OH 2002.

Finley, Ruth E. *Old Patchwork Quilts and the Women Who Made Them*. EPM Publications, McLean, VA, 1992.

Fons, Marianne and Liz Porter. *Quilter's Complete Guide*. Oxmoor House, Inc., and Leisure Arts, Inc., Birmingham, AL, 1993.

Fry, Gladys-Marie. *Stitched from the Soul: Slave Quilts from the Antebellum South*. University of North Carolina, Chapel Hill, 1990.

Goldsmith, Becky, and Linda Jenkins. *Flowering Favorites from Piece O' Cake Designs*. C&T Publishing, Inc., Lafayette, CA, 2003.

Gonzalez, Fran Iverson. *EQ5 Simplified*. The Electric Quilt Company, Bowling Green, OH, 2002.

Gordon, Maggi McCormick. *The Ultimate Quilting Book*. Collins & Brown, London, 1999.

George Braziller, *Grandes Heures of Jean, Duke of Berry*. George Braziller, Inc., NY, 1971.

Guerrier, Katharine. *The Quilter's Companion.* Creative Publishing International, Chanhassen, MN, 2003.

Gulati, Cara. *3-D Explosion, Simply Fabulous Art Quilt Illusions.* Doodle Press, Nicasio, CA, 2004.

Hanisko, Dorothy. *Simply Seminole.* The Quilt Digest Press, Lincolnwood, IL, 1997.

Hargrave, Harriet. *From Fiber To Fabric.* C&T Publishing, Inc., Lafayette, CA, 1997.

___. *Mastering Machine Appliqué, Mock Hand Appliqué and Other Techniques.* C&T Publishing, Lafayette, CA, 1991.

Havig, Bettina. *Carrie Hall Blocks.* University of Kansas. American Quilter's Society, Paducah, KY, 1999.

James, Michael. *The Quiltmaker's Handbook.* Prentice-Hall, Inc., Englewoods, NJ, 1978.

___. *The Second Quiltmaker's Handbook.* Leone Publications, Mountain View, CA, 1981.

Johnson-Srebro, Nancy. *Block Magic, Too!.* C&T Publishing, Inc., Lafayette, CA, 2003.

Kiracofe, Roderick, *The American Quilt: A History of Cloth and Comfort 1750–1950,* Clarkson Potter, NY, 2004.

Kough, Lynn G. *Quiltmaking for Beginners.* The Quilt Digest Press, Lincolnwood, IL, 2000.

Lane, Rose Wilder. *Woman's Day Book of American Needlework.* Simon and Schuster, NY, 1963.

Leisure Arts, Inc. *Beloved Land, Beloved Quilts.* Leisure Arts, Inc. Little Rock, AR, 2003.

Leman, Bonnie, and Judy Martin. *Taking The Math Out Of Making Patchwork Quilts.* Moon Over the Mountain Publishing Company, Denver, CO, 1981.

Levie, Eleanor, Jennifer Place, and Mary Seehafer Sears. *Country Living's Country Quilts.* Hearst Books, New York, NY, 1992.

McClun, Diana and Laura Nownes, *Quilts Galore!.* The Quilt Digest Press, San Francisco, CA, 1990.

___. *Quilts, Quilts, and More Quilts!.* C&T Publishing, Inc., Lafayette, CA, 1993.

___. *Quilts! Quilts!! Quilts!!!.* Quilt Digest Press, Lincolnwood, IL, 1998.

Mech, Susan Delaney, M.D. *Rx for Quilters.* C&T Publishing, Inc., Lafayette, CA, 2000.

Meredith Corporation. *Better Homes and Gardens 501 Quilt Blocks.* Meredith Corp., Des Moines, IA, 1994.

___. *Better Homes and Gardens Complete Guide to Quilting,* Meredith Corp., Des Moines, IA, 2002.

Michell, Marti. *Weekend Basket Quilts.* American School of Needlework, San Marcos, CA, 1993.

Miller, Priscilla. *Yo-Yo Quilts and Originals.* American School of Needlework, San Marcos, CA, 1992.

Montano, Judith Baker. *Crazy Quilt Handbook.* C&T Publishing, Inc., Lafayette, CA 1987.

Mullen, Jan. *Reverse Appliqué with No Brakez.* C&T Publishing, Inc., Lafayette, CA, 2003.

Nownes, Laura. *Cathedral Window.* The Quilt Digest Press, Gualala, CA, 1991.

Nickels, Sue. *Machine Appliqué.* American Quilter's Society, Paducah, KY, 2001.

Orlofsky, Patsy and Myron. *Quilts in America.* McGraw-Hill, NY, 1974.

Pahl, Ellen (editor). *The Quilter's Ultimate Visual Guide.* Rodale Press, Inc., Emmaus, PA, 1997.

Payne, Blanche. *History of Costume: from the Ancient Egyptians to the Twentieth Century.* Harper and Row, New York, NY, 1965.

Pellman, Rachel T. *Amish Quilt Patterns.* Good Books, Intercourse, Pennsylvania, 1984.

Perry, Gai. *Impressionist Palette, Quilt Color & Design.* C&T Publishing, Inc., Lafayette, CA, 1997.

___. *Impressionist Quilts.* C&T Publishing, Inc., Lafayette, CA, 1995.

Porcella, Yvonne. *Colors Changing Hue.* C&T Publishing, Inc., Lafayette, CA, 1994.

Reader's Digest. *Complete Guide to Sewing.* The Reader's Digest Association, Inc., Pleasantville, NY, 1978.

Ringle, Weeks, and Bill Kerr. *Color Harmony for Quilts.* Rockport Publishers, Inc., Gloucester, Massachusetts, 2002.

Root, Elizabeth. *Hawaiian Quilting.* Dover Publications, Inc., New York, NY, 1989.

Rounds, Jennifer (editor) and Catherine Comyns (editor). *A Floral Affair.* C&T Publishing, Inc., Lafayette, CA, 2003.

Sandbach, Kathy. *Show Me How to Create Quilting Designs.* C&T Publishing, Inc., Lafayette, CA, 2004.

___. *Show me how to Machine Quilt.* C&T Publishing, Inc., Lafayette, CA, 2002.

Schneider, Sally (editor). *Rodale's Successful Quilting Library, Sensational Sets & Borders.* Rodale Press, Inc., Emmaus, PA, 1998.

Seely, Ann and Joyce Stewart. *Color Magic for Quilters.* Rodale Press, Inc. Emmaus, PA, 1997.

Serrao, Poakalani and John Serrao. *Poakalani Hawaiian Quilt Cushion Patterns & Designs.* Mutual Publishing, Honolulu, HI, 1999.

Severson, Judy. *Flowers in Appliqué.* Quilt Digest Press, Chicago, IL, 1998.

Siber, Julie (editor). *Amish Quilts of Lancaster County.* Esprit De Corp., San Francisco, CA, 1990.

___. *Esprit Quilt Collection.* Esprit De Corp., San Francisco, CA, 1985

Sieber, Roy. *African Textiles and Decorative Arts.* Museum of Modern Art, NY, 1972.

Sienkiewicz, Elly. *The Best of Baltimore Beauties, Part II.* C&T Publishing, Inc., Lafayette, CA, 2002.

___. *Fancy Appliqué.* C&T Publishing, Inc., Lafayette, CA, 1999.

Sinema, Laurene. *Appliqué!!, The Complete Guide to Hand Appliqué,* The Quilt Digest Press. Gualala, CA, 1992.

Solomon, Anita Grossman. *Make It Simpler, Paper Piecing.* C&T Publishing, Inc., Lafayette, CA, 2003.

Soltys, Karen Costello (editor). *Rodale's Successful Quilting Library, Perfect Piecing.* Rodale Press, Inc., Emmaus, PA, 1997.

Swan, Susan Burrows. *Plain and Fancy.* Holt Rhinehart Winston, NY, 1977.

Taylor, Roderick. *Ottoman Embroidery.* Interlink Books, NY, 1993.

Townswick, Jane (editor). *Rodale's Successful Quilting Library, Choosing Quilting Designs.* Rodale Press, Inc., Emmaus, PA, 2001.

___. *Rodale's Successful Quilting Library, Favorite Techniques from the Experts,* Emmaus, PA, 2000.

Walner, Hari. *Trapunto by Machine.* C&T Publishing, Martinez, CA, 1996.

Webster, Marie D. *Quilts: Their Story and How to Make Them.* Santa Barbara, CA, 1990.

Wells, Valori. *Radiant New York Beauties.* C&T Publishing, Inc., Lafayette, CA, 2003.

Wilens, Patricia (editor). *Leisure Arts Presents Encyclopedia of Classic Quilt Patterns.* Oxmoor House, Inc., Birmingham, AL, 2001.

___. *Leisure Arts Presents Great American Quilts, Book 8.* Oxmoor House, Inc., Birmingham, AL, 2000.

Zieman, Nancy, and Natalie Sewell. *Landscape Quilts.* Oxmoor House, Inc., Birmingham, AL, 2001.

239

This index contains only the names and alternate names of blocks in the Pattern Gallery (p. 177–226). For information on quilting styles, techniques, and uses of the blocks, see the general index.